Swift Apprentice

Third Edition

By the raywenderlich.com Tutorial Team

Janie Clayton, Alexis Gallagher, Matt Galloway, Eli Ganim,
Ben Morrow, Cosmin Pupăză and Steven Van Impe

Swift Apprentice: Third Edition

Janie Clayton, Alexis Gallagher, Matt Galloway, Eli Ganim, Ben Morrow, Cosmin Pupăză and Steven Van Impe

ISBN: 978-1-942878-43-8

Dedications

"Here's to the crazy ones. Except Josh. He knows what he did."

— *Janie Clayton*

"To my wife, and her remarkable patience in the face of the rationally inexplicable features of my writing process."

— *Alexis Gallagher*

"To my amazing family who keep putting up with me spending my spare hours writing books like this."

— *Matt Galloway*

"To my loved ones: Moriah, Lia and Ari."

— *Eli Ganim*

"To the Swift community, both old and new — and to Brigette, who puts up with my long hours at the keyboard to help make this book possible."

— *Erik Kerber*

"For MawMaw. A talented cook, a loving smooch, a worthy opponent in chicken foot; a home weaver. Her blessing abides beyond her time."

— *Ben Morrow*

"To Oana, Sclip and Nori, for believing in me all the way."

— *Cosmin Pupăză*

About the authors

Janie Clayton is an independent iOS developer. She spent a year apprenticed to a super genius programming robots and learning the forgotten ways of long term software maintenance and development. Janie is the coauthor on several books on iOS and Swift development. Janie lives outside of Madison, Wisconsin with her attempted grumble of pugs and multitude of programming books. Janie writes her various musings on her blog at RedQueenCoder.com.

Alexis Gallagher is a software engineer who is always looking for the conceptual deep dive and always hoping to find pearls down at the bottom. When he's not coding, he's out and about in sunny San Francisco.

Matt Galloway is a software engineer with a passion for excellence. He stumbled into iOS programming when it first was a thing, and has never looked back. When not coding, he likes to brew his own beer.

Eli Ganim is an engineering manager at Facebook. He is passionate about teaching, writing, and sharing his knowledge with others.

Erik Kerber is a software developer in Minneapolis, MN, and the lead iOS developer for the Target app. He does his best to balance a life behind the keyboard with cycling, hiking, scuba diving, and traveling.

Ben Morrow delights in discovering the unspoken nature of the world. He'll tell you the surprising bits while on a walk. He produces beauty by drawing out the raw wisdom that exists within each of us.

Cosmin Pupăză is a software developer and tutorial writer from Romania. He has worked with more than a dozen programming languages over the years, but none of them has made such a great impact on himself as the advent of Swift. When not coding, he either plays the guitar or studies WWII history. Cosmin blogs about Swift at cosminpupaza.wordpress.com.

About the editors

Steven Van Impe is the technical editor of this book. Steven is a computer science lecturer at the University College of Ghent, Belgium. When he's not teaching, Steven can be found on his bike, rattling over cobblestones and sweating up hills, or relaxing around the table, enjoying board games with friends. You can find Steven on Twitter as @svanimpe.

Chris Belanger is the editor of this book. Chris is the Book Team Lead and Lead Editor for raywenderlich.com. He was a developer for nearly 20 years in various fields from e-health to aerial surveillance to industrial controls. If there are words to wrangle or a paragraph to ponder, he's on the case. When he kicks back, you can usually find Chris with guitar in hand, looking for the nearest beach. Twitter: @crispytwit.

Ray Fix is the final pass editor of this book. A passionate Swift educator, enthusiast and advocate, he is actively Swift to create Revolve--the next generation in research microscopy at Echo. He also serves as the iOS tutorials topics master at RayWenderlich.com. Ray is mostly-fluent in spoken and written Japanese and stays healthy by walking, jogging, and playing ultimate frisbee. When he is not doing one of those things, he is writing and dreaming of code in Swift.

Table of Contents:

Introduction

Welcome to the Swift Apprentice, fully updated for Swift 4!

In a little over three years, Swift has gone from being a secret project at Apple, Inc. to a full-blown, open source community driven language. It continues to refine its core goal of being a general purpose language that supports safety, speed and expressiveness.

Despite its advanced, industrial-strength nature, Swift is a great choice for the beginning programmer, since Xcode offers a sandbox-type environment where you can directly execute Swift statements to try out various components of the language — without having to create a whole app first.

Developers around the world use Swift to build thousands of amazing apps for the iPhone, iPad, Mac, Apple TV and the Apple Watch. That means what you learn in this book will still be useful as you expand your development skills and possibly work as an app developer someday.

You'll learn about basic things like constants, values and types, move up to more complicated items such as data structures, classes and enumerators, and finish off with some in-depth knowledge about protocol extensions, custom operators and protocol-oriented programming, many which are topics common to other programming languages, and some that Swift improves upon in novel ways.

Swift is also a lot of fun! It's easy to try out small bits of code and play around with different values as you test new ideas. Programming is a hands-on experience, and Swift makes it fast and easy to both follow along with this book, as well as explore on your own.

Who this book is for

If you're a complete beginner to programming, this is the book for you! There are short exercises and challenges throughout the book to give you some programming practice and test your knowledge along the way.

If you want to get right into iOS app development while learning bits of the Swift language as you go, we recommend you read through *The iOS Apprentice*. *The iOS Apprentice* and this book make very good companions — you can read them in parallel, or use this book as a reference to expand on topics you read about in *The iOS Apprentice*.

What you need

To follow along with this book, you'll need the following:

- **A Mac running macOS Sierra 10.12.6**, with the latest point release and security patches installed. This is so you can install the latest version of the required development tool: Xcode.
- **Xcode 9 or later.** Xcode is the main development tool for writing code in Swift. You need Xcode 9 at a minimum, since that version includes Swift 4. You can download the latest version of Xcode for free from the Mac App Store, here: apple.co/1FLn51R.

If you haven't installed the latest version of Xcode, be sure to do that before continuing with the book. The code covered in this book depends on Swift 4 and Xcode 9 — you may get lost if you try to work with an older version.

How to use this book

Each chapter of this book presents some theory on the topic at hand, along with plenty of Swift code to demonstrate the practical applications of what you're learning.

Since this is a book for beginners, we suggest reading it in order the first time. After that, the book will make a great reference for you to return to and refresh your memory on particular topics.

All the code in this book is platform-neutral; that means it isn't specific to iOS, macOS or any other platform. The code runs in **playgrounds**, which you'll learn about in the very first chapter.

As you read through the book, you can follow along and type the code into your own playground. That means you'll be able to play with the code by making changes and see the results immediately.

You'll find **mini-exercises** throughout the book, which are short exercises about the topic at hand. There are also **challenges** at the end of each chapter, which are either programming questions or longer coding exercises to test your knowledge.

You'll get the most out of this book if you follow along with these exercises and challenges.

What's in store

This book is divided into four sections. Each section has a short introduction that describes its chapters, their topics and the overarching themes of the section. Here's a brief overview of the book's sections:

Section I: Swift Basics

The first section of the book starts at the very beginning of the computing environment: first, how computers work, and then, how Swift's playgrounds feature works. With those logistics out of the way, you'll take a tour of the fundamentals of the Swift language and learn the basics of managing data, structuring your code, performing simple operations and calculations, working with types.

Section II: Collection Types

Stored data is a core component of any app, whether it's a list of friends in your social networking app or a set of unlockable characters in your hit game. In this section, you'll learn how to store collections of data in Swift.

Section III: Building Your Own Types

Swift comes with basic building blocks, but its real power is in the custom things you can build to model parts of your app. Swift has no idea about playable characters and monsters and power-ups, for example — these are things you need to build yourself! You'll learn how to do that in this section.

Section IV: Advanced Topics

The final section of the book covers more advanced topics in Swift. You'll learn about specific things, such as how to handle problems that come up as your code runs, as well as about more general things such as memory management, which will help you understand some of Swift's behind-the-scenes mechanisms.

Book source code and forums

You can get the source code for the book here:

www.raywenderlich.com/store/swift-apprentice/source-code

You'll find playgrounds with the code from the chapters, as well as solutions to the challenges for your reference.

We've also set up an official forum for the book at www.raywenderlich.com/forums. This is a great place to ask any questions you have about the book and the Swift language in general, or to submit any errors you might find.

PDF Version

We also have a PDF version of this book available, which can be handy if you want a soft copy to take with you, or you want to quickly search for a specific term within the book.

Buying the PDF version of the book also has a few extra benefits: free PDF updates each time we update the book, access to older PDF versions of the book, and you can download the PDF from anywhere, at anytime.

Visit our Swift Apprentice store page here: https://store.raywenderlich.com/products/swift-apprentice.

And since you purchased the print version of this book, you're eligible to upgrade to the PDF at a significant discount!

Simply email support@razeware.com with your receipt for the physical copy and we'll get you set up with the discounted PDF version of the book.

License

By purchasing *Swift Apprentice*, you have the following license:

- You are allowed to use and/or modify the source code in *Swift Apprentice* in as many apps as you want, with no attribution required.

Acknowledgments

We would like to thank many people for their assistance in making this book possible:

- **Our families:** For bearing with us in this crazy time as we worked all hours of the night to get this book ready for publication!
- **Everyone at Apple:** For producing the amazing hardware and software we know and love, and for creating an exciting new programming language that we can use to make apps for that hardware!
- **The Swift Community** For all the people, both inside and outside of Apple, who have worked very hard to make Swift the best computer language in the world.
- And most importantly, **the readers of raywenderlich.com — especially you!** Thank you so much for reading our site and purchasing this book. Your continued readership and support is what makes all of this possible!

About the cover

Flying fish have been known to soar 655 feet in a single flight, can reach heights of 20 ft above the water, and may fly as fast as 37 mph.

If you ever feel like a fish out of water trying to learn Swift, just think about the animals on the cover of this book — if they can adapt to a completely new environment, so can you! :]

Section I: Swift Basics

The chapters in this section will introduce you to the very basics of programming in Swift. From the fundamentals of how computers work all the way up to language structures, you'll cover enough of the language to be able to work with data and organize your code's behavior.

The section begins with some groundwork to get you started:

- **Chapter 1, Expressions, Variables & Constants**: This is it, your whirlwind introduction to the world of programming! You'll begin with an overview of computers and programming, and then say hello to Swift playgrounds, which are where you'll spend your coding time for the rest of this book. You'll learn some basics such as code comments, arithmetic operations, constants and variables. These are some of the fundamental building blocks of any language, and Swift is no different.
- **Chapter 2, Types & Operations**: You'll learn about handling different types, including strings which allow you to represent text. You'll learn about converting between types and you'll also be introduced to type inference which makes your life as a programmer a lot simpler. You'll learn about tuples which allow you to make your own types made up of multiple values of any type.

Once you have the basic data types in your head, it'll be time to *do* things with that data:

- **Chapter 3, Basic Control Flow**: You'll learn how to make decisions and repeat tasks in your programs by using syntax to control the flow. You'll also learn about **Booleans**, which represent true and false values, and how you can use these to compare data.
- **Chapter 4, Advanced Flow Control**: Continuing the theme of code not running in a straight line, you'll learn about another loop known as the `for` loop. You'll also learn about `switch` statements which are particularly powerful in Swift.
- **Chapter 5, Functions**: Functions are the basic building blocks you use to structure your code in Swift. You'll learn how to define functions to group your code into reusable units.

The final chapter of the section loops a very important data type:

- **Chapter 6, Optionals**: This chapter covers optionals, a special type in Swift that represents either a real value or the absence of a value. By the end of this chapter, you'll know why you need optionals and how to use them safely.

These fundamentals will get you Swiftly on your way, and before you know it, you'll be ready for the more advanced topics that follow. Let's get started!

Chapter 1: Expressions, Variables & Constants

By Matt Galloway

Welcome to the book! In this first chapter, you're going to learn a few basics. You'll learn how code works first. Then you'll learn about the tools you'll be using to write Swift code.

Then, you'll start your adventure into Swift by learning some basics such as code comments, arithmetic operations, constants and variables. These are some of the fundamental building blocks of any language, and Swift is no different.

First of all, you'll cover the basic workings of computers, because it really pays to have a grounding before you get into more complicated aspects of programming.

How a computer works

You may not believe me when I say it, but a computer is not very smart on its own. The power of computers is all derived from how they're programmed by people like you and me. If you want to successfully harness the power of a computer — and I assume you do, if you're reading this book — it's important to understand how computers work.

It may also surprise you to learn that computers themselves are rather simple machines. At the heart of a computer is a **Central Processing Unit** (**CPU**). This is essentially a math machine. It performs addition, subtraction, and other arithmetical operations on numbers. Everything you see when you operate your computer is all built upon a CPU crunching numbers many millions of times per second. Isn't it amazing what can come from just numbers?

The CPU stores the numbers it acts upon in small memory units called **registers**. The CPU is able to read numbers into registers from the computer's main memory, known as **Random Access Memory** (**RAM**). It's also able to write the number stored in a register back into RAM. This allows the CPU to work with large amounts of data that wouldn't all fit in the bank of registers.

Here is a diagram of how this works:

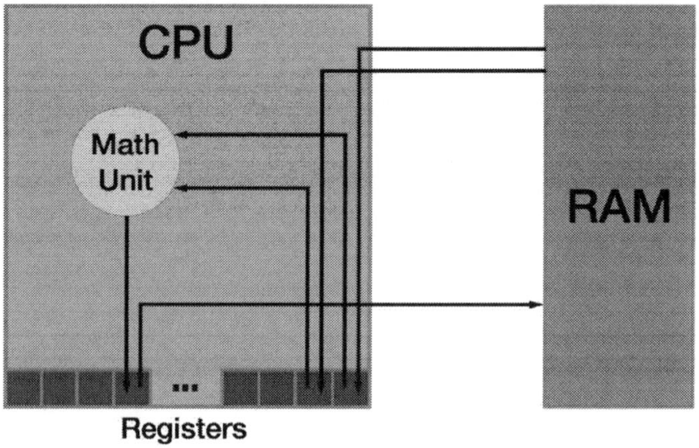

As the CPU pulls values from RAM into its registers, it uses those values in its math unit and stores the results back in another register.

Each time the CPU makes an addition, a subtraction, a read from RAM or a write to RAM, it's executing a single **instruction**. Each computer program is usually made up of thousands to millions of instructions. A complex computer program such as your operating system, macOS (yes, that's a computer program too!), may have many millions of instructions in total.

It's entirely possible to write individual instructions to tell a computer what to do, but for all but the simplest programs, it would be immensely time-consuming and tedious. This is because most computer programs aim to do much more than simple math — computer programs let you surf the internet, manipulate images, and allow you to chat with your friends.

Instead of writing individual instructions, you write **code** in a specific **programming language**, which in your case will be Swift. This code is put through a computer program called a **compiler**, which converts the code into instructions the CPU knows how to execute. Each line of code you write will turn into many instructions — some lines could end up being tens of instructions!

Representing numbers

As you know by now, numbers are a computer's bread and butter, the fundamental basis of everything it does. Whatever information you send to the compiler will eventually become a number. For example, each character within a block of text is represented by a number. You'll learn more about this in Chapter 3, which delves into types including **strings**, the computer term for a block of text.

Images are no exception. In a computer, each image is also represented by a series of numbers. An image is split into many thousands, or even millions, of picture elements called **pixels**, where each pixel is a solid color. If you look closely at your computer screen, you may be able to make out these blocks. That is unless you have a particularly high-resolution display where the pixels are incredibly small! Each of these solid color pixels is usually represented by three numbers: one for the amount of red, one for the amount of green and one for the amount of blue. For example, an entirely red pixel would be 100% red, 0% green and 0% blue.

The numbers the CPU works with are notably different from those you are used to. When you deal with numbers in day-to-day life, you work with them in **base 10**, otherwise known as the **decimal** system. Having used this numerical system for so long, you intuitively understand how it works. So that you can you can appreciate the CPU's point of view, consider how base 10 works.

The decimal or base 10 number **423** contains **three units**, **two tens** and **four hundreds**:

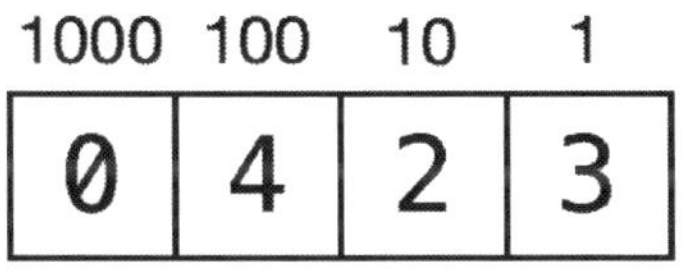

In the base 10 system, each digit of a number can have a value of 0, 1, 2, 3, 4, 5, 6, 7, 8 or 9, giving a total of 10 possible values for each digit. Yep, that's why it's called base 10!

But the true value of each digit depends on its position within the number. Moving from right to left, each digit gets multiplied by an increasing power of 10. So the multiplier for the far-right position is 10 to the power of 0, which is 1. Moving to the left, the next multiplier is 10 to the power of 1, which is 10. Moving again to the left, the next multiplier is 10 to the power of 2, which is 100. And so on.

This means each digit has a value ten times that of the digit to its right. The number **423** is equal to the following:

```
(0 * 1000) + (4 * 100) + (2 * 10) + (3 * 1) = 423
```

Binary numbers

Because you've been trained to operate in base 10, you don't have to think about how to read most numbers — it feels quite natural. But to a computer, base 10 is way too complicated! Computers are simple-minded, remember? They like to work with base 2.

Base 2 is often called **binary**, which you've likely heard of before. It follows that base 2 has only two options for each digit: 0 or 1.

Almost all modern computers use binary because at the physical level, it's easiest to handle only two options for each digit. In digital electronic circuitry, which is mostly what comprises a computer, the presence of an electrical voltage is 1 and the absence is 0 — that's base 2!

> **Note:** There have been computers both real and imagined that use the ternary numeral system, which has three possible values instead of two. Computer scientists, engineers and dedicated hackers continue to explore the possibilities of a base-3 computer. See https://en.wikipedia.org/wiki/Ternary_computer and http://hackaday.com/tag/ternary-computer/.

Here's a representation of the base 2 number 1101:

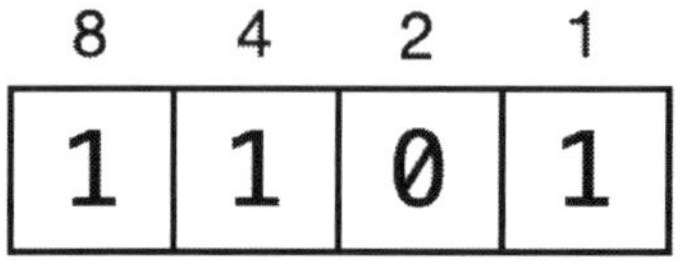

In the base 10 number system, the place values increase by a factor of 10: 1, 10, 100, 1000, etc. In base 2, they increase by a factor of 2: 1, 2, 4, 8, 16, etc. The general rule is to multiply each digit by an increasing power of the base number — in this case, powers of 2 — moving from right to left.

So the far-right digit represents (1 * 2^0), which is (1 * 1), which is 1. The next digit to the left represents (0 * 2^1), which is (0 * 2), which is 0. In the illustration above, you can see the powers of 2 on top of the blocks.

Put another way, every power of 2 either is (1) or isn't (0) present as a component of a binary number. The decimal version of a binary number is the sum of all the powers of 2 that make up that number. So the binary number 1101 is equal to:

```
(1 * 8) + (1 * 4) + (0 * 2) + (1 * 1) = 13
```

And if you wanted to convert the base 10 number 423 into binary, you would simply need to break down 423 into its component powers of 2. You would wind up with the following:

```
(1 * 256) + (1 * 128) + (0 * 64) + (1 * 32) + (0 * 16) + (0 * 8)
+ (1 * 4) + (1 * 2) + (1 * 1) = 423
```

As you can see by scanning the binary digits in the above equation, the resulting binary number is 110100111. You can prove to yourself that this is equal to 423 by doing the math!

The computer term given to each digit of a binary number is a **bit** (a contraction of "binary digit"). Eight bits make up a **byte**. Four bits is called a **nibble**, a play on words that shows even old-school computer scientists had a sense of humor.

A computer's limited memory means it can normally deal with numbers up to a certain length. Each register, for example, is usually 32 or 64 bits in length, which is why we speak of 32-bit and 64-bit CPUs.

Therefore, a 32-bit CPU can handle a maximum base-number of 4,294,967,295, which is the base 2 number `11111111111111111111111111111111`. That is 32 ones—count them!

It's possible for a computer to handle numbers that are larger than the CPU maximum, but the calculations have to be split up and managed in a special and longer way, much like the long multiplication you performed in school.

Hexadecimal numbers

As you can imagine, working with binary numbers can become quite tedious, because it can take a long time to write or type them. For this reason, in computer programming, we often use another number format known as **hexadecimal**, or **hex** for short. This is **base 16**.

Of course, there aren't 16 distinct numbers to use for digits; there are only 10. To supplement these, we use the first six letters, **a** through **f**.

They are equivalent to decimal numbers like so:

- `a` = `10`
- `b` = `11`
- `c` = `12`
- `d` = `13`
- `e` = `14`
- `f` = `15`

Here's a base 16 example using the same format as before:

4096	256	16	1
c	0	d	e

Notice first that you can make hexadecimal numbers look like words. That means you can have a little bit of fun. :]

Now the values of each digit refer to powers of 16. In the same way as before, you can convert this number to decimal like so:

```
(12 * 4096) + (0 * 256) + (13 * 16) + (14 * 1) = 49374
```

You translate the letters to their decimal equivalents and then perform the usual calculations.

But why bother with this?

Hexadecimal is important because each hexadecimal digit can represent precisely four binary digits. The binary number `1111` is equivalent to hexadecimal `f`. It follows that you can simply concatenate the binary digits representing each hexadecimal digit, creating a hexadecimal number that is shorter than its binary or decimal equivalents.

For example, consider the number `c0de` from above:

```
c = 1100
0 = 0000
d = 1101
e = 1110

c0de = 1100 0000 1101 1110
```

This turns out to be rather helpful, given how computers use long 32-bit or 64-bit binary numbers. Recall that the longest 32-bit number in decimal is 4,294,967,295. In hexadecimal, it is `ffffffff`. That's much more compact and clear.

How code works

Computers have a lot of constraints, and by themselves, they can only do a small number of things. The power that the computer programmer adds, through coding, is putting these small things together, in the right order, to produce something much bigger.

Coding is much like writing a recipe. You assemble ingredients (the data) and give the computer a step-by-step recipe for how to use them.

Here's an example:

```
Step 1. Load photo from hard drive.
Step 2. Resize photo to 400 pixels wide by 300 pixels high.
Step 3. Apply sepia filter to photo.
Step 4. Print photo.
```

This is what's known as **pseudo-code**. It isn't written in a valid computer programming language, but it represents the **algorithm** that you want to use. In this case, the algorithm takes a photo, resizes it, applies a filter and then prints it. It's a relatively straightforward algorithm, but it's an algorithm nonetheless!

Swift code is just like this: a step-by-step list of instructions for the computer. These instructions will get more complex as you read through this book, but the principle is the same: You are simply telling the computer what to do, one step at a time.

Each programming language is a high-level, pre-defined way of expressing these steps. The compiler knows how to interpret the code you write and convert it into instructions that the CPU can execute.

There are many different programming languages, each with its own advantages and disadvantages. Swift is an extremely modern language. It incorporates the strengths of many other languages while ironing out some of their weaknesses. In years to come, programmers will look back on Swift as being old and crusty, too. But for now, it's an extremely exciting language because it is quickly evolving.

This has been a brief tour of computer hardware, number representation and code, and how they all work together to create a modern program. That was a lot to cover in one section! Now it's time to learn about the tools you'll use to write in Swift as you follow along with this book.

Playgrounds

The set of tools you use to write software is often referred to as the **toolchain**. The part of the toolchain into which you write your code is known as the **Integrated Development Environment** (**IDE**). The most commonly used IDE for Swift is called Xcode, and that's what you'll be using.

Xcode includes a handy feature called a **playground**, which allows you to quickly write and test code without needing to build a complete app. You'll use playgrounds throughout the book to practice coding, so it's important to understand how they work. That's what you'll learn during the rest of this chapter.

Creating a playground

When you open Xcode, it will greet you with the following welcome screen:

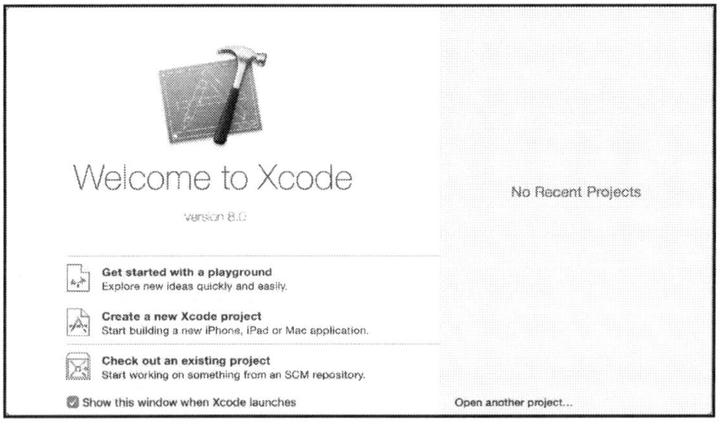

If you don't see this screen, it's most likely because the "Show this window when Xcode launches" option was unchecked. You can also open the screen by pressing **Command-Shift-1** or clicking **Window\Welcome to Xcode** from the menu bar.

From the welcome screen, you can jump quickly into a playground by clicking on **Get started with a playground**. Click on that now and Xcode will present you with a choice of templates.

The platform you choose simply defines which version of the template Xcode will use to create the playground. Currently, your options are **iOS**, **macOS** or **tvOS**. Each platform comes with its own environment set up and ready for you to begin playing around with code. For the purposes of this book, choose whichever platform you wish. You won't be writing any platform-specific code; instead, you'll be learning the core principles of the Swift language.

Select the **Blank** template and click **Next**. Xcode will now ask you to name the playground and select a location to save it. The name is merely cosmetic and for your own use; when you create your playgrounds, feel free to choose names that will help you remember what they're about. For example, while you're working through Chapter 2, you may want to name your playground **Chapter2**.

Click **Create** to create and save the playground. Xcode then presents you with the playground, like so:

Even blank playgrounds don't start entirely empty but have some basic starter code to get you going. Don't worry — you'll soon learn what this code means.

Playgrounds overview

At first glance, a playground may look like a rather fancy text editor. Well, here's some news for you: It is essentially just that!

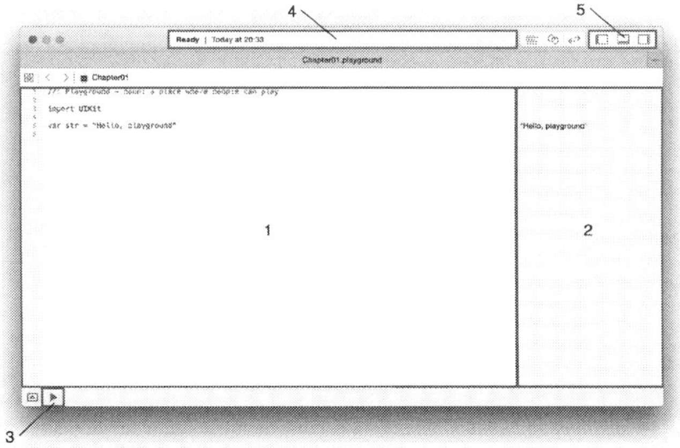

The previous screenshot highlights the first and most important things to know about:

1. **Source editor**: This is the area in which you'll write your Swift code. It's much like a text editor such as Notepad or TextEdit. You'll notice the use of what's known as a monospaced font, meaning all characters are the same width. This makes the code much easier to read and format.
2. **Results sidebar**: This area shows the results of your code. You'll learn more about how code is executed as you read through the book. The results sidebar will be the main place you'll look to confirm your code is working as expected.
3. **Execution control**: Playgrounds execute automatically by default, meaning you can write code and immediately see the output. This control allows you to execute the playground again. Holding down the button allows you to switch between automatic execution and manual execution modes.
4. **Activity viewer**: This shows the status of the playground. In the screenshot, it shows that the playground has finished executing and is ready to handle more code in the source editor. When the playground is executing, this viewer will indicate this with a spinner.
5. **Panel controls**: These toggle switches show and hide three panels, one that appears on the left, one on the bottom and one on the right. The panels each display extra information that you may need to access from time to time. You'll usually keep them hidden, as they are in the screenshot. You'll learn more about each of these panels as you move through the book.

Playgrounds execute the code in the source editor from top to bottom. Every time you change the code, the playground will re-execute everything. You can also force a re-execution by clicking **Editor\Execute Playground**. Alternatively, you can use the execution control.

You can turn on line numbers on the left side of the source editor by clicking **Xcode\Preferences...\Text Editing\Line Numbers**. Line numbers can be very useful when you want to refer to parts of your code.

Once the playground execution is finished, Xcode updates the results sidebar to show the results of the corresponding line in the source editor. You'll see how to interpret the results of your code as you work through the examples in this book.

Getting started with Swift

Now that you know how computers work and know what this "playground" thing is, it's time to start writing some Swift!

You may wish to follow along with your own playground. Simply create one and type in the code as you go!

First up is something that helps you organize your code. Read on!

Code comments

The Swift compiler generates executable code from your source code. To accomplish this, it uses a detailed set of rules you will learn about in this book. Sometimes these details can obscure the big picture of *why* you wrote your code a certain way or even what problem you are solving. To prevent this, it's good to document what you wrote so that the next human who passes by will be able to make sense of your work. That next human, after all, may be a future you.

Swift, like most other programming languages, allows you to document your code through the use of what are called **comments**. These allow you to write any text directly along side your code which is ignored by the compiler.

The first way to write a comment is like so:

```
// This is a comment. It is not executed.
```

This is a **single line comment**.

You could stack these up like so to allow you to write paragraphs:

```
// This is also a comment.
// Over multiple lines.
```

However, there is a better way to write comments which span multiple lines. Like so:

```
/* This is also a comment.
   Over many..
   many...
   many lines. */
```

This is a **multi-line comment**. The start is denoted by `/*` and the end is denoted by `*/`. Simple!

Swift also allows you to nest comments, like so:

```
/* This is a comment.

 /* And inside it
 is
 another comment.
 */
```

```
Back to the first.
*/
```

This might not seem particularly interesting, but it may be if you have seen other programming languages. Many do not allow you to nest comments like this as when it sees the first `*/` it thinks you are closing the first comment.

You should use code comments where necessary to document your code, explain your reasoning, or simply to leave jokes for your colleagues. :]

Printing out

It's also useful to see the results of what your code is doing. In Swift, you can achieve this through the use of the `print` command.

`print` will output whatever you want to the **debug area** (sometimes referred to as the console).

For example, consider the following code:

```
print("Hello, Swift Apprentice reader!")
```

This will output a nice message to the debug area, like so:

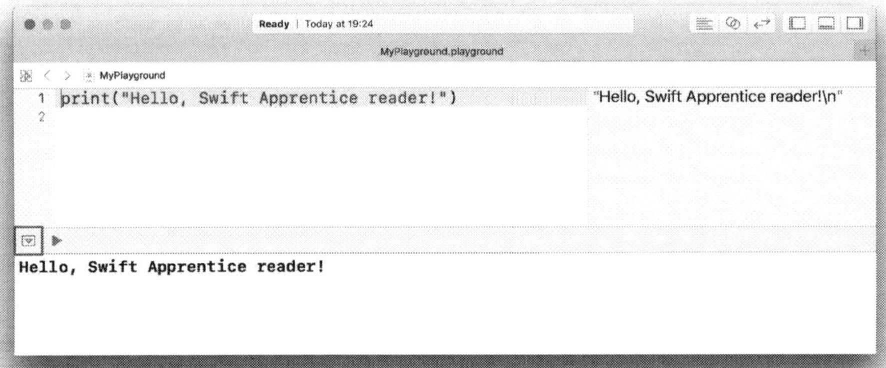

You can hide or show the debug area using the button highlighted with the red box in the picture above. You can also click **View\Debug Area\Show Debug Area** to do the same thing.

Arithmetic operations

When you take one or more pieces of data and turn them into another piece of data, this is known as an **operation**.

The simplest way to understand operations is to think about arithmetic. The addition operation takes two numbers and converts them into the sum of the two numbers. The subtraction operation takes two numbers and converts them into the difference of the two numbers.

You'll find simple arithmetic all over your apps; from tallying the number of "likes" on a post, to calculating the correct size and position of a button or a window, numbers are indeed everywhere!

In this section, you'll learn about the various arithmetic operations that Swift has to offer by considering how they apply to numbers. In later chapters, you see operations for types other than numbers.

Simple operations

All operations in Swift use a symbol known as the **operator** to denote the type of operation they perform. Consider the four arithmetic operations you learned in your early school days: addition, subtraction, multiplication and division. For these simple operations, Swift uses the following operators:

- Add: +
- Subtract: -
- Multiply: *
- Divide: /

These operators are used like so:

```
2 + 6
10 - 2
2 * 4
24 / 3
```

Each of these lines is what is known as an **expression**. An expression has a value. In these cases, all four expressions have the same value: 8. You write the code to perform these arithmetic operations much as you would write it if you were using pen and paper.

In your playground, you can see the values of these expressions in the right-hand bar, known as the **results sidebar**.

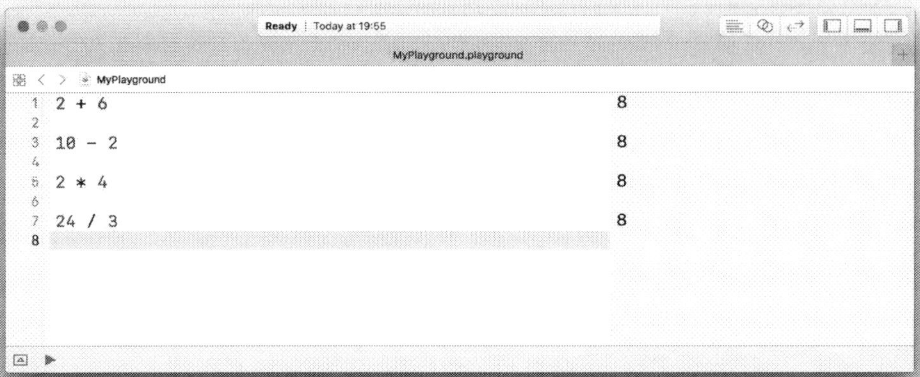

If you want, you can remove the whitespace surrounding the operator:

```
2+6
```

Removing the whitespace is an all or nothing, you can't mix styles. For example:

```
2+6   // OK
2 + 6 // OK
2 +6  // ERROR
2+ 6  // ERROR
```

It's often easier to read expressions if you have white space on either side of the operator.

Decimal numbers

All of the operations above have used whole numbers, more formally known as **integers**. However, as you will know, not every number is whole.

As an example, consider the following:

```
22 / 7
```

This, you may be surprised to know, results in the number 3. This is because if you only use integers in your expression, Swift makes the result an integer also. In this case, the result is rounded down to the next integer.

You can tell Swift to use decimal numbers by changing it to the following:

```
22.0 / 7.0
```

This time, the result is 3.142857142857143 as expected.

The remainder operation

The four operations you've seen so far are easy to understand because you've been doing them for most of your life. Swift also has more complex operations you can use, all of them standard mathematical operations, just less common ones. Let's turn to them now.

The first of these is the **remainder** operation, also called the modulo operation. In division, the denominator goes into the numerator a whole number of times, plus a remainder. This remainder is exactly what the remainder operation gives. For example, 10 modulo 3 equals 1, because 3 goes into 10 three times, with a remainder of 1.

In Swift, the remainder operator is the `%` symbol, and you use it like so:

```
28 % 10
```

In this case, the result equals `8`, because 10 goes into 28 twice with a remainder of 8. If you want to compute the same thing using decimal numbers you do it like so:

```
(28.0).truncatingRemainder(dividingBy: 10.0)
```

This computes divides 28 by 10 and then **truncates** the result, chopping off any extra decimals and returns the remainder of that. The result is identical to `%` when there are no decimals.

Shift operations

The **shift left** and **shift right** operations take the binary form of a decimal number and shift the digits left or right, respectively. Then they return the decimal form of the new binary number.

For example, the decimal number 14 in binary, padded to 8 digits, is `00001110`. Shifting this left by two places results in `00111000`, which is 56 in decimal.

Here's an illustration of what happens during this shift operation:

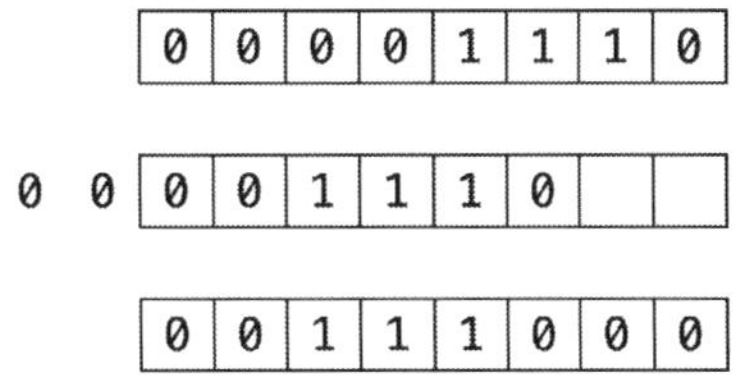

The digits that come in to fill the empty spots on the right become `0`. The digits that fall off the end on the left are lost.

Shifting right is the same, but the digits move to the right.

The operators for these two operations are as follows:

- Shift left: <<
- Shift right: >>

These are the first operators you've seen that contain more than one character. Operators can contain any number of characters, in fact.

Here's an example that uses both of these operators:

```
1 << 3

32 >> 2
```

Both of these values equal the number 8.

One reason for using shifts is to make multiplying or dividing by powers of two easy. Notice that shifting left by one is the same as multiplying by two, shifting left by two is the same as multiplying by four, and so on. Likewise, shifting right by one is the same as dividing by two, shifting right by two is the same as dividing by four, and so on.

In the old days, code often made use of this trick because shifting bits is much simpler for a CPU to do than complex multiplication and division arithmetic. Therefore the code was quicker if it used shifting. However these days, CPUs are much faster and compilers can even convert multiplication and division by powers of two into shifts for you. So you'll see shifting only for binary twiddling, which you probably won't see unless you become an embedded systems programmer!

Order of operations

Of course, it's likely that when you calculate a value, you'll want to use multiple operators. Here's an example of how to do this in Swift:

```
((8000 / (5 * 10)) - 32) >> (29 % 5)
```

Note the use of parentheses, which in Swift serve two purposes: to make it clear to anyone reading the code — including yourself — what you meant, and to disambiguate. For example, consider the following:

```
350 / 5 + 2
```

Does this equal 72 (350 divided by 5, plus 2) or 50 (350 divided by 7)? Those of you who paid attention in school will be screaming "72!" And you would be right!

Swift uses the same reasoning and achieves this through what's known as **operator precedence**. The division operator (/) has a higher precedence than the addition operator (+), so in this example, the code executes the division operation first.

If you wanted Swift to do the addition first — that is, to return 50 — then you could use parentheses like so:

```
350 / (5 + 2)
```

The precedence rules follow the same that you learned in math at school. Multiply and divide have the same precedence, higher than add and subtract which also have the same precedence.

Math functions

Swift also has a vast range of math functions for you to use when necessary. You never know when you need to pull out some trigonometry, especially when you're a pro at Swift and writing those complex games!

> **Note:** Not all of these functions are part of Swift. Some are provided by the operating system. Don't remove the import statement that comes as part of the playground template or Xcode will tell you it can't find these functions.

For example, consider the following:

```
sin(45 * Double.pi / 180)
// 0.7071067811865475

cos(135 * Double.pi / 180)
// -0.7071067811865475
```

These compute the sine and cosine respectively. Notice how both make use of `Double.pi` which is a constant Swift provides us, ready-made with pi to as much precision as is possible by the computer. Neat!

Then there's this:

```
(2.0).squareRoot()
// 1.414213562373095
```

This computes the square root of 2. Did you know that sin(45°) equals 1 over the square root of 2?

Not to mention these would be a shame:

```
max(5, 10)
// 10

min(-5, -10)
// -10
```

These compute the maximum and minimum of two numbers respectively.

If you're particularly adventurous you can even combine these functions like so:

```
max((2.0).squareRoot(), Double.pi / 2)
// 1.570796326794897
```

Naming data

At its simplest, computer programming is all about manipulating data. Remember, everything you see on your screen can be reduced to numbers that you send to the CPU. Sometimes you yourself represent and work with this data as various types of numbers, but other times the data comes in more complex forms such as text, images and collections.

In your Swift code, you can give each piece of data a name you can use to refer to it later. The name carries with it an associated **type** that denotes what sort of data the name refers to, such as text, numbers, or a date.

You'll learn about some of the basic types in this chapter, and you'll encounter many other types throughout the rest of this book.

Constants

Take a look at this:

```
let number: Int = 10
```

This declares a constant called `number` which is of type `Int`. Then it sets the value of the constant to the number `10`.

> **Note:** Thinking back to operators, here's another one. The equals sign, =, is known as the **assignment operator**.

The type `Int` can store integers. The way you store decimal numbers is like so:

```
let pi: Double = 3.14159
```

This is similar to the `Int` constant, except the name and the type are different. This time, the constant is a `Double`, a type that can store decimals with high precision.

There's also a type called `Float`, short for floating point, that stores decimals with lower precision than `Double`. In fact, `Double` has about double the precision of `Float`, which is why it's called `Double` in the first place. A `Float` takes up less memory than a `Double` but generally, memory use for numbers isn't a huge issue and you'll see `Double` used in most places.

Once you've declared a constant, you can't change its data. For example, consider the following code:

```
number = 0
```

This code produces an error:

```
Cannot assign to value: 'number' is a 'let' constant
```

In Xcode, you would see the error represented this way:

Constants are useful for values that aren't going to change. For example, if you were modeling an airplane and needed to keep track of the total number of seats available, you could use a constant.

You might even use a constant for something like a person's age. Even though their age will change as their birthday comes, you might only be concerned with their age at this particular instant.

Variables

Often you want to change the data behind a name. For example, if you were keeping track of your bank account balance with deposits and withdrawals, you might use a variable rather than a constant.

If your program's data never changed, then it would be a rather boring program! But as you've seen, it's not possible to change the data behind a constant.

When you know you'll need to change some data, you should use a variable to represent that data instead of a constant. You declare a variable in a similar way, like so:

```
var variableNumber: Int = 42
```

Only the first part of the statement is different: You declare constants using `let`, whereas you declare variables using `var`.

Once you've declared a variable, you're free to change it to whatever you wish, as long as the type remains the same. For example, to change the variable declared above, you could do this:

```
variableNumber = 0
variableNumber = 1_000_000
```

To change a variable, you simply assign it a new value.

> **Note:** In Swift, you can optionally use underscores to make larger numbers more human-readable. The quantity and placement of the underscores is up to you.

This is a good time to take a closer look at the results sidebar of the playground. When you type the code above into a playground, you'll see that the results sidebar on the right shows the current value of `variableNumber` at each line:

`var variableNumber: Int = 42`	42
`variableNumber = 0`	0
`variableNumber = 1_000_000`	1,000,000

The results sidebar will show a relevant result for each line if one exists. In the case of a variable or constant, the result will be the new value, whether you've just declared a constant, or declared or reassigned a variable.

Using meaningful names

Always try to choose meaningful names for your variables and constants. Good names can acts as documentation and make your code easy to read.

A good name *specifically* describes the role of variable or constant. Here are some examples of good names:

- `personAge`
- `numberOfPeople`
- `gradePointAverage`

Often a bad name is simply not descriptive enough. Here are some examples of bad names:

- `a`
- `temp`
- `average`

The key is to ensure that you'll understand what the variable or constant refers to when you read it again later. Don't make the mistake of thinking you have an infallible memory! It's common in computer programming to look back at your own code as early as a day or two later and have forgotten what it does. Make it easier for yourself by giving your variables and constants intuitive, precise names.

Also, note how the names above are written. In Swift, it is common to **camel case** names. For variables and constants, follow these rules to properly case your names:

- Start with a lowercase letter.
- If the name is made up of multiple words, join them together and start every other word with an uppercase letter.
- If one of these words is an abbreviation, write the entire abbreviation in the same case (e.g.: `sourceURL` and `urlDescription`)

In Swift, you can even use the full range of Unicode characters. For example, you could declare a variable like so:

```
var 🐶💩: Int = -1
```

That might make you laugh, but use caution with special characters like these. They are harder to type and therefore may end up causing you more pain than amusement.

Special characters like these probably make more sense in *data* that you store rather than in Swift code; you'll learn more about Unicode in Chapter 9, "Strings."

Increment and decrement

A common operation that you will need is to be able to increment or decrement a variable. In Swift, this is achieved like so:

```
var counter: Int = 0

counter += 1
// counter = 1
```

```
counter -= 1
// counter = 0
```

The `counter` variable begins as `0`. The increment sets its value to `1`, and then the decrement sets its value back to `0`.

These operators are similar to the assignment operator (=), except they also perform an addition or subtraction. They take the current value of the variable, add or subtract the given value and assign the result to the variable.

In other words, the code above is shorthand for the following:

```
var counter: Int = 0
counter = counter + 1
counter = counter - 1
```

Similarly, the *= and /= operators do the equivalent for multiplication and division, respectively:

```
counter = 10

counter *= 3  // same as counter = counter * 3
// counter = 30

counter /= 2  // same as counter = counter / 2
// counter = 15
```

Mini-exercises

If you haven't been following along with the code in Xcode, now's the time to create a new playground and try some exercises to test yourself!

1. Declare a constant of type `Int` called `myAge` and set it to your age.
2. Declare a variable of type `Double` called `averageAge`. Initially, set it to your own age. Then, set it to the average of your age and my own age of `30`.
3. Create a constant called `testNumber` and initialize it with whatever integer you'd like. Next, create another constant called `evenOdd` and set it equal to `testNumber` modulo 2. Now change `testNumber` to various numbers. What do you notice about `evenOdd`?
4. Create a variable called `answer` and initialize it with the value `0`. Increment it by `1`. Add `10` to it. Multiply it by `10`. Then, shift it to the right by `3`. After all of these operations, what's the answer?

Key points

- Computers, at their most fundamental level, perform simple mathematics.
- A programming language allows you to write code, which the compiler converts into instructions that the CPU can execute.
- Computers operate on numbers in base 2 form, otherwise known as binary.
- The IDE you use to write Swift code is named Xcode.
- By providing immediate feedback about how code is executing, playgrounds allow you to write and test Swift code quickly and efficiently.
- Code comments are denoted by a line starting with `//` or multiple lines bookended with `/*` and `*/`.
- Code comments can be used to document your code.
- You can use `print` to write things to the debug area.
- The arithmetic operators are:

```
Add: +
Subtract: -
Multiply: *
Divide: /
Remainder: %
```

- Constants and variables give names to data.
- Once you've declared a constant, you can't change its data, but you can change a variable's data at any time.
- Always give variables and constants meaningful names to save yourself and your colleagues headaches later.
- Operators to perform arithmetic and then assign back to the variable:

```
Add and assign: +=
Subtract and assign: -=
Multiply and assign: *=
Divide and assign: /=
```

Where to go from here?

In this chapter, you've only dealt with only numbers, both integers and decimals. Of course, there's more to the world of code than that! In the next chapter, you're going to learn about more types such as strings, which allow you to store text.

Challenges

Before moving on, here are some challenges to test your knowledge of variables and constants. You can try the code in a playground to check your answers.

1. Declare a constant `exercises` with value 9 and a variable `exercisesSolved` with value 0. Increment this variable every time you solve an exercise (including this one).

2. Given the following code:

```
age = 16
print(age)
age = 30
print(age)
```

Declare `age` so that it compiles. Did you use `var` or `let`?

3. Consider the following code:

```
let a: Int = 46
let b: Int = 10
```

Work out what `answer` equals when you replace the final line of code above with each of these options:

```
// 1
let answer1: Int = (a * 100) + b
// 2
let answer2: Int = (a * 100) + (b * 100)
// 3
let answer3: Int = (a * 100) + (b / 10)
```

4. Add parentheses to the following calculation. The parentheses should show the order in which the operations are performed and should not alter the result of the calculation.

```
5 * 3 - 4 / 2 * 2
```

5. Declare two constants `a` and `b` of type `Double` and assign both a value. Calculate the average of `a` and `b` and store the result in a constant named `average`.

6. A temperature expressed in °C can be converted to °F by multiplying by 1.8 then incrementing by 32. In this challenge, do the reverse: convert a temperature from °F to °C. Declare a constant named `fahrenheit` of type `Double` and assign it a value. Calculate the corresponding temperature in °C and store the result in a constant named `celcius`.

7. Suppose the squares on a chessboard are numbered left to right, top to bottom, with 0 being the top-left square and 63 being the bottom-right square. Rows are numbered top to bottom, 0 to 7. Columns are numbered left to right, 0 to 7. Declare a constant `position` and assign it a value between 0 and 63. Calculate the corresponding row and column numbers and store the results in constants named `row` and `column`.

8. A circle is made up of 2π radians, corresponding with 360 degrees. Declare a constant `degrees` of type `Double` and assign it an initial value. Calculate the corresponding angle in radians and store the result in a constant named `radians`.

9. Declare four constants named `x1`, `y1`, `x2` and `y2` of type `Double`. These constants represent the 2-dimensional coordinates of two points. Calculate the distance between these two points and store the result in a constant named `distance`.

Chapter 2: Types & Operations

By Matt Galloway

Now that you know how to perform basic operations and manipulate data using operations, it's time to learn more about **types**. Formally, a **type** describes a set of values and the operations that can be performed on them.

In this chapter, you'll learn about handling different types, including strings which allow you to represent text. You'll learn about converting between types and you'll also be introduced to type inference which makes your life as a programmer a lot simpler.

Finally, you'll learn about tuples which allow you to make your own types made up of multiple values of any type.

Type conversion

Sometimes you'll have data in one format and need to convert it to another. The naïve way to attempt this would be like so:

```
var integer: Int = 100
var decimal: Double = 12.5
integer = decimal
```

Swift will complain if you try to do this and spit out an error on the third line:

```
Cannot assign value of type 'Double' to type 'Int'
```

Some programming languages aren't as strict and will perform conversions like this automatically. Experience shows this kind of automatic conversion is a source of software bugs and often hurts performance. Swift disallows you from assigning a value of one type to another and avoids these issues.

Remember, computers rely on us programmers to tell them what to do. In Swift, that includes being explicit about type conversions. If you want the conversion to happen, you have to say so!

Instead of simply assigning, you need to explicitly say that you want to convert the type. You do it like so:

```
integer = Int(decimal)
```

The assignment on the third line now tells Swift unequivocally that you want to convert from the original type, `Double`, to the new type, `Int`.

> **Note:** In this case, assigning the decimal value to the integer results in a loss of precision: The `integer` variable ends up with the value 12 instead of `12.5`. This is why it's important to be explicit. Swift wants to make sure you know what you're doing and that you may end up losing data by performing the type conversion.

Operators with mixed types

So far, you've only seen operators acting independently on integers or doubles. But what if you have an integer that you want to multiply by a double?

You might think you could do it like this:

```
let hourlyRate: Double = 19.5
let hoursWorked: Int = 10
let totalCost: Double = hourlyRate * hoursWorked
```

If you try that, you'll get an error on the final line:

```
Binary operator '*' cannot be applied to operands of type
'Double' and 'Int'
```

This is because in Swift, you can't apply the * operator to mixed types. This rule also applies to the other arithmetic operators. It may seem surprising at first, but Swift is being rather helpful.

Swift forces you to be explicit about what you mean when you want an `Int` multiplied by a `Double`, because the result can be only *one* type. Do you want the result to be an `Int`, converting the `Double` to an `Int` before performing the multiplication? Or do you

want the result to be a `Double`, converting the `Int` to a `Double` before performing the multiplication?

In this example, you want the result to be a `Double`. You don't want an `Int`, because in that case, Swift would convert the `hourlyRate` constant into an `Int` to perform the multiplication, rounding it down to 19 and losing the precision of the `Double`.

You need to tell Swift you want it to consider the `hoursWorked` constant to be a `Double`, like so:

```
let totalCost: Double = hourlyRate * Double(hoursWorked)
```

Now, each of the operands will be a `Double` when Swift multiplies them, so `totalCost` is a `Double` as well.

Type inference

Up to this point in this book, each time you've seen a variable or constant declared it's been accompanied by a type annotation. You may be asking yourself why you need to bother writing the `: Int` and `: Double`, since the right hand side of the assignment *is already* an `Int` or a `Double`. It's redundant, to be sure; your crazy-clever brain can see this without too much work.

It turns out the Swift compiler can deduce this as well. It doesn't need you to tell it the type all the time — it can figure it out on its own. This is done through a process called **type inference**. Not all programming languages have this, but Swift does, and it's a key component of Swift's power as a language.

So, you can simply drop the type in most places where you see one.

For example, consider the following constant declaration:

```
let typeInferredInt = 42
```

Sometimes it's useful to check the inferred type of a variable or constant. You can do this in a playground by holding down the **Option** key and clicking on the variable or constant's name. Xcode will display a popover like this:

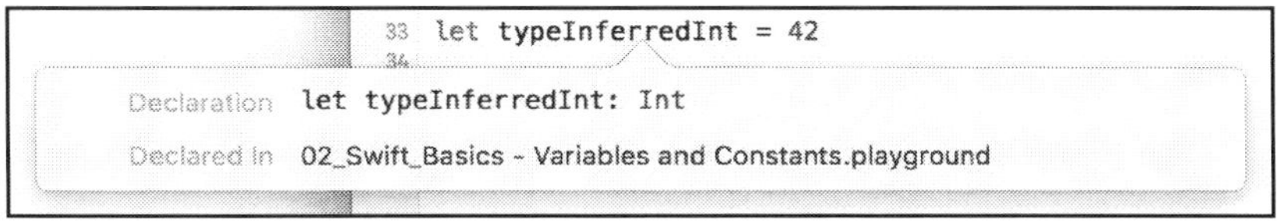

Xcode tells you the inferred type by giving you the declaration you would have had to use if there were no type inference. In this case, the type is `Int`.

It works for other types, too:

```
let typeInferredDouble = 3.14159
```

Option-clicking on this reveals the following:

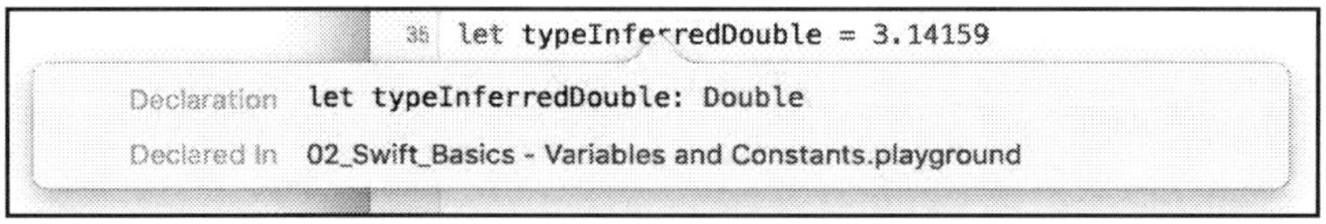

You can see from this that type inference isn't magic. Swift is simply doing what your brain does very easily. Programming languages that don't use type inference can often feel verbose, because you need to specify the often obvious type each time you declare a variable or constant.

> **Note:** In later chapters, you'll learn about more complex types where sometimes Swift can't infer the type. That's a pretty rare case though, and you'll see type inference used for most of the code examples in this book — except in cases where we want to highlight the type for you.

Sometimes you want to define a constant or variable and ensure it's a certain type, even though what you're assigning to it is a different type. You saw earlier how you can convert from one type to another. For example, consider the following:

```
let wantADouble = 3
```

Here, Swift infers the type of `wantADouble` as `Int`. But what if you wanted `Double` instead?

The first thing you could do is the following:

```
let actuallyDouble = Double(3)
```

This is like you saw before with type conversion.

Another option would be to not use type inference at all and do the following:

```
let actuallyDouble: Double = 3
```

There is a third option, like so:

```
let actuallyDouble = 3 as Double
```

This uses a new keyword you haven't seen before, `as`. It also performs a type conversion, and you will see this throughout the book.

> **Note:** Literal values like 3 don't have a type. It's only when using them in an expression or assigning them to a constant or variable that Swift infers a type for them.
>
> A literal number value that doesn't contain a decimal point can be used as an `Int` as well as a `Double`. This is why you're allowed to assign the value `3` to constant `actuallyDouble`.
>
> Literal number values that *do* contain a decimal point cannot be integers. This means we could have avoided this entire discussion had we started with
>
> ```
> let wantADouble = 3.0
> ```
>
> Sorry! :]

Mini-exercises

1. Create a constant called `age1` and set it equal to `42`. Create a constant called `age2` and set it equal to `21`. Check using Option-click that the type for both has been inferred correctly as `Int`.
2. Create a constant called `avg1` and set it equal to the average of `age1` and `age2` using the naïve operation `(age1 + age2) / 2`. Use Option-click to check the type and check the result of `avg1`. Why is it wrong?
3. Correct the mistake in the above exercise by converting `age1` and `age2` to type `Double` in the formula. Use Option-click to check the type and check the result of `avg1`. Why is it now correct?

Strings

Numbers are essential in programming, but they aren't the only type of data you need to work with in your apps. Text is also an extremely common data type, such as people's names, their addresses, or even the words of a book. All of these are examples of text that an app might need to handle.

Most computer programming languages store text in a data type called a **string**. This chapter introduces you to strings, first by giving you background on the concept of strings and then by showing you how to use them in Swift.

How computers represent strings

Computers think of strings as a collection of individual **characters**. In Chapter 1 of this book, you learned that numbers are the language of CPUs, and all code, in whatever programming language, can be reduced to raw numbers. Strings are no different!

That may sound very strange. How can characters be numbers? At its base, a computer needs to be able to translate a character into the computer's own language, and it does so by assigning each character a different number. This forms a two-way mapping from character to number that is called a **character set**.

When you press a character key on your keyboard, you are actually communicating the number of the character to the computer. Your word processor application converts that number into a picture of the character and finally, presents that picture to you.

Unicode

In isolation, a computer is free to choose whatever character set mapping it likes. If the computer wants the letter **a** to equal the number 10, then so be it. But when computers start talking to each other, they need to use a common character set. If two computers used different character sets, then when one computer transferred a string to the other, they would end up thinking the strings contained different characters.

There have been several standards over the years, but the most modern standard is **Unicode**. It defines the character set mapping that almost all computers use today.

> **Note:** You can read more about Unicode at its official website, http://unicode.org/.

As an example, consider the word **cafe**. The Unicode standard tells us that the letters of this word should be mapped to numbers like so:

c	a	f	e
99	97	102	101

The number associated with each character is called a **code point**. So in the example above, **c** uses code point 99, **a** uses code point 97, and so on.

Of course, Unicode is not just for the simple Latin characters used in English, such as **c**, **a**, **f** and **e**. It also lets you map characters from languages around the world. The word **cafe**, as you're probably aware, is derived from French, in which it's written as **café**.

Unicode maps these characters like so:

c	a	f	é
99	97	102	233

And here's an example using Chinese characters (this, according to Google translate, means "Computer Programming"):

电	脑	编	程
30005	33041	32534	31243

You've probably heard of emojis, which are small pictures you can use in your text. These pictures are, in fact, just normal characters and are also mapped by Unicode. For example:

💩	😀
128169	128512

This is only two characters. The code points for these are very large numbers, but each is still only a single code point. The computer considers these as no different than any other two characters.

> **Note:** The word "emoji" comes from Japanese, where "e" means picture and "moji" means character.

Strings in Swift

Swift, like any good programming language, can work directly with characters and strings. It does so through the data types `Character` and `String`, respectively. In this section, you'll learn about these data types and how to work with them.

Characters and strings

The `Character` data type can store a single character. For example:

```
let characterA: Character = "a"
```

This stores the character **a**. It can hold any character — even an emoji:

```
let characterDog: Character = "🐶"
```

But this data type is designed to hold only single characters. The `String` data type, on the other hand, stores multiple characters. For example:

```
let stringDog: String = "Dog"
```

It's as simple as that! The right-hand side of this expression is what's known as a **string literal**; it's the Swift syntax for representing a string.

Of course, type inference applies here as well. If you remove the type in the above declaration, then Swift does the right thing and makes the `stringDog` a `String` constant:

```
let stringDog = "Dog" // Inferred to be of type String
```

> **Note:** There's no such thing as a character literal in Swift. A character is simply a string of length one. However, Swift infers the type of any string literal to be `String`, so if you want a `Character` instead, you must make the type explicit.

Concatenation

You can do much more than create simple strings. Sometimes you need to manipulate a string, and one common way to do so is to combine it with another string.

In Swift, you do this in a rather simple way: by using the addition operator. Just as you can add numbers, you can add strings:

```
var message = "Hello" + " my name is "
let name = "Matt"
message += name // "Hello my name is Matt"
```

You need to declare `message` as a variable rather than a constant because you want to modify it. You can add string literals together, as in the first line, and you can add string variables or constants together, as in the last line.

It's also possible to add characters to a string. However, Swift's strictness with types means you have to be explicit when doing so, just as you have to be when you work with numbers if one is an `Int` and the other is a `Double`.

To add a character to a string, you do this:

```
let exclamationMark: Character = "!"
message += String(exclamationMark) // "Hello my name is Matt!"
```

With this code, you explicitly convert the `Character` to a `String` before you add it to `message`.

Interpolation

You can also build up a string by using **interpolation**, which is a special Swift syntax that lets you build a string in a way that's easy to read:

```
message = "Hello my name is \(name)!" // "Hello my name is
Matt!"
```

As I'm sure you'll agree, this is much more readable than the example from the previous section. It's an extension of the string literal syntax, whereby you replace certain parts of the string with other values. You enclose the value you want to insert in parentheses preceded by a backslash.

This syntax works in the same way to build a string from other data types, such as numbers:

```
let oneThird = 1.0 / 3.0
let oneThirdLongString = "One third is \(oneThird) as a
decimal."
```

Here, you use a `Double` in the interpolation. At the end of this code, your `oneThirdLongString` constant will contain the following:

```
One third is 0.3333333333333333 as a decimal.
```

Of course, it would actually take infinite characters to represent one third as a decimal, because it's a repeating decimal. String interpolation with a `Double` gives you no way to control the precision of the resulting string.

This is an unfortunate consequence of using string interpolation: It's simple to use, but offers no ability to customize the output.

Multi-line strings

Swift has a neat way to express strings that contain multiple lines. This can be rather useful when you need to put a very long string in your code.

You do it like so:

```
let bigString = """
  You can have a string
  that contains multiple
  lines
  by
  doing this.
  """
print(bigString)
```

The three double-quotes signify that this is a multi-line string. Handily, the first and final new lines do not become part of the string. This makes it more flexible as you don't have to have the three double-quotes on the same line as the string.

In the case above, it will print the following:

```
You can have a string
that contains multiple
lines
by
doing this.
```

Notice that the two-space margin in the multiline string literal is stripped out of the result. Swift looks at number of leading spaces on the final three double-quotes line. Using this as a baseline, Swift requires that all lines above it have at least that much space so it can remove it from each line. This lets you format your code with pretty indentation without effecting the output.

Mini-exercises

1. Create a string constant called `firstName` and initialize it to your first name. Also create a string constant called `lastName` and initialize it to your last name.

2. Create a string constant called `fullName` by adding the `firstName` and `lastName` constants together, separated by a space.

3. Using interpolation, create a string constant called `myDetails` that uses the `fullName` constant to create a string introducing yourself. For example, my string would read: `"Hello, my name is Matt Galloway."`.

Tuples

Sometimes data comes in pairs or triplets. An example of this is a pair of (x, y) coordinates on a 2D grid. Similarly, a set of coordinates on a 3D grid is comprised of an x-value, a y-value and a z-value. In Swift, you can represent such related data in a very simple way through the use of a *tuple*.

A tuple is a type that represents data composed of more than one value of any type. You can have as many values in your tuple as you like. For example, you can define a pair of 2D coordinates where each axis value is an integer, like so:

```
let coordinates: (Int, Int) = (2, 3)
```

The type of `coordinates` is `(Int, Int)`. The types of the values within the tuple, in this case `Int`, are separated by commas and surrounded by parentheses. The code for creating the tuple is much the same, with each value separated by commas and surrounded by parentheses.

Type inference can infer tuple types too:

```
let coordinates = (2, 3)
```

You could similarly create a tuple of `Double` values, like so:

```
let coordinatesDoubles = (2.1, 3.5)
// Inferred to be of type (Double, Double)
```

Or you could mix and match the types comprising the tuple, like so:

```
let coordinatesMixed = (2.1, 3)
// Inferred to be of type (Double, Int)
```

And here's how to access the data inside a tuple:

```
let x1 = coordinates.0
let y1 = coordinates.1
```

You can reference each item in the tuple by its position in the tuple, starting with zero. So in this example, `x1` will equal `2` and `y1` will equal `3`.

> **Note:** Starting with zero is a common practice in computer programming and is called **zero indexing**. You'll see this again in Chapter 7, "Arrays, Dictionaries, Sets".

In the previous example, it may not be immediately obvious that the first value, at index `0`, is the x-coordinate and the second value, at index `1`, is the y-coordinate. This is another demonstration of why it's important to *always* name your variables in a way that avoids confusion.

Fortunately, Swift allows you to name the individual parts of a tuple, and you can be explicit about what each part represents. For example:

```
let coordinatesNamed = (x: 2, y: 3)
// Inferred to be of type (x: Int, y: Int)
```

Here, the code annotates the values of `coordinatesNamed` to contain a label for each part of the tuple.

Then, when you need to acccss each part of the tuple, you can access it by its name:

```
let x2 = coordinatesNamed.x
let y2 = coordinatesNamed.y
```

This is much clearer and easier to understand. More often than not, it's helpful to name the components of your tuples.

If you want to access multiple parts of the tuple at the same time, as in the examples above, you can also use a shorthand syntax to make it easier:

```
let coordinates3D = (x: 2, y: 3, z: 1)
let (x3, y3, z3) = coordinates3D
```

This declares three new constants, `x3`, `y3` and `z3`, and assigns each part of the tuple to them in turn. The code is equivalent to the following:

```
let coordinates3D = (x: 2, y: 3, z: 1)
let x3 = coordinates3D.x
let y3 = coordinates3D.y
let z3 = coordinates3D.z
```

If you want to ignore a certain element of the tuple, you can replace the corresponding part of the declaration with an underscore. For example, if you were performing a 2D calculation and wanted to ignore the z-coordinate of `coordinates3D`, then you'd write the following:

```
let (x4, y4, _) = coordinates3D
```

This line of code only declares `x4` and `y4`. The _ is special and simply means you're ignoring this part for now.

> **Note:** You'll find that you can use the underscore (also called the wildcard operator) throughout Swift to ignore a value.

Mini-exercises

1. Declare a constant tuple that contains three `Int` values followed by a `Double`. Use this to represent a date (month, day, year) followed by an average temperature for that date.
2. Change the tuple to name the constituent components. Give them names related to the data that they contain: `month`, `day`, `year` and `averageTemperature`.
3. In one line, read the day and average temperature values into two constants. You'll need to employ the underscore to ignore the month and year.
4. Up until now, you've only seen constant tuples. But you can create variable tuples, too. Change the tuple you created in the exercises above to a variable by using `var` instead of `let`. Now change the average temperature to a new value.

A whole lot of number types

You've been using `Int` to represent whole numbers. An `Int` is represented with 64 bits on most modern hardware and with 32 bits on older, or more resource constrained systems. Swift provides many more number types that use different amounts of storage. For whole numbers, you can use the explicit **signed** types `Int8`, `Int16`, `Int32`, `Int64`. These types consume 1, 2, 4, and 8 bytes of storage respectively. Each of these types use 1 bit to represent the sign.

If you are only dealing with non-negative values there are a set of explicit **unsigned** types that you can use. These include `UInt8`, `UInt16`, `UInt32` and `UInt64`. While you cannot represent negative values with these, the extra 1 bit lets you represent values that are twice as big as their **signed** counterparts.

Here is a summary of the different integer types and their storage size in bytes. Most of the time you will just want to use an `Int`. These become useful if your code is interacting with another piece of software that uses one of these more exact sizes or if you need to optimize for storage size.

Type	Minimum value	Maximum value	Storage size
Int8	-128	127	1
UInt8	0	255	1
Int16	-32768	32767	2
UInt16	0	65535	2
Int32	-2147483648	2147483647	4
UInt32	0	4294967295	4
Int64	-9223372036854775808	9223372036854775807	8
UInt64	0	18446744073709551615	8

You've been using `Double` to represent fractional numbers. Swift offers a `Float` type which has less range and precision than `Double` but requires half as much storage. Modern hardware has been optimized for `Double` so it is the one that you should reach for unless you have good reason not to.

Type	Minimum value	Maximum value	Precision	Storage size
Float	1.175494E-38	3.402823E+38	6 digits	4
Double	2.225073e-308	1.797693E+308	15 digits	8

Most of the time you will just use `Int` and `Double` to represent numbers but every once in a while you might encounter the other types.

For example, suppose you need to add together an `Int16` with a `UInt8` and an `Int32`. You can do that like so:

```
let a: Int16 = 12
let b: UInt8 = 255
let c: Int32 = -100000

let answer = Int(a) + Int(b) + Int(c)  // answer is an Int
```

A peek behind the curtains: Protocols

Even though there are a dozen different numeric types, they are pretty easy to understand and use. This is because they all roughly support the same operations. In other words, once you know how to use an `Int`, using any one of the flavors is very straight-forward.

One of the truly great features of Swift is that it formalizes the idea of type commonality using what are known as **protocols**. By learning a protocol, you instantly understand how an entire family of types that use that protocol work.

In the case of integers, the functionality can be diagrammed like so:

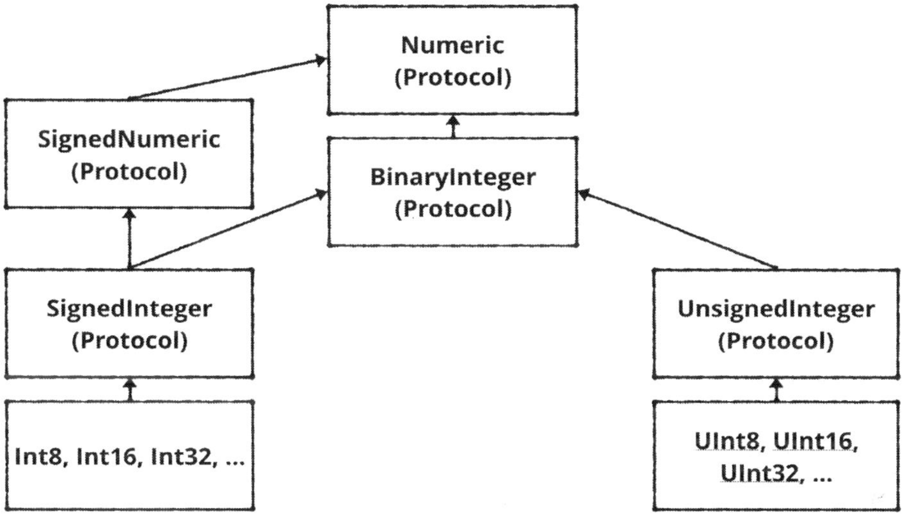

The arrows indicate conformance to (sometimes called *adoption of*) a protocol. While this graph does not show all of the protocols that integer types conform to, it gives you insight about how things are organized.

Swift is the first protocol-based language. As you begin to understand the protocols that underly the types, you can leverage the system in ways not possible with other languages.

By the end of this book you will be hooking into existing protocols and even creating new ones of your own.

Key points

- Type conversion allows you to convert values of one type into another.
- Type conversion is required when using an operator, such as the basic arithmetic operators (+, -, *, /), with mixed types.
- Type inference allows you to omit the type when Swift already knows it.
- **Unicode** is the standard for mapping characters to numbers.
- A single mapping in Unicode is called a **code point**.
- The `Character` data type stores single characters. The `String` data type stores collections of characters, or strings.
- You can combine strings by using the addition operator.

- You can use **string interpolation** to build a string in-place.
- You can use tuples to group data into a single data type.
- Tuples can either be unnamed or named. Their elements are accessed with index numbers for unnamed tuples, or programmer given names for named tuples.
- There are many kinds of numeric types with different storage and precision capabilities.
- Protocols are how types are organized in Swift.

Where to go from here?

Types are a fundamental part of programming. They're what allow you to correctly store your data. You've seen a few more here, including strings and tuples as well as a bunch of numeric types. Later on in the book you'll learn how to define your own types with **structs**, **enums** and **classes**.

In the next chapter, you'll learn about Boolean logic and simple control flow. This is required for any program to be able to make decisions about how the program should proceed based on the data it's manipulating.

Give the following challenges a try to solidify your knowledge and you'll be ready to move on!

Challenges

1. Create a constant called `coordinates` and assign a tuple containing two and three to it.
2. Create a constant called `namedCoordinate` with a `row` and `column` component.
3. Which of the following are valid statements?

```
let character: Character = "Dog"
let character: Character = "🐶"
let string: String = "Dog"
let string: String = "🐶"
```

4. Is this valid code?

```
let tuple = (day: 15, month: 8, year: 2015)
```

```
let day = tuple.Day
```

5. What is wrong with the following code?

```
let name = "Matt"
name += " Galloway"
```

6. What is the type of the constant named `value`?

```
let tuple = (100, 1.5, 10)
let value = tuple.1
```

7. What is the value of the constant named `month`?

```
let tuple = (day: 15, month: 8, year: 2015)
let month = tuple.month
```

8. What is the value of the constant named `summary`?

```
let number = 10
let multiplier = 5
let summary = "\(number) multiplied by \(multiplier) equals \
(number * multiplier)"
```

9. What is the sum of `a` and `b`, minus `c`?

```
let a = 4
let b: Int32 = 100
let c: UInt8 = 12
```

10. What is the numeric difference between `Double.pi` and `Float.pi`?

Chapter 3: Basic Control Flow

By Matt Galloway

When writing a computer program, you need to be able to tell the computer what to do in different scenarios. For example, a calculator app would need to do one thing if the user tapped the addition button and another thing if the user tapped the subtraction button.

In computer-programming terms, this concept is known as **control flow**. It is so named because the flow of the program is controlled by various methods. In this chapter, you'll learn how to make decisions and repeat tasks in your programs by using syntax to control the flow. You'll also learn about **Booleans**, which represent true and false values, and how you can use these to compare data.

Comparison operators

You've seen a few types now, such as `Int`, `Double` and `String`. Here you'll learn about another type, one that will let you compare values through the **comparison operators**.

When you perform a comparison, such as looking for the greater of two numbers, the answer is either *true* or *false*. Swift has a data type just for this! It's called a `Bool`, which is short for Boolean, after a rather clever man named George Boole who invented an entire field of mathematics around the concept of true and false.

This is how you use a Boolean in Swift:

```
let yes: Bool = true
let no: Bool = false
```

And because of Swift's type inference, you can leave off the type annotation:

```
let yes = true
let no = false
```

A Boolean can only be either true or false, denoted by the keywords `true` and `false`. In the code above, you use the keywords to set the state of each constant.

Boolean operators

Booleans are commonly used to compare values. For example, you may have two values and you want to know if they're equal: either they are (true) or they aren't (false).

In Swift, you do this using the **equality operator**, which is denoted by ==:

```
let doesOneEqualTwo = (1 == 2)
```

Swift infers that `doesOneEqualTwo` is a `Bool`. Clearly, 1 does not equal 2, and therefore `doesOneEqualTwo` will be `false`.

Similarly, you can find out if two values are *not* equal using the `!=` operator:

```
let doesOneNotEqualTwo = (1 != 2)
```

This time, the comparison is true because 1 does not equal 2, so `doesOneNotEqualTwo` will be `true`.

The prefix `!` operator, also called the not-operator, toggles true to false and false to true. Another way to write the above is:

```
let alsoTrue = !(1 == 2)
```

Because 1 does not equal 2, `(1 == 2)` is `false`, and then `!` flips it to `true`.

Two more operators let you determine if a value is greater than (>) or less than (<) another value. You'll likely know these from mathematics:

```
let isOneGreaterThanTwo = (1 > 2)
let isOneLessThanTwo = (1 < 2)
```

And it's not rocket science to work out that `isOneGreaterThanTwo` will equal `false` and `isOneLessThanTwo` will equal `true`.

There's also an operator that lets you test if a value is less than *or* equal to another value: <=. It's a combination of < and ==, and will therefore return `true` if the first value is either less than the second value or equal to it.

Similarly, there's an operator that lets you test if a value is greater than or equal to another — you may have guessed that it's >=.

Boolean logic

Each of the examples above tests just one condition. When George Boole invented the Boolean, he had much more planned for it than these humble beginnings. He invented Boolean logic, which lets you combine multiple conditions to form a result.

One way to combine conditions is by using **AND**. When you AND together two Booleans, the result is another Boolean. If both input Booleans are `true`, then the result is `true`. Otherwise, the result is `false`.

George Boole

In Swift, the operator for Boolean AND is &&, used like so:

```
let and = true && true
```

In this case, `and` will be `true`. If either of the values on the right was `false`, then `and` would be `false`.

Another way to combine conditions is by using **OR**. When you OR together two Booleans, the result is `true` if *either* of the input Booleans is `true`. Only if *both* input Booleans are `false` will the result be `false`.

In Swift, the operator for Boolean OR is `||`, used like so:

```
let or = true || false
```

In this case, `or` will be `true`. If both values on the right were `false`, then `or` would be `false`. If both were `true`, then `or` would still be `true`.

In Swift, Boolean logic is usually applied to multiple conditions. Maybe you want to determine if two conditions are true; in that case, you'd use AND. If you only care about whether one of two conditions is true, then you'd use OR.

For example, consider the following code:

```
let andTrue = 1 < 2 && 4 > 3
let andFalse = 1 < 2 && 3 > 4

let orTrue = 1 < 2 || 3 > 4
let orFalse = 1 == 2 || 3 == 4
```

Each of these tests two separate conditions, combining them with either AND or OR.

It's also possible to use Boolean logic to combine more than two comparisons. For example, you can form a complex comparison like so:

```
let andOr = (1 < 2 && 3 > 4) || 1 < 4
```

The parentheses disambiguates the expression. First Swift evaluates the sub-expression inside the parentheses, and then it evaluates the full expression, following these steps:

```
1. (1 < 2 && 3 > 4) || 1 < 4
2. (true && false) || true
3. false || true
4. true
```

String equality

Sometimes you want to determine if two strings are equal. For example, a children's game of naming an animal in a photo would need to determine if the player answered correctly.

In Swift, you can compare strings using the standard equality operator, ==, in exactly the same way as you compare numbers. For example:

```
let guess = "dog"
let dogEqualsCat = guess == "cat"
```

Here, `dogEqualsCat` is a Boolean that in this case equals `false`, because `"dog"` does not equal `"cat"`. Simple!

Just as with numbers, you can compare not just for equality, but also to determine is one value is greater than or less that another value. For example:

```
let order = "cat" < "dog"
```

This syntax checks if one string comes before another alphabetically. In this case, `order` equals `true` because `"cat"` comes before `"dog"`.

Note: You will learn more about string equality in Chapter 9: Strings. There are some interesting things that crop up when strings contain special characters.

Mini-exercises

1. Create a constant called `myAge` and set it to your age. Then, create a constant named `isTeenager` that uses Boolean logic to determine if the age denotes someone in the age range of 13 to 19.
2. Create another constant named `theirAge` and set it to my age, which is 30. Then, create a constant named `bothTeenagers` that uses Boolean logic to determine if both you and I are teenagers.
3. Create a constant named `reader` and set it to your name as a string. Create a constant named `author` and set it to my name, Matt Galloway. Create a constant named `authorIsReader` that uses string equality to determine if `reader` and `author` are equal.
4. Create a constant named `readerBeforeAuthor` which uses string comparison to determine if `reader` comes before `author`.

The if statement

The first and most common way of controlling the flow of a program is through the use of an **`if` statement**, which allows the program to do something only *if* a certain condition is true. For example, consider the following:

```
if 2 > 1 {
  print("Yes, 2 is greater than 1.")
}
```

This is a simple `if` statement. If the condition is true, then the statement will execute the code between the braces. If the condition is false, then the statement won't execute the code between the braces. It's as simple as that!

You can extend an `if` statement to provide code to run in case the condition turns out to be false. This is known as the **else clause**. Here's an example:

```
let animal = "Fox"

if animal == "Cat" || animal == "Dog" {
  print("Animal is a house pet.")
```

```
} else {
  print("Animal is not a house pet.")
}
```

Here, if `animal` equals either `"Cat"` or `"Dog"`, then the statement will run the first block of code. If `animal` does not equal either `"Cat"` or `"Dog"`, then the statement will run the block inside the `else` part of the `if` statement, printing the following to the debug area:

```
Animal is not a house pet.
```

But you can go even further than that with `if` statements. Somtimes you want to check one condition, then another. This is where **`else-if`** comes into play, nesting another `if` statement in the `else` clause of a previous `if` statement.

You can use it like so:

```
let hourOfDay = 12
let timeOfDay: String

if hourOfDay < 6 {
  timeOfDay = "Early morning"
} else if hourOfDay < 12 {
  timeOfDay = "Morning"
} else if hourOfDay < 17 {
  timeOfDay = "Afternoon"
} else if hourOfDay < 20 {
  timeOfDay = "Evening"
} else if hourOfDay < 24 {
  timeOfDay = "Late evening"
} else {
  timeOfDay = "INVALID HOUR!"
}
print(timeOfDay)
```

These nested `if` statements test multiple conditions one by one until a true condition is found. Only the code associated with that first true condition is executed, regardless of whether subsequent `else-if` conditions are true. In other words, the order of your conditions matters!

You can add an `else` clause at the end to handle the case where none of the conditions are true. This `else` clause is optional if you don't need it; in this example you *do* need it, to ensure that `timeOfDay` has a valid value by the time you print it out.

In this example, the `if` statement takes a number representing an hour of the day and converts it to a string representing the part of the day to which the hour belongs.

Working with a 24-hour clock, the statements are checked in order, one at a time:

- The first check is to see if the hour is less than 6. If so, that means it's early morning.
- If the hour is not less than 6, the statement continues to the first `else-if`, where it checks the hour to see if it's less than 12.
- Then in turn, as conditions prove false, the statement checks the hour to see if it's less than 17, then less than 20, then less than 24.
- Finally, if the hour is out of range, the statement prints that information to the console.

In the code above, the `hourOfDay` constant is `12`. Therefore, the code will print the following:

```
Afternoon
```

Notice that even though both the `hourOfDay < 20` and `hourOfDay < 24` conditions are also true, the statement only executes the first block whose condition is true; in this case, the block with the `hourOfDay < 17` condition.

Short circuiting

An important fact about `if` statements is what happens when there are multiple Boolean conditions separated by ANDs (&&) or ORs (||).

Consider the following code:

```
if 1 > 2 && name == "Matt Galloway" {
  // ...
}
```

The first condition of the `if` statement, `1 > 2` is `false`. Therefore the whole expression cannot ever be `true`. So Swift will not even bother to check the second part of the expression, namely the check of `name`.

Similarly, consider the following code:

```
if 1 < 2 || name == "Matt Galloway" {
  // ...
}
```

Since `1 < 2` is `true`, the whole expression must be `true` as well. Therefore once again, the check of `name` is not executed. This will come in handy later on when you start dealing with more complex data types.

Encapsulating variables

`if` statements introduce a new concept **scope**, which is a way to encapsulate variables through the use of braces.

Imagine you want to calculate the fee to charge your client. Here's the deal you've made:

> You earn $25 for every hour up to 40 hours, and $50 for every hour thereafter.

Using Swift, you can calculate your fee in this way:

```
var hoursWorked = 45

var price = 0
if hoursWorked > 40 {
  let hoursOver40 = hoursWorked - 40
  price += hoursOver40 * 50
  hoursWorked -= hoursOver40
}
price += hoursWorked * 25

print(price)
```

This code takes the number of hours and checks if it's over 40. If so, the code calculates the number of hours over 40 and multiplies that by $50, then adds the result to the price. The code then subtracts the number of hours over 40 from the hours worked. It multiplies the remaining hours worked by $25 and adds that to the total price.

In the example above, the result is as follows:

```
1250
```

The interesting thing here is the code inside the `if` statement. There is a declaration of a new constant, `hoursOver40`, to store the number of hours over 40. Clearly, you can use it inside the `if` statement. But what happens if you try to use it at the end of the above code?

```
...

print(price)
print(hoursOver40)
```

This would result in the following error:

```
Use of unresolved identifier 'hoursOver40'
```

This error informs you that you're only allowed to use the `hoursOver40` constant within the scope in which it was created. In this case, the `if` statement introduced a new scope, so when that scope is finished, you can no longer use the constant.

However, each scope can use variables and constants from its parent scope. In the example above, the scope inside of the `if` statement uses the `price` and `hoursWorked` variables, which you created in the parent scope.

The ternary conditional operator

Now I want to introduce a new operator, one you didn't see in Chapter 2. It's called the **ternary conditional operator** and it's related to `if` statements.

If you wanted to determine the minimum and maximum of two variables, you could use `if` statements, like so:

```
let a = 5
let b = 10

let min: Int
if a < b {
  min = a
} else {
  min = b
}

let max: Int
if a > b {
  max = a
} else {
  max = b
}
```

By now you know how this works, but it's a lot of code. Wouldn't it be nice if you could shrink this to just a couple of lines? Well, you can, thanks to the ternary conditional operator!

The ternary conditional operator takes a condition and returns one of two values, depending on whether the condition was true or false. The syntax is as follows:

```
(<CONDITION>) ? <TRUE VALUE> : <FALSE VALUE>
```

You can use this operator to rewrite your long code block above, like so:

```
let a = 5
let b = 10

let min = a < b ? a : b
let max = a > b ? a : b
```

In the first example, the condition is `a < b`. If this is true, the result assigned back to `min` will be the value of `a`; if it's false, the result will be the value of `b`.

I'm sure you'll agree that's much simpler! This is a useful operator that you'll find yourself using regularly.

> **Note:** Because finding the greater or smaller of two numbers is such a common operation, the Swift standard library provides two functions for this purpose: `max` and `min`. If you were paying attention earlier in the book, then you'll recall you've already seen these.

Mini-exercises

1. Create a constant named `myAge` and initialize it with your age. Write an `if` statement to print out `Teenager` if your age is between 13 and 19, and `Not a teenager` if your age is not between 13 and 19.
2. Create a constant named `answer` and use a ternary condition to set it equal to the result you print out for the same cases in the above exercise. Then print out `answer`.

Loops

Loops are Swift's way of executing code multiple times. In this section, you'll learn about one type of loop: the `while` loop. If you know another programming language, you'll find the concepts and maybe even the syntax to be familiar.

While loops

A **`while` loop** repeats a block of code while a condition is true. You create a `while` loop this way:

```
while <CONDITION> {
  <LOOP CODE>
}
```

The loop checks the condition for every iteration. If the condition is `true`, then the loop executes and moves on to another iteration. If the condition is `false`, then the loop stops. Just like `if` statements, `while` loops introduce a scope.

The simplest `while` loop takes this form:

```
while true {
}
```

This is a `while` loop that never ends because the condition is always `true`. Of course, you would never write such a `while` loop, because your program would spin forever! This situation is known as an **infinite loop**, and while it might not cause your program to crash, it will very likely cause your computer to freeze.

Here's a more useful example of a `while` loop:

```
var sum = 1

while sum < 1000 {
  sum = sum + (sum + 1)
}
```

This code calculates a mathematical sequence, up to the point where the value is greater than `1000`.

The loop executes as follows:

- **Before iteration 1:** `sum` = 1, loop condition = true
- **After iteration 1:** `sum` = 3, loop condition = true
- **After iteration 2:** `sum` = 7, loop condition = true
- **After iteration 3:** `sum` = 15, loop condition = true
- **After iteration 4:** `sum` = 31, loop condition = true
- **After iteration 5:** `sum` = 63, loop condition = true
- **After iteration 6:** `sum` = 127, loop condition = true
- **After iteration 7:** `sum` = 255, loop condition = true
- **After iteration 8:** `sum` = 511, loop condition = true
- **After iteration 9:** `sum` = 1023, loop condition = false

After the ninth iteration, the `sum` variable is `1023`, and therefore the loop condition of `sum < 1000` becomes false. At this point, the loop stops.

Repeat-while loops

A variant of the `while` loop is called the **repeat-while loop**. It differs from the `while` loop in that the condition is evaluated *at the end* of the loop rather than at the beginning.

You construct a `repeat-while` loop like this:

```
repeat {
  <LOOP CODE>
} while <CONDITION>
```

Here's the example from the last section, but using a `repeat-while` loop:

```
sum = 1

repeat {
  sum = sum + (sum + 1)
} while sum < 1000
```

In this example, the outcome is the same as before. However, that isn't always the case — you might get a different result with a different condition.

Consider the following `while` loop:

```
sum = 1

while sum < 1 {
  sum = sum + (sum + 1)
}
```

Consider the corresponding `repeat-while` loop, which uses the same condition:

```
sum = 1

repeat {
  sum = sum + (sum + 1)
} while sum < 1
```

In the case of the regular `while` loop, the condition `sum < 1` is `false` right from the start. That means the body of the loop won't be reached! The value of `sum` will equal `1` because the loop won't execute any iterations.

In the case of the `repeat-while` loop, `sum` will equal `3` because the loop executes once.

Breaking out of a loop

Sometimes you want to break out of a loop early. You can do this using the `break` statement, which immediately stops the execution of the loop and continues on to the code after the loop.

For example, consider the following code:

```
sum = 1

while true {
  sum = sum + (sum + 1)
  if sum >= 1000 {
    break
  }
}
```

Here, the loop condition is `true`, so the loop would normally iterate forever. However, the `break` means the `while` loop will exit once the sum is greater than or equal to `1000`.

You've seen how to write the same loop in different ways, demonstrating that in computer programming, there are often many ways to achieve the same result.

You should choose the method that's easiest to read and conveys your intent in the best way possible. This is an approach you'll internalize with enough time and practice.

Mini-exercises

1. Create a variable named `counter` and set it equal to `0`. Create a while loop with the condition `counter < 10` which prints out `counter is X` (where `X` is replaced with `counter` value) and then increments `counter` by `1`.

2. Create a variable named `counter` and set it equal to `0`. Create another variable named `roll` and set it equal to `0`. Create a `repeat-while` loop.

   Inside the loop, set `roll` equal to `Int(arc4random_uniform(6))` which means to pick a random number between `0` and `5`. Then increment `counter` by `1`.

   Finally, print `After X rolls, roll is Y` where `X` is the value of `counter` and `Y` is the value of `roll`. Set the loop condition such that the loop finishes when the first `0` is rolled.

Key points

- You use the Boolean data type `Bool` to represent true and false.
- The comparison operators, all of which return a Boolean, are:

```
Equal: `==`
Not equal: `!=`
Less than: `<`
Greater than: `>`
Less than or equal: `<=`
Greater than or equal: `>=`
```

- You can use Boolean logic to combine comparison conditions.
- You use `if` statements to make simple decisions based on a condition.
- You use `else` and `else-if` within an `if` statement to extend the decision-making beyond a single condition.
- Short circuiting ensures that only the minimal required parts of a Boolean expression are evaluated.
- You can use the ternary operator in place of simple `if` statements.
- Variables and constants belong to a certain scope, beyond which you cannot use them. A scope inherits visible variables and constants from its parent.
- `while` loops allow you to perform a certain task a number of times until a condition is met.
- The `break` statement lets you break out of a loop.

Where to go from here?

Apps very rarely run all the way through the same way every time; depending on what data comes in from the internet or from user input, your code will need to make decisions on which path to take. With `if` and `else`, you can have your code make decisions on what to do based on some condition.

In the next chapter, you'll see how to use more advanced control flow statements. This will involve more loops like the `while` loop you saw in this chapter, and a new construct called the `switch` statement.

Challenges

1. What's wrong with the following code?

```
let firstName = "Matt"

if firstName == "Matt" {
  let lastName = "Galloway"
} else if firstName == "Ray" {
  let lastName = "Wenderlich"
}
let fullName = firstName + " " + lastName
```

2. In each of the following statements, what is the value of the Boolean `answer` constant?

```
let answer = true && true
let answer = false || false
let answer = (true && 1 != 2) || (4 > 3 && 100 < 1)
let answer = ((10 / 2) > 3) && ((10 % 2) == 0)
```

3. Suppose the squares on a chessboard are numbered left to right, top to bottom, with 0 being the top-left square and 63 being the bottom-right square. Rows are numbered top to bottom, 0 to 7. Columns are numbered left to right, 0 to 7. Given a current position on the chessboard, expressed as a row and column number, calculate the next position on the chessboard, again expressed as a row and column number. The ordering is determined by the numbering from 0 to 63. The position after 63 is again 0.

4. Given the coefficients a, b and c, calculate the solutions to a quadratic equation with these coefficients. Take into account the different number of solutions (0, 1 or 2). If you need a math refresher, this Wikipedia article on the quadratic equation will help: https://en.wikipedia.org/wiki/Quadratic_formula.

5. Given a month (represented with a `String` in all lowercase) and the current year (represented with an `Int`), calculate the number of days in the month. Remember that because of leap years, "february" has 29 days when the year is a multiple of 4 but not a multiple of 100. February also has 29 days when the year is a multiple of 400.

6. Given a number, determine if this number is a power of 2. (Hint: you can use `log2(number)` to find the base 2 logarithm of `number`. `log2(number)` will return a whole number if `number` is a power of two. You can also solve the problem using a loop and no logarithm.)

7. Print a table of the first 10 powers of 2.

8. Given a number n, calculate the n-th Fibonacci number. (Recall Fibonacci is 1, 1, 2, 3, 5, 8, 13, ... Start with 1 and 1 and add these values together to get the next value. The next value is the sum of the previous two. So the next value in this case is 8+13 = 21.)

9. Given a number n, calculate the factorial of n. (Example: 4 factorial is equal to 1 * 2 * 3 * 4.)

10. Given a number between 2 and 12, calculate the odds of rolling this number using two six-sided dice. Compute it by exhaustively looping through all of the combinations and counting the fraction of outcomes that give you that value. Don't use a formula.

Chapter 4: Advanced Control Flow

By Matt Galloway

In the previous chapter, you learned how to control the flow of execution using the decision-making powers of `if` statements and the `while` loop. In this chapter, you'll continue to learn how to control the flow of execution. You'll learn about another loop known as the `for` loop.

Loops may not sound very interesting, but they're very common in computer programs. For example, you might have code to download an image from the cloud; with a loop, you could run that multiple times to download your entire photo library. Or if you have a game with multiple computer-controlled characters, you might need a loop to go through each one and make sure it knows what to do next.

You'll also learn about `switch` statements, which are particularly powerful in Swift. They let you inspect a value and decide what to do based on that value. They're incredibly powerful when used with some advanced Swift features such as pattern matching.

Countable ranges

Before you dive into the `for` loop statement, you need to know about the **Countable Range** data types, which let you represent a sequence of countable integers. Let's look at two types of ranges.

First, there's **countable closed range**, which you represent like so:

```
let closedRange = 0...5
```

The three dots (`...`) indicate that this range is closed, which means the range goes from 0 to 5 inclusive. That's the numbers `(0, 1, 2, 3, 4, 5)`.

Second, there's **countable half-open range**, which you represent like so:

```
let halfOpenRange = 0..<5
```

Here, you replace the three dots with two dots and a less-than sign (`..<`). Half-open means the range goes from 0 up to, but not including, 5. That's the numbers `(0, 1, 2, 3, 4)`.

Both open and half-open ranges must always be increasing. In other words, the second number must always be greater than or equal to the first.

Countable ranges are commonly used in both `for` loops and `switch` statements, which means that throughout the rest of the chapter, you'll use ranges as well!

For loops

In the previous chapter you looked at `while` loops. Now that you know about ranges, it's time to look at another type of loop: the **`for` loop**. This is probably the most common loop you'll see, and you'll use it to run code a certain number of times.

You construct a `for` loop like this:

```
for <CONSTANT> in <COUNTABLE RANGE> {
  <LOOP CODE>
}
```

The loop begins with the `for` keyword, followed by a name given to the loop constant (more on that shortly), followed by `in`, followed by the range to loop through.

Here's an example:

```
let count = 10
var sum = 0
for i in 1...count {
  sum += i
}
```

In the code above, the `for` loop iterates through the range 1 to `count`. At the first iteration, `i` will equal the first element in the range: 1. Each time around the loop, `i` will increment until it's equal to `count`; the loop will execute one final time and then finish.

> **Note:** If you'd used a half-open range, the the last iteration would see `i` equal to `count - 1`.

Inside the loop, you add `i` to the `sum` variable; it runs 10 times to calculate the sequence `1 + 2 + 3 + 4 + 5 + ...` all the way up to 10.

Here are the values of the constant `i` and variable `sum` for each iteration:

- **Start of iteration 1:** `i` = 1, `sum` = 0
- **Start of iteration 2:** `i` = 2, `sum` = 1
- **Start of iteration 3:** `i` = 3, `sum` = 3
- **Start of iteration 4:** `i` = 4, `sum` = 6
- **Start of iteration 5:** `i` = 5, `sum` = 10
- **Start of iteration 6:** `i` = 6, `sum` = 15
- **Start of iteration 7:** `i` = 7, `sum` = 21
- **Start of iteration 8:** `i` = 8, `sum` = 28
- **Start of iteration 9:** `i` = 9, `sum` = 36
- **Start of iteration 10:** `i` = 10, `sum` = 45
- **After iteration 10:** `sum` = 55

In terms of scope, the `i` constant is only visible inside the scope of the `for` loop, which means it's not available outside of the loop.

> **Note:** If you're mathematically astute, you might notice that this example computes **triangle numbers**. Here's a quick explanation: http://bbc.in/1O89TGP

Xcode's playground gives you a handy way to visualize such an iteration. Hover over the `sum += i` line in the results pane, and you'll see a white dot on the right.

Hover over that dot to reveal a plus (+) button:

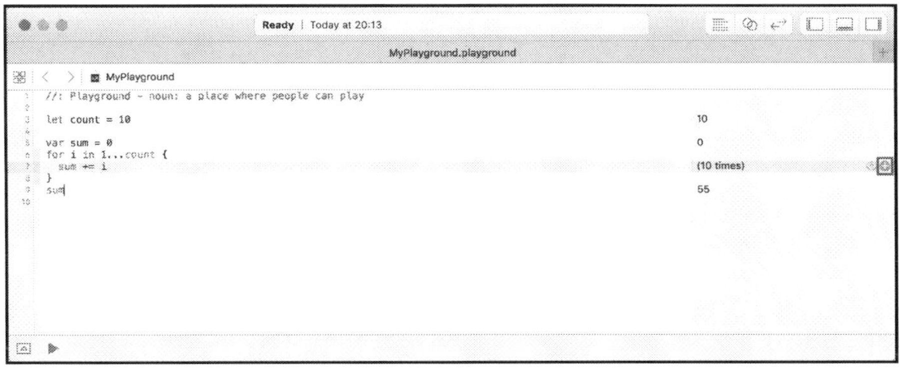

Click this plus (+) button and Xcode will display a graph underneath the line within the playground code editor:

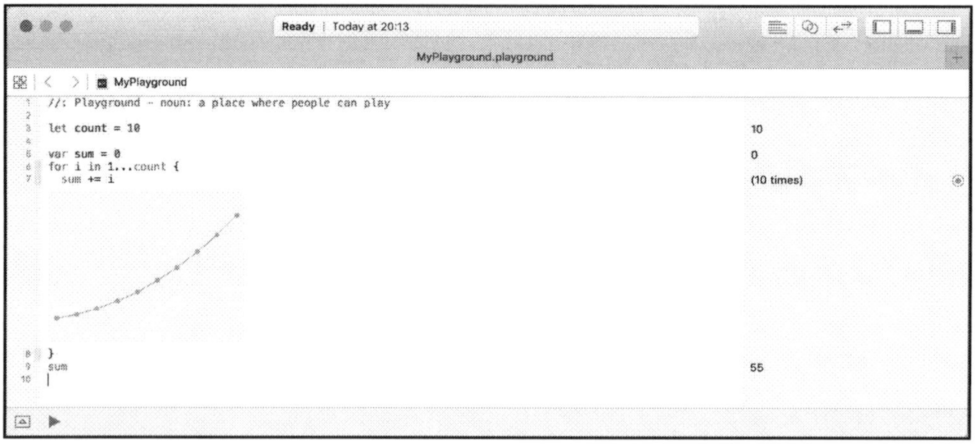

This graph lets you visualize the `sum` variable as the loop iterates.

Finally, sometimes you only want to loop a certain number of times, and so you don't need to use the loop constant at all. In that case, you can employ the underscore to indicate you're ignoring it, like so:

```
sum = 1
var lastSum = 0

for _ in 0..<count {
  let temp = sum
  sum = sum + lastSum
  lastSum = temp
}
```

This code doesn't require a loop constant; the loop simply needs to run a certain number of times. In this case, the range is 0 up to, but not including, `count` and is half-open. This is the usual way of writing loops that run a certain number of times.

It's also possible to only perform the iteration under certain conditions. For example, imagine you wanted to compute a sum similar to that of triangle numbers, but only for odd numbers:

```
sum = 0
for i in 1...count where i % 2 == 1 {
  sum += i
}
```

The previous loop has a `where` clause in the `for` loop statement. The loop still runs through all values in the range 1 to `count`, but it will only execute the loop's code block when the `where` condition is true; in this case, where `i` is odd.

Continue and labeled statements

Sometimes you'd like to skip a loop iteration for a particular case without breaking out of the loop entirely. You can do this with the `continue` statement, which immediately ends the current iteration of the loop and starts the next iteration.

> **Note:** In many cases, you can use the simpler `where` clause you just learned about. The `continue` statement gives you a higher level of control, letting you decide where and when you want to skip an iteration.

Take the example of an 8 by 8 grid, where each cell holds a value of the row multiplied by the column. It looks much line a multiplication table, doesn't it?

	0	1	2	3	4	5	6	7
0	0	0	0	0	0	0	0	0
1	0	1	2	3	4	5	6	7
2	0	2	4	6	8	10	12	14
3	0	3	6	9	12	15	18	21
4	0	4	8	12	16	20	24	28
5	0	5	10	15	20	25	30	35
6	0	6	12	18	24	30	36	42
7	0	7	14	21	28	35	42	49

Let's say you wanted to calculate the sum of all cells but exclude all even rows, as shown below:

	0	1	2	3	4	5	6	7
0								
1	0	1	2	3	4	5	6	7
2								
3	0	3	6	9	12	15	18	21
4								
5	0	5	10	15	20	25	30	35
6								
7	0	7	14	21	28	35	42	49

Using a `for` loop, you can achieve this as follows:

```
sum = 0

for row in 0..<8 {
  if row % 2 == 0 {
    continue
  }

  for column in 0..<8 {
    sum += row * column
  }
}
```

When the row modulo 2 equals 0, the row is even. In this case, `continue` makes the `for` loop skip to the next row.

Just like `break`, `continue` works with both `for` loops and `while` loops.

The second code example will calculate the sum of all cells, excluding those where the column is greater than or equal to the row.

To illustrate, it should sum the following cells:

	0	1	2	3	4	5	6	7
0								
1	0							
2	0	2						
3	0	3	6					
4	0	4	8	12				
5	0	5	10	15	20			
6	0	6	12	18	24	30		
7	0	7	14	21	28	35	42	

Using a `for` loop, you can achieve this as follows:

```
sum = 0

rowLoop: for row in 0..<8 {
  columnLoop: for column in 0..<8 {
    if row == column {
      continue rowLoop
    }
    sum += row * column
  }
}
```

The previous code block makes use of **labeled statements**, labeling the two loops as `rowLoop` and the `columnLoop`, respectively. When the row equals the column inside the inner `columnLoop`, the outer `rowLoop` will continue.

You can use labeled statements like these with `break` to break out of a certain loop. Normally, `break` and `continue` work on the innermost loop, so you need to use labeled statements if you want to manipulate an outer loop.

Mini-exercises

1. Create a constant named `range` and set it equal to a range starting at 1 and ending with 10 inclusive. Write a `for` loop which iterates over this range and prints the square of each number.
2. Write a `for` loop to iterate over the same range as in the exercise above and print the square root of each number. You'll need to type convert your loop constant.
3. Above, you saw a `for` loop which iterated over only the even rows like so:

```
sum = 0
for row in 0..<8 {
  if row % 2 == 0 {
    continue
  }
  for column in 0..<8 {
    sum += row * column
  }
}
```

Change this to use a `where` clause on the first `for` loop to skip even rows instead of using `continue`. Check that the sum is 448 as in the initial example.

Switch statements

You can also control flow via the `switch` statement. It executes different code depending on the value of a variable or constant. Here's a `switch` statement that acts on an integer:

```
let number = 10

switch number {
case 0:
  print("Zero")
default:
  print("Non-zero")
}
```

In this example, the code will print the following:

```
Non-zero
```

The purpose of this `switch` statement is to determine whether or not a number is zero. It will get more complex — I promise!

To handle a specific case, you use `case` followed by the value you want to check for, which in this case is `0`. Then, you use `default` to signify what should happen for all other values.

Here's another example:

```
switch number {
case 10:
  print("It's ten!")
default:
  break
}
```

This time you check for 10, in which case, you print a message. Nothing should happen for other values. When you want nothing to happen for a case, you use the `break` statement. This tells Swift that you *meant* to not write any code here and that nothing should happen. Cases can never be empty, so you *must* write some code, even if it's just a `break`!

Of course, `switch` statements also work with data types other than integers. They work with any data type!

Here's an example of switching on a string:

```
let string = "Dog"

switch string {
case "Cat", "Dog":
  print("Animal is a house pet.")
default:
  print("Animal is not a house pet.")
}
```

This will print the following:

```
Animal is a house pet.
```

In this example, you provide two values for the case, meaning that if the value is equal to either "Cat" or "Dog", then the statement will execute the case.

Advanced switch statements

You can also give your switch statements more than one case. In the previous chapter, you saw an if statement that used multiple else clauses to convert an hour of the day to a string describing that part of the day. You could rewrite that more succinctly with a switch statement, like so:

```
let hourOfDay = 12
let timeOfDay: String

switch hourOfDay {
case 0, 1, 2, 3, 4, 5:
  timeOfDay = "Early morning"
case 6, 7, 8, 9, 10, 11:
  timeOfDay = "Morning"
case 12, 13, 14, 15, 16:
  timeOfDay = "Afternoon"
case 17, 18, 19:
  timeOfDay = "Evening"
case 20, 21, 22, 23:
  timeOfDay = "Late evening"
default:
  timeOfDay = "INVALID HOUR!"
}

print(timeOfDay)
```

This code will print the following:

```
Afternoon
```

Remember ranges? Well, you can use ranges to simplify this switch statement. You can rewrite the above code using ranges:

```
switch hourOfDay {
case 0...5:
  timeOfDay = "Early morning"
case 6...11:
  timeOfDay = "Morning"
case 12...16:
  timeOfDay = "Afternoon"
case 17...19:
  timeOfDay = "Evening"
case 20..<24:
```

```
  timeOfDay = "Late evening"
default:
  timeOfDay = "INVALID HOUR!"
}
```

This is more succinct than writing out each value individually for all cases.

When there are multiple cases, the statement will execute the first one that matches. You'll probably agree that this is more succinct and more clear than using an `if` statement for this example.

It's slightly more precise as well, because the `if` statement method didn't address negative numbers, which here are correctly deemed to be invalid.

It's also possible to match a case to a condition based on a property of the value. As you learned in Chapter 2, you can use the modulo operator to determine if an integer is even or odd. Consider this code:

```
switch number {
case let x where x % 2 == 0:
  print("Even")
default:
  print("Odd")
}
```

This will print the following:

```
Even
```

This `switch` statement uses the `let-where` syntax, meaning the case will match only when a certain condition is true. The `let` part binds a value to a name, while the `where` part provides a Boolean condition that must be true for the case to match.

In this example, you've designed the case to match if the value is even — that is, if the value modulo 2 equals 0.

The method by which you can match values based on conditions is known as **pattern matching**.

In the previous example, the binding introduced a unnecessary constant `x`; it's simply another name for `number`.

You are allowed to use `number` in the `where` clause and replace the binding with an underscore to ignore it.

```
switch number {
case _ where number % 2 == 0:
  print("Even")
default:
  print("Odd")
}
```

Partial matching

Another way you can use `switch` statements with matching to great effect is as follows:

```
let coordinates = (x: 3, y: 2, z: 5)

switch coordinates {
case (0, 0, 0): // 1
  print("Origin")
case (_, 0, 0): // 2
  print("On the x-axis.")
case (0, _, 0): // 3
  print("On the y-axis.")
case (0, 0, _): // 4
  print("On the z-axis.")
default:        // 5
  print("Somewhere in space")
}
```

This `switch` statement makes use of **partial matching**. Here's what each case does, in order:

1. Matches precisely the case where the value is `(0, 0, 0)`. This is the origin of 3D space.
2. Matches y=0, z=0 and any value of x. This means the coordinate is on the x-axis.
3. Matches x=0, z=0 and any value of y. This means the coordinate is on the y-axis.
4. Matches x=0, y=0 and any value of z. This means the coordinate is on the z-axis.
5. Matches the remainder of coordinates.

You're using the underscore to mean that you don't care about the value. If you don't want to ignore the value, then you can bind it and use it in your `switch` statement.

Here's an example of how to do this:

```
switch coordinates {
case (0, 0, 0):
  print("Origin")
case (let x, 0, 0):
  print("On the x-axis at x = \(x)")
```

```
case (0, let y, 0):
  print("On the y-axis at y = \(y)")
case (0, 0, let z):
  print("On the z-axis at z = \(z)")
case let (x, y, z):
  print("Somewhere in space at x = \(x), y = \(y), z = \(z)")
}
```

Here, the axis cases use the `let` syntax to pull out the pertinent values. The code then prints the values using string interpolation to build the string.

Notice how you don't need a default in this `switch` statement. This is because the final case is essentially the default; it matches anything, because there are no constraints on any part of the tuple. If the `switch` statement exhausts all possible values with its cases, then no default is necessary.

Also notice how you could use a single `let` to bind all values of the tuple: `let (x, y, z)` is the same as `(let x, let y, let z)`.

Finally, you can use the same `let-where` syntax you saw earlier to match more complex cases. For example:

```
switch coordinates {
case let (x, y, _) where y == x:
  print("Along the y = x line.")
case let (x, y, _) where y == x * x:
  print("Along the y = x^2 line.")
default:
  break
}
```

Here, you match the "y equals x" and "y equals x squared" lines.

And those are the basics of `switch` statements!

Mini-exercises

1. Write a switch statement that takes an age as an integer and prints out the life stage related to that age. You can make up the life stages, or use my categorization as follows: 0-2 years, Infant; 3-12 years, Child; 13-19 years, Teenager; 20-39, Adult; 40-60, Middle aged; 61+, Elderly.

2. Write a `switch` statement that takes a tuple containing a string and an integer. The string is a name, and the integer is an age. Use the same cases that you used in the previous exercise and `let` syntax to print out the name followed by the life stage. For example, for myself it would print out `"Matt is an adult."`.

Key points

- You can use **ranges** to create a sequence of numbers, incrementing to move from one value to another.
- **Closed ranges** include both the start and end values.
- **Half-open ranges** include the start value and stop one before the end value.
- **For loops** allow you to iterate over a range.
- The **continue** statement lets you finish the current iteration of a loop and begin the next iteration.
- **Labeled statements** let you use `break` and `continue` on an outer loop.
- You use **switch** statements to decide which code to run depending on the value of a variable or constant.
- The power of a `switch` statement comes from leveraging **pattern matching** to compare values using complex rules.

Where to go from here?

You've learned about the core language features for dealing with data over these past few chapters, from data types to variables, then on to decision-making with Booleans and loops with ranges. In the next chapter you'll learn one of the key ways to make your code more reusable and easy to read through the use of functions.

Challenges

1. In the following `for` loop, what will be the value of `sum`, and how many iterations will happen?

```
var sum = 0
for i in 0...5 {
  sum += i
}
```

2. In the `while` loop below, how many instances of "a" will there be in `aLotOfAs`? Hint: `aLotOfAs.count` tells you how many characters are in the string `aLotOfAs`.

```
var aLotOfAs = ""
while aLotOfAs.count < 10 {
  aLotOfAs += "a"
}
```

3. Consider the following `switch` statement:

```
switch coordinates {
case let (x, y, z) where x == y && y == z:
  print("x = y = z")
case (_, _, 0):
  print("On the x/y plane")
case (_, 0, _):
  print("On the x/z plane")
case (0, _, _):
  print("On the y/z plane")
default:
  print("Nothing special")
}
```

What will this code print when `coordinates` is each of the following?

```
let coordinates = (1, 5, 0)
let coordinates = (2, 2, 2)
let coordinates = (3, 0, 1)
let coordinates = (3, 2, 5)
let coordinates = (0, 2, 4)
```

4. A closed range can never be empty. Why?
5. Print a countdown from 10 to 0. (Note: do not use the `reversed()` method, which will be introduced later.)
6. Print 0.0, 0.1, 0.2, 0.3, 0.4, 0.5, 0.6, 0.7, 0.8, 0.9, 1.0. (Note: do not use the `stride(from:by:to:)` function, which will be introduced later.)

Chapter 5: Functions

By Matt Galloway

Functions are a core part of many programming languages. Simply put, a function lets you define a block of code that performs a task. Then, whenever your app needs to execute that task, you can run the function instead of having to copy and paste the same code everywhere.

In this chapter, you'll learn how to write your own functions, and see firsthand how Swift makes them easy to use.

Function basics

Imagine you have an app that frequently needs to print your name. You can write a function to do this:

```
func printMyName() {
  print("My name is Matt Galloway.")
}
```

The code above is known as a **function declaration**. You define a function using the `func` keyword. After that comes the name of the function, followed by parentheses. You'll learn more about the need for these parentheses in the next section.

After the parentheses comes an opening brace, followed by the code you want to run in the function, followed by a closing brace. With your function defined, you can use it like so:

```
printMyName()
```

This prints out the following:

```
My name is Matt Galloway.
```

If you suspect that you've already used a function in previous chapters, you're correct! `print`, which prints the text you give it to the console, is indeed a function.

This leads nicely into the next section, in which you'll learn how to pass data to a function and get data back in return.

Function parameters

In the previous example, the function simply prints out a message. That's great, but sometimes you want to **parameterize** your function, which lets the function perform differently depending on the data passed into it via its **parameters**.

As an example, consider the following function:

```
func printMultipleOfFive(value: Int) {
  print("\(value) * 5 = \(value * 5)")
}
printMultipleOfFive(value: 10)
```

Here, you can see the definition of one parameter inside the parentheses after the function name, named `value` and of type `Int`. In any function, the parentheses contain what's known as the **parameter list**. These parentheses are required both when declaring and when invoking the function, even if the parameter list is empty.

This function will print out any given multiple of five. In the example, you call the function with an **argument** of 10, so the function prints the following:

```
10 * 5 = 50
```

> **Note:** Take care not to confuse the terms "parameter" and "argument". A function declares its *parameters* in its parameter list. When you call a function, you provide values as *arguments* for the functions parameters.

You can take this one step further and make the function more general. With two parameters, the function can print out a multiple of any two values.

```
func printMultipleOf(multiplier: Int, andValue: Int) {
  print("\(multiplier) * \(andValue) = \(multiplier *
andValue)")
}
printMultipleOf(multiplier: 4, andValue: 2)
```

There are now two parameters inside the parentheses after the function name: one named `multiplier` and the other named `andValue`, both of type `Int`.

Notice that you need to apply the labels in the parameter list to the arguments when you call a function. In the example above you need to put `multiplier:` before the multiplier and `andValue:` before the value to be multiplied.

In Swift, you should try to make your function calls read like a sentence. In the example above, you would read the last line of code like this:

Print multiple of multiplier 4 and value 2

You can make this even clearer by giving a parameter a different external name. For example, you can change the name of the `andValue` parameter:

```
func printMultipleOf(multiplier: Int, and value: Int) {
  print("\(multiplier) * \(value) = \(multiplier * value)")
}
printMultipleOf(multiplier: 4, and: 2)
```

You assign a different external name by writing it in front of the parameter name. In this example, the internal name of the parameter is now `value` while the external name (the argument label) in the function call is now `and`. You can read the new call as:

Print multiple of multiplier 4 and 2

If you want to have no external name at all, then you can employ the underscore _, as you've seen in previous chapters:

```
func printMultipleOf(_ multiplier: Int, and value: Int) {
  print("\(multiplier) * \(value) = \(multiplier * value)")
}
printMultipleOf(4, and: 2)
```

This makes it even more readable. The function call now reads like so:

```
Print multiple of 4 and 2
```

You could, if you so wished, take this even further and use _ for all parameters, like so:

```
func printMultipleOf(_ multiplier: Int, _ value: Int) {
  print("\(multiplier) * \(value) = \(multiplier * value)")
}
printMultipleOf(4, 2)
```

In this example, all parameters have no external name. But this illustrates how you use the underscore wisely. Here, your expression is still understandable, but more complex functions that take many parameters can become confusing and unwieldy with no external parameter names. Imagine if a function took five parameters!

You can also give default values to parameters:

```
func printMultipleOf(_ multiplier: Int, _ value: Int = 1) {
  print("\(multiplier) * \(value) = \(multiplier * value)")
}
printMultipleOf(4)
```

The difference is the `= 1` after the second parameter, which means that if no value is provided for the second parameter, it defaults to `1`.

Therefore, this code prints the following:

```
4 * 1 = 4
```

It can be useful to have a default value when you expect a parameter to be one particular value the majority of the time, and it will simplify your code when you call the function.

Return values

All of the functions you've seen so far have performed a simple task: printing something out. Functions can also return a value. The caller of the function can assign the return value to a variable or constant, or use it directly in an expression.

This means you can use a function to manipulate data. You simply take in data through parameters, manipulate it and then return it.

Here's how you define a function that returns a value:

```
func multiply(_ number: Int, by multiplier: Int) -> Int {
  return number * multiplier
}
let result = multiply(4, by: 2)
```

To declare that a function returns a value, you add a -> followed by the type of the return value after the set of parentheses and before the opening brace. In this example, the function returns an `Int`.

Inside the function, you use a `return` statement to return the value. In this example, you return the product of the two parameters.

It's also possible to return multiple values through the use of tuples:

```
func multiplyAndDivide(_ number: Int, by factor: Int)
                   -> (product: Int, quotient: Int) {
  return (number * factor, number / factor)
}
let results = multiplyAndDivide(4, by: 2)
let product = results.product
let quotient = results.quotient
```

This function returns *both* the product and quotient of the two parameters: It returns a tuple containing two `Int` values with appropriate member value names.

The ability to return multiple values through tuples is one of the many things that makes it such a pleasure to work with Swift. And it turns out to be a very useful feature, as you'll see shortly.

Advanced parameter handling

Function parameters are constants by default, which means they can't be modified.

To illustrate this point, consider the following code:

```
func incrementAndPrint(_ value: Int) {
  value += 1
  print(value)
}
```

This results in an error:

```
Left side of mutating operator isn't mutable: 'value' is a 'let'
constant
```

The parameter value is the equivalent of a constant declared with let. Therefore, when the function attempts to increment it, the compiler emits an error.

An important point to note is that Swift copies the value before passing it to the function, a behavior known as **pass-by-value**.

> **Note**: Pass-by-value and making copies is the standard behavior for all of the types you've seen so far in this book. You'll see another way for things to be passed into functions in Chapter 14, "Classes".

Usually you want this behavior. Ideally, a function doesn't alter its parameters. If it did, then you couldn't be sure of the parameters' values and you might make incorrect assumptions in your code, leading to the wrong data.

Sometimes you *do* want to let a function change a parameter directly, a behavior known as **copy-in copy-out** or **call by value result**. You do it like so:

```
func incrementAndPrint(_ value: inout Int) {
  value += 1
  print(value)
}
```

inout before the parameter type indicates that this parameter should be copied in, that local copy used within the function, and copied back out when the function returns.

You need to make a slight tweak to the function call to complete this example. Add an ampersand (&) before the argument, which makes it clear at the call site that you are using copy-in copy-out:

```
var value = 5
incrementAndPrint(&value)
print(value)
```

Now the function can change the value however it wishes.

This example will print the following:

```
6
6
```

The function increments value, which retains its modified data after the function finishes. The value goes *in* to the function and comes back *out* again, thus the keyword inout.

Under certain conditions, the compiler can simplify copy-in copy-out to what is called *pass-by-reference*. The argument value isn't copied into the parameter. Instead, the parameter will hold a reference to the memory of original value. This optimization satisfies all requirements of copy-in copy-out while removing the need for copies.

Overloading

Did you notice how you used the same function name for several different functions in the previous examples?

```
func printMultipleOf(multiplier: Int, andValue: Int)
func printMultipleOf(multiplier: Int, and value: Int)
func printMultipleOf(_ multiplier: Int, and value: Int)
func printMultipleOf(_ multiplier: Int, _ value: Int)
```

This is called **overloading** and lets you define similar functions using a single name.

However, the compiler must still be able to tell the difference between these functions. Whenever you call a function, it should always be clear which function you're calling. This is usually achieved through a difference in the parameter list:

- A different number of parameters.
- Different parameter types.
- Different external parameter names, such as the case with `printMultipleOf`.

You can also overload a function name based on a different return type, like so:

```
func getValue() -> Int {
  return 31
}

func getValue() -> String {
  return "Matt Galloway"
}
```

Here, there are two functions called `getValue()`, which return different types. One an `Int` and the other a `String`.

Using these is a little more complicated. Consider the following:

```
let value = getValue()
```

How does Swift know which `getValue()` to call? The answer is, it doesn't. And it will print the following error:

```
error: ambiguous use of 'getValue()'
```

There's no way of knowing which one to call. It's a chicken and egg situation. It's unknown what type `value` is, so Swift doesn't know which `getValue()` to call or what the return type of `getValue()` should be.

To fix this, you can declare what type you want `value` to be, like so:

```
let valueInt: Int = getValue()
let valueString: String = getValue()
```

This will correctly call the `Int` version of `getValue()` in the first instance, and the `String` version of `getValue()` in the second instance.

It's worth noting that overloading should be used with care. Only use overloading for functions that are related and similar in behavior. When only the return type is overloaded, as in the above example, you loose type inference and so is not recommended.

Mini-exercises

1. Write a function named `printFullName` that takes two strings called `firstName` and `lastName`. The function should print out the full name defined as `firstName + " " + lastName`. Use it to print out your own full name.
2. Change the declaration of `printFullName` to have no external name for either parameter.
3. Write a function named `calculateFullName` that returns the full name as a string. Use it to store your own full name in a constant.
4. Change `calculateFullName` to return a tuple containing both the full name and the length of the name. You can find a string's length by using the `count` property. Use this function to determine the length of your own full name.

Functions as variables

This may come as a surprise, but functions in Swift are simply another data type. You can assign them to variables and constants just as you can any other type of value, such as an `Int` or a `String`.

To see how this works, consider the following function:

```
func add(_ a: Int, _ b: Int) -> Int {
  return a + b
}
```

This function takes two parameters and returns the sum of their values.

You can assign this function to a variable, like so:

```
var function = add
```

Here, the name of the variable is `function` and its type is inferred as `(Int, Int) -> Int` from the `add` function you assign to it.

Notice how the function type `(Int, Int) -> Int` is written in the same way you write the parameter list and return type in a function declaration. Here, the `function` variable is of a function type that takes two `Int` parameters and returns an `Int`.

Now you can use the `function` variable in just the same way you'd use `add`, like so:

```
function(4, 2)
```

This returns 6.

Now consider the following code:

```
func subtract(_ a: Int, _ b: Int) -> Int {
  return a - b
}
```

Here, you declare another function that takes two `Int` parameters and returns an `Int`. You can set the `function` variable from before to your new `subtract` function, because the parameter list and return type of `subtract` are compatible with the type of the `function` variable.

```
function = subtract
function(4, 2)
```

This time, the call to `function` returns 2.

The fact that you can assign functions to variables comes in handy because it means you can pass functions to other functions. Here's an example of this in action:

```
func printResult(_ function: (Int, Int) -> Int, _ a: Int, _ b:
Int) {
  let result = function(a, b)
  print(result)
}
printResult(add, 4, 2)
```

`printResult` takes three parameters:

1. `function` is of a function type that takes two `Int` parameters and returns an `Int`, declared like so: `(Int, Int) -> Int`.

2. `a` is of type `Int`.
3. `b` is of type `Int`.

`printResult` calls the passed-in function, passing into it the two `Int` parameters. Then it prints the result to the console:

```
6
```

It's extremely useful to be able to pass functions to other functions, and it can help you write reusable code. Not only can you pass data around to manipulate, but passing functions as parameters also means you can be flexible about what code executes.

The land of no return

There are some functions which are designed to never, ever, return. This may sound confusing, but consider the example of a function that is designed to crash an application. This may sound strange, but if an application is about to work with corrupt data, it's often best to crash rather than continue in an unknown and potentially dangerous state.

Another example of a non-returning function is one which handles an event loop. An event loop is at the heart of every modern application which takes input from the user and displays things on a screen. The event loop services requests coming from the user, then passes these events to the application code, which in turn causes the information to be displayed on the screen. The loop then cycles back and services the next event.

These event loops are often started in an application by calling a function which is known to never return. Once you're coding iOS or Mac apps, think back to this paragraph when you encounter `UIApplicationMain` or `NSApplicationMain`.

Swift has a way to tell the compiler that a function is known to never return. It is done like so:

```
func noReturn() -> Never {
}
```

Notice the special return type `Never`. This is what indicates that this function will never return.

If you wrote this code you would get the following error:

```
Return from a 'noreturn' function
```

Understandable! Thanks Swift!

A crude, but honest, implementation of a function that wouldn't return would be as follows:

```
func infiniteLoop() -> Never {
  while true {
  }
}
```

You may be wondering why bother with this special return type. It's useful because by the compiler knowing that the function won't ever return, it can make certain optimizations when generating the code to call the function. Essentially, the code which calls the function doesn't need to bother doing anything after the function call, because it knows that this function will never end before the application is terminated.

Writing good functions

There are many ways to solve problems with functions. The best (easiest to use and understand) functions do *one simple task* rather than trying to do many. This makes them easier to mix and match and assemble into more complex behaviors. Good functions also have a well defined set of inputs that produce the same output every time. This makes them easier to reason about and test in isolation. Keep these rules-of-thumb in mind as you create functions.

Key points

- You use a **function** to define a task, which you can execute as many times as you like without having to write the code multiple times.
- Functions can take zero or more **parameters** and optionally return a value.
- You can add an external name to a function parameter to change the label you use in a function call, or you can use an underscore to denote no label.
- Parameters are passed as constants, unless you mark them as `inout`, in which case they are copied-in and copied-out.

- Functions can have the same name with different parameters. This is called overloading.
- Functions can have a special `Never` return type to inform Swift that this function will never exit.
- You can assign functions to variables and pass them to other functions.
- Strive to create functions that are clearly named and have one job with repeatable inputs and outputs.

Where to go from here?

Functions are the first step in grouping small pieces of code together into a larger unit.

In the next chapter you'll learn about **optionals**, which are an important part of Swift's syntactic arsenal. Before you move on, check out the challenges ahead as you'll need to understand functions before understanding some of the upcoming topics!

Challenges

Challenge 1: Looping with stride functions

In the last chapter you wrote some `for` loops with countable ranges. Countable ranges are limited in that they must always be increasing by one. The Swift `stride(from:to:by:)` and `stride(from:through:by:)` functions let you loop much more flexibly. For example, if you wanted to loop from 10 to 20 by 4's you can write:

```
for index in stride(from: 10, to: 22, by: 4) {
  print(index)
}
// prints 10, 14, 18

for index in stride(from: 10, through: 22, by: 4) {
  print(index)
}
// prints 10, 14, 18, and 22
```

- What is the difference between the two stride function overloads?
- Write a loop that goes from 10.0 to (and including) 9.0, decrementing by 0.1.

Challenge 2: It's prime time

When I'm acquainting myself with a programming language, one of the first things I do is write a function to determine whether or not a number is prime. That's your second challenge.

First, write the following function:

```
func isNumberDivisible(_ number: Int, by divisor: Int) -> Bool
```

You'll use this to determine if one number is divisible by another. It should return `true` when `number` is divisible by `divisor`.

Hint: You can use the modulo (%) operator to help you out here.

Next, write the main function:

```
func isPrime(_ number: Int) -> Bool
```

This should return `true` if `number` is prime, and `false` otherwise. A number is prime if it's only divisible by 1 and itself. You should loop through the numbers from 1 to the number and find the number's divisors. If it has any divisors other than 1 and itself, then the number isn't prime. You'll need to use the `isNumberDivisible(_:by:)` function you wrote earlier.

Use this function to check the following cases:

```
isPrime(6) // false
isPrime(13) // true
isPrime(8893) // true
```

Hint 1: Numbers less than 0 should not be considered prime. Check for this case at the start of the function and return early if the number is less than 0.

Hint 2: Use a `for` loop to find divisors. If you start at 2 and end before the number itself, then as soon as you find a divisor, you can return `false`.

Hint 3: If you want to get *really* clever, you can simply loop from 2 until you reach the square root of `number`, rather than going all the way up to `number` itself. I'll leave it as an exercise for you to figure out why. It may help to think of the number 16, whose square root is 4. The divisors of 16 are 1, 2, 4, 8 and 16.

Challenge 3: Recursive functions

In this challenge, you're going to see what happens when a function calls *itself*, a behavior called **recursion**. This may sound unusual, but it can be quite useful.

You're going to write a function that computes a value from the **Fibonacci sequence**. Any value in the sequence is the sum of the previous two values. The sequence is defined such that the first two values equal 1. That is, `fibonacci(1) = 1` and `fibonacci(2) = 1`.

Write your function using the following declaration:

```
func fibonacci(_ number: Int) -> Int
```

Then, verify you've written the function correctly by executing it with the following numbers:

```
fibonacci(1)  // = 1
fibonacci(2)  // = 1
fibonacci(3)  // = 2
fibonacci(4)  // = 3
fibonacci(5)  // = 5
fibonacci(10) // = 55
```

Hint 1: For values of `number` less than 0, you should return 0.

Hint 2: To start the sequence, hard-code a return value of 1 when `number` equals 1 or 2.

Hint 3: For any other value, you'll need to return the sum of calling `fibonacci` with `number - 1` and `number - 2`.

Chapter 6: Optionals

By Matt Galloway

All the variables and constants you've dealt with so far have had concrete values. When you had a string variable, like `var name`, it had a string value associated with it, like `"Matt Galloway"`. It could have been an empty string, like `""`, but nevertheless, there was a value to which you could refer.

That's one of the built-in safety features of Swift: If the type says `Int` or `String`, then there's an actual integer or string there, guaranteed.

This chapter will introduce you to the concept of **optionals**, a special Swift type that can represent not just a value, but also the absence of a value. By the end of this chapter, you'll know why you need optionals and how to use them safely.

Introducing nil

Sometimes, it's useful to be able to represent the absence of a value. Imagine a scenario where you need to refer to a person's identifying information; you want to store the person's name, age and occupation. Name and age are both things that must have a value — everyone has them. But not everyone is employed, so the absence of a value for occupation is something you need to be able to handle.

Without knowing about optionals, this is how you might represent the person's name, age and occupation:

```
var name = "Matt Galloway"
var age = 30
var occupation = "Software Developer & Author"
```

But what if I become unemployed? Maybe I've won the lottery and want to give up work altogether (I wish!). This is when it would be useful to be able to refer to the absence of a value.

Why couldn't you just use an empty string? You *could*, but optionals are a much better solution. Read on to see why.

Sentinel values

A valid value that represents a special condition such as the absence of a value is known as a **sentinel value**. That's what your empty string would be in the previous example.

Let's look at another example. Say your code requests something from a server, and you use a variable to store any returned error code:

```
var errorCode = 0
```

In the success case, you represent the lack of an error with a zero. That means `0` is a sentinel value.

Just like the empty string for occupation, this works, but it's potentially confusing for the programmer. `0` might actually be a valid error code — or could be in the future, if the server changed how it responded. Either way, you can't be completely confident that the server didn't return an error without consulting the documentation.

In these two examples, it would be much better if there were a special type that could represent the absence of a value. It would then be explicit when a value exists and when one doesn't.

Nil is the name given to the absence of a value, and you're about to see how Swift incorporates this concept directly into the language in a rather elegant way.

Some other programming languages simply use sentinel values. Some, like Objective-C, have the concept of `nil`, but it is merely a synonym for zero. It is just another sentinel value.

Swift introduces a whole new type, **optional**, that handles the possibility a value could be `nil`. If you're handling a non-optional type, then you're guaranteed to have a value and don't need to worry about the existence of a valid value. Similarly, if you are using an optional type then you know you must handle the `nil` case. It removes the ambiguity introduced by using sentinel values.

Introducing optionals

Optionals are Swift's solution to the problem of representing both a value and the absence of a value. An optional is allowed to hold either a value *or* `nil`.

Think of an optional as a box: it either contains a value, or it doesn't. When it doesn't contain a value, it's said to contain `nil`. The box itself always exists; it's always there for you to open and look inside.

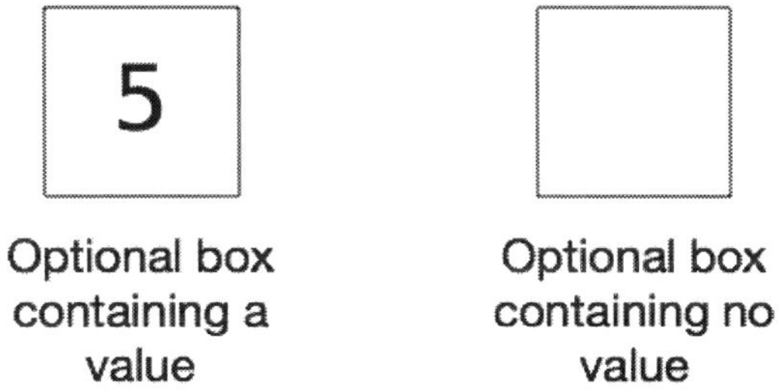

A string or an integer, on the other hand, doesn't have this box around it. Instead there's always a value, such as `"hello"` or 42. Remember, non-optional types are guaranteed to have an actual value.

> **Note:** Those of you who've studied physics may be thinking about Schroedinger's cat right now. Optionals are a little bit like that, except it's not a matter of life and death!

You declare a variable of an optional type by using the following syntax:

```
var errorCode: Int?
```

The only difference between this and a standard declaration is the question mark at the end of the type. In this case, `errorCode` is an "optional `Int`". This means the variable itself is like a box containing either an `Int` or `nil`.

> **Note:** You can add a question mark after any type to create an optional type. This optional type is said to *wrap* the regular non-optional type. For example, optional type `String?` wraps type `String`. In other words: an optional box of type `String?` holds either a `String` or `nil`.

> Also, note how an optional type must be made explicit using a type annotation (here `: Int?`). Optional types can never be inferred from initialization values, as those values are of a regular, non-optional type, or `nil`, which can be used with any optional type.

Setting the value is simple. You can either set it to an `Int`, like so:

```
errorCode = 100
```

Or you can set it to `nil`, like so:

```
errorCode = nil
```

This diagram may help you visualize what's happening:

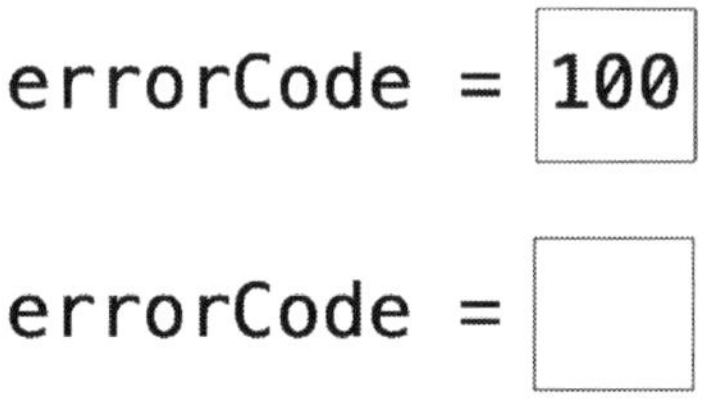

The optional box always exists. When you assign `100` to the variable, you're filling the box with the value. When you assign `nil` to the variable, you're emptying the box.

Take a few minutes to think about this concept. The box analogy will be a big help as you go through the rest of the chapter and begin to use optionals.

Mini-exercises

1. Make an optional `String` called `myFavoriteSong`. If you have a favorite song, set it to a string representing that song. If you have more than one favorite song or no favorite, set the optional to `nil`.
2. Create a constant called `parsedInt` and set it equal to `Int("10")` which tries to parse the string `10` and convert it to an `Int`. Check the type of `parsedInt` using Option-Click. Why is it an optional?
3. Change the string being parsed in the above exercise to a non-integer (try `dog` for example). What does `parsedInt` equal now?

Unwrapping optionals

It's all well and good that optionals exist, but you may be wondering how you can look inside the box and manipulate the value it contains.

Take a look at what happens when you print out the value of an optional:

```
var result: Int? = 30
print(result)
```

This prints the following:

```
Optional(30)
```

Note: You will also see a warning on this line which says "Expression implicitly coerced from 'Int?' to Any". This is because Swift warns that you're using an optional in the place of the `Any` type as it's something that usually means you did something wrong. To silence the warning here you can change the code to `print(result as Any)`.

That isn't really what you wanted — although if you think about it, it makes sense. Your code has printed the box. The result says, "`result` is an optional that contains the value `30`".

To see how an optional type is different from a non-optional type, see what happens if you try to use `result` as if it were a normal integer:

```
print(result + 1)
```

This code triggers an error:

```
Value of optional type 'Int?' not unwrapped; did you mean to use
'!' or '?'?
```

It doesn't work because you're trying to add an integer to a box — not to the value inside the box, but to the box itself. That doesn't make sense!

Force unwrapping

The error message gives an indication of the solution: It tells you that the optional is `not unwrapped`. You need to unwrap the value from its box. It's like Christmas!

Let's see how that works. Consider the following declarations:

```
var authorName: String? = "Matt Galloway"
var authorAge: Int? = 30
```

There are two different methods you can use to unwrap these optionals. The first is known as **force unwrapping**, and you perform it like so:

```
var unwrappedAuthorName = authorName!
print("Author is \(unwrappedAuthorName)")
```

This code prints:

```
Author is Matt Galloway
```

Great! That's what you'd expect.

The exclamation mark after the variable name tells the compiler that you want to look inside the box and take out the value. The result is a value of the wrapped type. This means `unwrappedAuthorName` is of type `String`, not `String?`.

The use of the word "force" and the exclamation mark `!` probably conveys a sense of danger to you, and it should. You should use force unwrapping sparingly. To see why, consider what happens when the optional doesn't contain a value:

```
authorName = nil
print("Author is \(authorName!)")
```

This code produces the following runtime error:

```
fatal error: unexpectedly found nil while unwrapping an Optional
value
```

The error occurs because the variable contains no value when you try to unwrap it. What's worse is that you get this error at runtime rather than compile time – which means you'd only notice the error if you happened to execute this code with some invalid input. Worse yet, if this code were inside an app, the runtime error would cause the app to crash!

How can you play it safe?

To stop the runtime error here, you could wrap the code that unwraps the optional in a check, like so:

```
if authorName != nil {
  print("Author is \(authorName!)")
} else {
  print("No author.")
}
```

The `if` statement checks if the optional contains `nil`. If it doesn't, that means it contains a value you can unwrap.

The code is now safe, but it's still not perfect. If you rely on this technique, you'll have to remember to check for `nil` every time you want to unwrap an optional. That will start to become tedious, and one day you'll forget and once again end up with the possibility of a runtime error.

Back to the drawing board, then!

Optional binding

Swift includes a feature known as **optional binding**, which lets you safely access the value inside an optional. You use it like so:

```
if let unwrappedAuthorName = authorName {
  print("Author is \(unwrappedAuthorName)")
} else {
  print("No author.")
}
```

You'll immediately notice that there are no exclamation marks here. This optional binding gets rid of the optional type. If the optional contains a value, this value is unwrapped and stored in, or *bound to*, the constant `unwrappedAuthorName`. The `if` statement then executes the first block of code, within which you can safely use `unwrappedAuthorName`, as it's a regular non-optional `String`.

If the optional doesn't contain a value, then the `if` statement executes the `else` block. In that case, the `unwrappedAuthorName` variable doesn't even exist.

You can see how optional binding is much safer than force unwrapping, and you should use it whenever an optional might be `nil`. Force unwrapping is only appropriate when an optional *is guaranteed* contain a value.

Because naming things is so hard, it's common practice to give the unwrapped constant the same name as the optional (thereby *shadowing* that optional):

```
if let authorName = authorName {
  print("Author is \(authorName)")
} else {
  print("No author.")
}
```

You can even unwrap multiple values at the same time, like so:

```
if let authorName = authorName,
   let authorAge = authorAge {
  print("The author is \(authorName) who is \(authorAge) years
old.")
} else {
  print("No author or no age.")
}
```

This code unwraps two values. It will only execute the `if` part of the statement when both optionals contain a value.

You can combine unwrapping multiple optionals with additional boolean checks. For example:

```
if let authorName = authorName,
   let authorAge = authorAge,
   authorAge >= 40 {
  print("The author is \(authorName) who is \(authorAge) years
old.")
} else {
  print("No author or no age or age less than 40.")
}
```

Here, you unwrap `name` and `age`, and check that `age` is greater than or equal to 40. The expression in the `if` statement will only be `true` if `name` is non-nil, *and* `age` is non-nil, *and* `age` is greater than or equal to 40.

Now you know how to safely look inside an optional and extract its value, if one exists.

Mini-exercises

1. Using your `myFavoriteSong` variable from earlier, use optional binding to check if it contains a value. If it does, print out the value. If it doesn't, print `"I don't have a favorite song."`
2. Change `myFavoriteSong` to the opposite of what it is now. If it's `nil`, set it to a string; if it's a string, set it to `nil`. Observe how your printed result changes.

Introducing guard

Sometimes you want to check a condition and only continue executing a function if the condition is true, such as when you use optionals. Imagine a function that fetches some data from the network. That fetch might fail if the network is down. The usual way to encapsulate this behavior is using an optional, which has a value if the fetch succeeds, and `nil` otherwise.

Swift has a useful and powerful feature to help in situations like this: the **`guard` statement**.

Consider the following function:

```
func calculateNumberOfSides(shape: String) -> Int? {
  switch shape {
  case "Triangle":
    return 3
  case "Square":
    return 4
  case "Rectangle":
    return 4
  case "Pentagon":
    return 5
  case "Hexagon":
    return 6
  default:
    return nil
  }
}
```

This function takes a shape name and returns the number of sides that shape has. If the shape isn't known, or you pass something that isn't a shape, then it returns `nil`.

You could use this function like so:

```
func maybePrintSides(shape: String) {
  let sides = calculateNumberOfSides(shape: shape)

  if let sides = sides {
    print("A \(shape) has \(sides) sides.")
  } else {
    print("I don't know the number of sides for \(shape).")
  }
}
```

There's nothing wrong with this, and it would work.

However the same logic could be written with a guard statement like so:

```
func maybePrintSides(shape: String) {
  guard let sides = calculateNumberOfSides(shape: shape) else {
    print("I don't know the number of sides for \(shape).")
    return
  }

  print("A \(shape) has \(sides) sides.")
}
```

The guard statement comprises `guard` followed by a condition that can include both Boolean expressions and optional bindings, followed by `else`, followed by a block of code. The block of code covered by the `else` will execute if the condition is *false*.

The block of code that executes in the case of the condition being false *must* return. If you accidentally forget, the compiler will stop you — this is the true beauty of the guard statement.

You may hear programmers talking about the "happy path" through a function; this is the path you'd expect to happen most of the time. Any other path followed would be due to an error, or another reason why the function should return earlier than expected.

Guard statements ensure the happy path remains on the left hand side of the code; this is usually regarded as a good thing as it makes code more readable and understandable.

Also, because the guard statement must return in the false case, the Swift compiler knows that if the condition was true, anything checked in the guard statement's condition *must* be true for the remainder of the function. This means the compiler can make certain optimizations. You don't need to understand how these optimizations work, or even what they are, since Swift is designed to be user-friendly and fast.

Nil coalescing

There's one final and rather handy way to unwrap an optional. You use it when you want to get a value out of the optional *no matter what* — and in the case of `nil`, you'll use a default value. This is called **nil coalescing**.

Here's how it works:

```
var optionalInt: Int? = 10
var mustHaveResult = optionalInt ?? 0
```

The nil coalescing happens on the second line, with the double question mark (`??`), known as the **nil coalescing operator**. This line means `mustHaveResult` will equal either the value inside `optionalInt`, or `0` if `optionalInt` contains `nil`. In this example, `mustHaveResult` contains the concrete `Int` value of `10`.

The previous code is equivalent to the following:

```
var optionalInt: Int? = 10
var mustHaveResult: Int
if let unwrapped = optionalInt {
  mustHaveResult = unwrapped
} else {
  mustHaveResult = 0
}
```

Set the `optionalInt` to `nil`, like so:

```
optionalInt = nil
mustHaveResult = optionalInt ?? 0
```

Now `mustHaveResult` equals `0`.

Key points

- `nil` represents the absence of a value.
- Non-optional variables and constants must always have a non-`nil` value.
- **Optional** variables and constants are like boxes that can contain a value *or* be empty (`nil`).
- To work with the value inside an optional, you must first unwrap it from the optional.
- The safest ways to unwrap an optional's value is by using **optional binding** or **nil coalescing**. Use **forced unwrapping** only when appropriate, as it could produce a runtime error.

Where to go from here?

Optionals are a core Swift feature that helps make the language safe and easy to use. You'll find yourself using them throughout your code, making your code safe by ensuring that the absence of values is handled explicitly. This is something that you'll hopefully come to admire over the course of your Swift experience!

In particular, look forward to using them in Section II, where you'll learn about collections.

Challenges

You've learned the theory behind optionals and seen them in practice. Now it's your turn to play!

Challenge 1: You be the compiler

Which of the following are valid statements?

```
var name: String? = "Ray"
var age: Int = nil
let distance: Float = 26.7
var middleName: String? = nil
```

Challenge 2: Divide and conquer

First, create a function that returns the number of times an integer can be divided by another integer without a remainder. The function should return `nil` if the division doesn't produce a whole number. Name the function `divideIfWhole`.

Then, write code that tries to unwrap the optional result of the function. There should be two cases: upon success, print `"Yep, it divides \(answer) times"`, and upon failure, print `"Not divisible :["`.

Finally, test your function:

1. Divide 10 by 2. This should print `"Yep, it divides 5 times."`
2. Divide 10 by 3. This should print `"Not divisible :[."`

Hint 1: Use the following as the start of the function signature:

```
func divideIfWhole(_ value: Int, by divisor: Int)
```

You'll need to add the return type, which will be an optional!

Hint 2: You can use the modulo operator (`%`) to determine if a value is divisible by another; recall that this operation returns the remainder from the division of two numbers. For example, `10 % 2 = 0` means that 10 is divisible by 2 with no remainder, whereas `10 % 3 = 1` means that 10 is divisible by 3 with a remainder of 1.

Challenge 3: Refactor and reduce

The code you wrote in the last challenge used `if` statements. In this challenge, refactor that code to use nil coalescing instead. This time, make it print `"It divides X times"` in all cases, but if the division doesn't result in a whole number, then `X` should be `0`.

Challenge 4: Nested optionals

Consider the following nested optional. It corresponds to a number inside a box inside a box inside a box.

```
let number: Int??? = 10
```

If you print `number` you get the following:

```
print(number)
// Optional(Optional(Optional(10)))

print(number!)
// Optional(Optional(10))
```

Do the following:

1. Fully force unwrap and print `number`.
2. Optionally bind and print `number` with `if let`.
3. Write a function `printNumber(_ number: Int???)` that uses `guard` to print the number only if it is bound.

Section II: Collection Types

So far, you've mostly seen data in the form of single elements. Although tuples can have multiple pieces of data, you have to specify the size up front; a tuple with three strings is a completely different type from a tuple with two strings, and converting between them isn't trivial. In this section, you'll learn about **collection types** in Swift. Collections are flexible "containers" that let you store any number of values together.

There are several collection types in Swift, but three important ones are arrays, dictionaries and sets. You'll learn about these here:

- **Chapter 7, Arrays, Dictionaries, and Sets**

Next you'll learn how to apply custom operations and loop over collection types with:

- **Chapter 8, Collection Iterations With Closures**

Finally, you will revisit strings, which are actually bi-directional collections of unicode characters in:

- **Chapter 9, Strings**

The collection types have similar interfaces but very different use cases. As you read through these chapters, keep the differences in mind, and you'll begin to develop a feel for which type you should use when.

As part of exploring the differences between the collection types, you'll also consider performance: how quickly the collections can perform certain operations, such as adding to the collection or searching through it.

The usual way to talk about performance is with **big-O notation**. If you're not familiar with it already, read on for a brief introduction.

Introducing big-O notation

Big-O notation is a way to describe **running time**, or how long an operation takes to complete. The idea is that the exact time an operation takes isn't important; it's the relative difference in scale that matters.

Imagine you have a list of names in some random order, and you have to look up the first name on the list. It doesn't matter whether the list has a single name or a million names — glancing at the very first name always takes the same amount of time. That's an example of a **constant time** operation, or **O(1)** in big-O notation.

Now say you have to find a particular name on the list. You need to scan through the list and look at every single name until you either find a match or reach the end. Again, we're not concerned with the exact amount of time this takes, just the relative time compared to other operations.

To figure out the running time, think in terms of units of work. You need to look at every name, so consider there to be one "unit" of work per name. If you had 100 names, that's 100 units of work. What if you double the number of names to 200? How does that change the amount of work? The answer is it *also* doubles the amount of work. Similarly, if you quadruple the number of names, that quadruples the amount of work.

This is an example of a **linear time** operation, or ***O*(N)** in big-O notation. The size of the input is the variable N, which means the amount of time the operation takes is also N. There's a direct, linear relationship between the input size (the number of names in the list) and the time it will take to search for one name.

You can see why constant time operations have the number 1 in *O*(1). They're just a single unit of work, no matter what!

You can read more about big-O notation by searching the Web. You'll only need constant time and linear time in this book, but there are other such **time complexities** out there.

Big-O notation is particularly important when dealing with collection types, because collections can store very large amounts of data, and you need to be aware of running times when you add, delete or edit values.

For example, if collection type A has constant-time searching and collection type B has linear-time searching, which you choose to use will depend on how much searching you're planning to do.

Chapter 7: Arrays, Dictionaries, Sets

By Eli Ganim

As discussed in the introduction to this section, collections are flexible "containers" that let you store any number of values together. Before discussing these collections, you need to understand the concept of *mutable* vs *immutable* collections.

Mutable versus immutable collections

Just like the previous types you've read about, such as `Int` or `String`, when you create a collection you must declare it as either a constant or a variable.

If the collection doesn't need to change after you've created it, you should make it immutable by declaring it as a constant with `let`. Alternatively, if you need to add, remove or update values in the collection, then you should create a mutable collection by declaring it as a variable with `var`.

Arrays

Arrays are the most common collection type you'll run into in Swift. Arrays are typed, just like regular variables and constants, and store multiple values like a simple list.

Before you create your first array, take some time to consider in detail what an array is and why you might want to use one.

What is an array?

An array is an ordered collection of values of the same type. The elements in the array are **zero-indexed**, which means the index of the first element is 0, the index of the second element is 1, and so on. Knowing this, you can work out that the last element's index is the number of values in the array less 1.

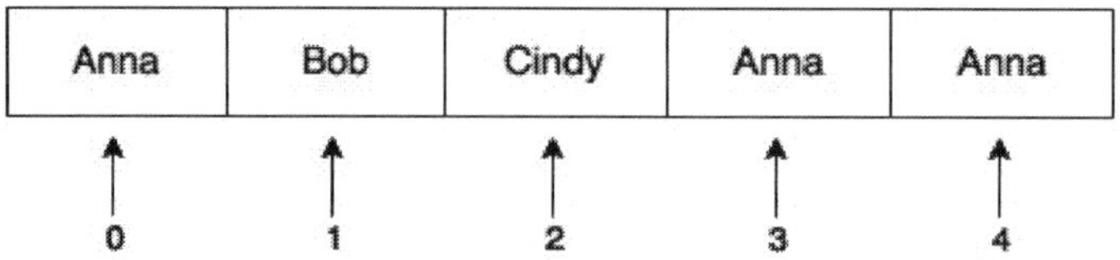

There are five elements in this array, at indices 0–4.

All values are of type `String`, so you can't add non-string types to an array that holds strings. Notice that the same value can appear multiple times.

When are arrays useful?

Arrays are useful when you want to store your items in a particular order. You may want the elements sorted, or you may need to fetch elements by index without iterating through the entire array.

For example, if you were storing high score data, then order would matter. You would want the highest score to come first in the list (i.e. at index 0) with the next-highest score after that, and so on.

Creating arrays

The easiest way to create an array is by using an **array literal**. This is a concise way to provide array values. An array literal is a list of values separated by commas and surrounded by square brackets.

```
let evenNumbers = [2, 4, 6, 8]
```

Since the array literal only contains integers, Swift infers the type of `evenNumbers` to be an array of `Int` values. This type is written as `[Int]`. The type inside the square brackets defines the type of values the array can store, which the compiler will enforce when you add elements to the array.

If you try to add a string, for example, the compiler will return an error and your code won't compile.

An empty array can be created using the empty array literal `[]`. Because the compiler isn't able to infer a type from this, you need to use a type annotation to make the type explicit:

```
var subscribers: [String] = []
```

It's also possible to create an array with all of its values set to a default value:

```
let allZeros = Array(repeating: 0, count: 5) // [0, 0, 0, 0, 0]
```

It's good practice to declare arrays that aren't going to change as constants. For example, consider this array:

```
let vowels = ["A", "E", "I", "O", "U"]
```

`vowels` is an array of strings and its values can't be changed. But that's fine, since the list of vowels doesn't tend to change very often!

Accessing elements

Being able to create arrays is useless unless you know how to fetch values from an array. In this section, you'll learn several different ways to access elements in an array.

Using properties and methods

Imagine you're creating a game of cards, and you want to store the players' names in an array. The list will need to change as players join or leave the game, so you need to declare a mutable array:

```
var players = ["Alice", "Bob", "Cindy", "Dan"]
```

In this example, `players` is a mutable array because you assigned it to a variable.

Before the game starts, you need to make sure there are enough players. You can use the `isEmpty` *property* to check if there's at least one player:

```
print(players.isEmpty)
// > false
```

> **Note:** You'll learn all about properties in Chapter 11, "Properties". For now, just think of them as variables that are built in to values. To access a property, place a dot after the name of the constant or variable that holds the value and follow it by the name of the property you want to access.

The array isn't empty, but you need at least two players to start a game. You can get the number of players using the `count` property:

```
if players.count < 2 {
  print("We need at least two players!")
} else {
  print("Let's start!")
}
// > Let's start!
```

It's time to start the game! You decide that the order of play is by the order of names in the array. How would you get the first player's name?

Arrays provide the `first` property to fetch the first object of an array:

```
var currentPlayer = players.first
```

Printing the value of `currentPlayer` reveals something interesting:

```
print(currentPlayer as Any)
// > Optional("Alice")
```

The property `first` actually returns an *optional*, because if the array were empty, `first` would return `nil`. The `print()` method realizes `currentPlayer` is optional and generates a warning. To suppress the warning, simply add `as Any` to the type to be printed.

Similarly, arrays have a `last` property that returns the last value in an array, or `nil` if the array is empty:

```
print(players.last as Any)
// > Optional("Dan")
```

Another way to get values from an array is by calling `min()`. This *method* returns the element with the lowest *value* in the array — not the lowest index! If the array contained strings, then it would return the string that's the lowest in alphabetical order, which in this case is `"Alice"`:

```
currentPlayer = players.min()
print(currentPlayer as Any)
```

```
// > Optional("Alice")
```

> **Note:** You'll learn all about methods in Chapter 12, "Methods". For now, just think of them as functions that are built in to values. To call a method, place a dot after the name of the constant or variable that holds the value and follow it by the name of the method you want to call. Just like with functions, don't forget to include the parameter list, even if it's empty, when calling a method.

Obviously, `first` and `min()` will not always return the same value. For example:

```
print([2, 3, 1].first as Any)
// > Optional(2)
print([2, 3, 1].min() as Any)
// > Optional(1)
```

As you might have guessed, arrays also have a `max()` method.

> **Note:** The `first` and `last` properties and the `min()` and `max()` methods aren't unique to arrays. Every collection type has these properties and methods, in addition to a plethora of others. You'll learn more about this behavior when you read about protocols in Chapter 16, "Protocols".

Now that you know how to get the first player, you'll announce who that player is:

```
if let currentPlayer = currentPlayer {
  print("\(currentPlayer) will start")
}
// > Alice will start
```

You use `if let` to unwrap the optional you got back from `min()`; otherwise, the statement would print `Optional("Alice") will start`, which is not what you want.

These properties and methods are helpful if you want to get the first, last, minimum or maximum elements. But what if the element you want can't be obtained with one of these properties or methods?

Using subscripting

The most convenient way to access elements in an array is by using the subscript syntax. This syntax lets you access any value directly by using its index inside square brackets:

```
var firstPlayer = players[0]
print("First player is \(firstPlayer)")
// > First player is "Alice"
```

Because arrays are zero-indexed, you use index 0 to fetch the first object. You can use a greater index to get the next elements in the array, but if you try to access an index that's beyond the size of the array, you'll get a runtime error.

```
var player = players[4]
// > fatal error: Index out of range
```

You receive this error because `players` contains only four strings. Index 4 represents the fifth element, but there *is* no fifth element in this array.

When you use subscripts, you don't have to worry about optionals, since trying to access a non-existing index doesn't return `nil`; it simply causes a runtime error.

Using countable ranges to make an ArraySlice

You can use the subscript syntax with countable ranges to fetch more than a single value from an array. For example, if you'd like to get the next two players, you could do this:

```
let upcomingPlayersSlice = players[1...2]
print(upcomingPlayersSlice[1], upcomingPlayersSlice[2])
// > "Bob Cindy\n"
```

The constant `upcomingPlayersSlice` is actually an `ArraySlice` of the original array. The reason for this type difference is to make clear that `upcomingPlayersSlice` shares storage with `players`.

The range you used is `1...2`, which represents the second and third items in the array. You can use an index here as long as the start value is smaller than or equal to the end value and both within the bounds of the array.

It is also easy to make a brand-new, zero-indexed `Array` from an `ArraySlice` like so:

```
let upcomingPlayersArray = Array(players[1...2])
print(upcomingPlayersArray[0], upcomingPlayersArray[1])
// > "Bob Cindy\n"
```

Checking for an element

You can check if there's at least one occurrence of a specific element in an array by using `contains(_:)`, which returns `true` if it finds the element in the array, and `false` otherwise.

You can use this strategy to write a function that checks if a given player is in the game:

```
func isEliminated(player: String) -> Bool {
  return !players.contains(player)
}
```

Now you can use this function any time you need to check if a player has been eliminated:

```
print(isEliminated(player: "Bob"))
// > false
```

You could even test for the existence of an element in a specific range using an `ArraySlice`:

```
players[1...3].contains("Bob") // true
```

Now that you can get data *out* of your arrays, it's time to look at mutable arrays and how to change their values.

Modifying arrays

You can make all kinds of changes to mutable arrays, such as adding and removing elements, updating existing values, and moving elements around into a different order. In this section, you'll see how to work with the array to match up what's going on with your game.

Appending elements

If new players want to join the game, they need to sign up and add their names to the array. Eli is the first player to join the existing four players. You can add Eli to the end of the array using the `append(_:)` method:

```
players.append("Eli")
```

If you try to append anything other than a string, the compiler will show an error. Remember, arrays can only store values of the same type. Also, `append(_:)` only works with mutable arrays.

The next player to join the game is Gina. You can append her to the game another way, by using the += operator:

```
players += ["Gina"]
```

The right-hand side of this expression is an array with a single element: the string `"Gina"`. By using +=, you're appending the elements of that array to `players`. Now the array looks like this:

```
print(players)
// > ["Alice", "Bob", "Cindy", "Dan", "Eli", "Gina"]
```

Here, you added a single element to the array, but you can see how easy it would be to append *multiple* items using the += operator by adding more names after Gina's.

Inserting elements

An unwritten rule of this card game is that the players' names have to be in alphabetical order. This list is missing a player that starts with the letter F. Luckily, Frank has just arrived. You want to add him to the list between Eli and Gina. To do that, you can use the `insert(_:at:)` method:

```
players.insert("Frank", at: 5)
```

The `at` argument defines where you want to add the element. Remember that the array is zero-indexed, so index 5 is Gina's index, causing her to move up as Frank takes her place.

Removing elements

During the game, the other players caught Cindy and Gina cheating. They should be removed from the game! You know that Gina is last in the players list, so you can remove her easily with the `removeLast()` method:

```
var removedPlayer = players.removeLast()
print("\(removedPlayer) was removed")
// > Gina was removed
```

This method does two things: It removes the last element and then returns it, in case you need to print it or store it somewhere else — like in an array of cheaters!

To remove Cindy from the game, you need to know the exact index where her name is stored. Looking at the list of players, you see that she's third in the list, so her index is 2.

```
removedPlayer = players.remove(at: 2)
print("\(removedPlayer) was removed")
// > Cindy was removed
```

But how would you get the index of an element if you didn't already know it? There's a method for that! `index(of:)` returns the *first index* of the element, because the array might contain multiple copies of the same value. If the method doesn't find the element, it returns `nil`.

Mini-exercise

Use `index(of:)` to determine the position of the element `"Dan"` in `players`.

Updating elements

Frank has decided everyone should call him Franklin from now on. You could remove the value `"Frank"` from the array and then add `"Franklin"`, but that's too much work for a simple task. Instead, you should use the subscript syntax to update the name.

```
print(players)
// > ["Alice", "Bob", "Dan", "Eli", "Frank"]
players[4] = "Franklin"
print(players)
// > ["Alice", "Bob", "Dan", "Eli", "Franklin"]
```

Be careful to not use an index beyond the bounds of the array, or your code will crash.

As the game continues, some players are eliminated, and new ones come to replace them. You can also use subscripting with ranges to update multiple values in a single line of code:

```
players[0...1] = ["Donna", "Craig", "Brian", "Anna"]
print(players)
// > ["Donna", "Craig", "Brian", "Anna", "Dan", "Eli",
"Franklin"]
```

This code replaces the first two players, Alice and Bob, with the four players in the new players array. As you can see, the size of the range doesn't have to be equal to the size of the array that holds the values you're adding.

Moving elements

Take a look at this mess! The `players` array contains names that start with A to F, but they aren't in the correct order, and that violates the rules of the game.

You can try to fix this situation by moving values one by one to their correct positions:

```
let playerAnna = players.remove(at: 3)
players.insert(playerAnna, at: 0)
print(players)
// > ["Anna", "Donna", "Craig", "Brian", "Dan", "Eli",
"Franklin"]
```

...or by swapping elements, by using `swapAt(_:_:)`:

```
players.swapAt(1, 3)
print(players)
// > ["Anna", "Brian", "Craig", "Donna", "Dan", "Eli",
"Franklin"]
```

This works for a few elements, but to sort the entire array, you should use `sort()`:

```
players.sort()
print(players)
// > ["Anna", "Brian", "Craig", "Dan", "Donna", "Eli",
"Franklin"]
```

If you'd like to leave the original array untouched and return a sorted *copy* instead, use `sorted()` instead of `sort()`.

Iterating through an array

It's getting late, so the players decide to stop for the night and continue tomorrow. In the meantime, you'll keep their scores in a separate array. You'll investigate a better approach for this when you learn about dictionaries, but for now you can continue to use arrays:

```
let scores = [2, 2, 8, 6, 1, 2, 1]
```

Before the players leave, you want to print the names of those still in the game. You can do this using the `for-in` loop you read about in Chapter 4, "Advanced Control Flow":

```
for player in players {
  print(player)
}
// > Anna
// > Brian
// > Craig
// > Dan
// > Donna
// > Eli
// > Franklin
```

This code goes over all the elements of `players`, from index 0 up to `players.count - 1` and prints their values. In the first iteration, `player` is equal to the first element of the array; in the second iteration, it's equal to the second element of the array; and so on, until the loop has printed all the elements in the array.

If you need the index of each element, you can iterate over the return value of the array's `enumerated()` method, which returns tuples with each element's index and value:

```
for (index, player) in players.enumerated() {
  print("\(index + 1). \(player)")
}
// > 1. Anna
// > 2. Brian
// > 3. Craig
// > 4. Dan
// > 5. Donna
// > 6. Eli
// > 7. Franklin
```

Now you can use the technique you've just learned to write a function that takes an array of integers as its input and returns the sum of its elements:

```
func sumOfElements(in array: [Int]) -> Int {
  var sum = 0
  for number in array {
    sum += number
  }
  return sum
}
```

You could use this function to calculate the sum of the players' scores:

```
print(sumOfElements(in: scores))
// > 22
```

Mini-exercise

Write a `for-in` loop that prints the players' names and scores.

Running time for array operations

Arrays are stored as a continuous block in memory. That means if you have ten elements in an array, the ten values are all stored one next to the other. With that in mind, here's the performance cost of various array operations:

Accessing elements: The cost of fetching an element is $O(1)$. Since all the values are sequential, it's easy to use *random access* and fetch a value at a particular index; all the compiler needs to know is where the array starts and what index you want to fetch.

Inserting elements: The complexity of adding an element depends on the position in which you add the new element:

- If you add to the beginning of the array, Swift requires *O*(N) because it has to shift all of the elements over by one to make room.
- Likewise, if you add to the middle of the array, all values from that index on need to be shifted over. Doing so will require `N/2` operations, therefore the running time is *O*(N).
- If you add to the end of the array using `append` and there's room, it will take *O*(1). If there isn't room, Swift will need to make space somewhere else and copy the entire array over before adding the new element, which will take *O*(N). The average case is *O*(1) though, because arrays are not full most of the time.

Deleting elements: Deleting an element leaves a gap where the removed element was. All elements in the array have to be sequential, so this gap needs to be closed by shifting elements forward.

The complexity is similar to inserting elements: If you're removing an element from the end, it's an *O*(1) operation. Otherwise the complexity is *O*(N).

Searching for an element: If the element you're searching for is the first element in the array, then the search will end after a single operation. If the element doesn't exist, you need to perform `N` operations until you realize that the element is not found. On average, searching for an element will take `N/2` operations, therefore searching has a complexity of *O*(N).

As you learn about dictionaries and sets, you'll see how their performance characteristics differ from arrays. That could give you a hint on which collection type to use for your particular case.

Key points

- **Arrays** are ordered collections of values of the same type.
- Use **subscripting** or one of the many properties and methods to access and update elements.
- Be wary of accessing an index that's out of bounds.

Dictionaries

A dictionary is an unordered collection of pairs, where each pair is comprised of a **key** and a **value**.

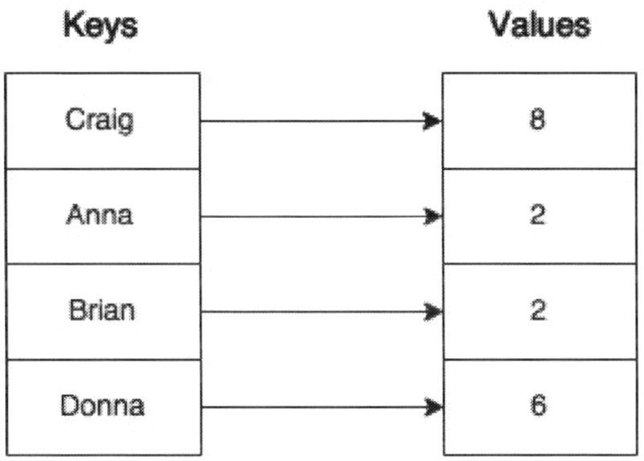

As shown in the diagram above, keys are unique. The same key can't appear twice in a dictionary, but different keys may point to the same value. All keys have to be of the same type, and all values have to be of the same type.

Dictionaries are useful when you want to look up values by means of an identifier. For example, the table of contents of this book maps chapter names to their page numbers, making it easy to skip to the chapter you want to read.

How is this different from an array? With an array, you can only fetch a value by its index, which has to be an integer, and all indexes have to be sequential. In a dictionary, the keys can be of any type and in no particular order.

Creating dictionaries

The easiest way to create a dictionary is by using a **dictionary literal**. This is a list of key-value pairs separated by commas, enclosed in square brackets.

For your card game from earlier, instead of using the two arrays to map players to their scores, you can use a dictionary literal:

```
var namesAndScores = ["Anna": 2, "Brian": 2, "Craig": 8,
"Donna": 6]
print(namesAndScores)
// > ["Craig": 8, "Anna": 2, "Donna": 6, "Brian": 2]
```

In this example, the type of the dictionary is inferred to be `[String: Int]`. This means `namesAndScores` is a dictionary with strings as keys and integers as values.

When you print the dictionary, you see there's no particular order to the pairs. Remember that, unlike arrays, dictionaries are unordered!

The empty dictionary literal looks like this: `[:]`. You can use that to empty an existing dictionary like so:

```
namesAndScores = [:]
```

...or create a new dictionary, like so:

```
var pairs: [String: Int] = [:]
```

The type annotation is required here, as the compiler can't infer the type of the dictionary from the empty dictionary literal.

After you create a dictionary, you can define its capacity:

```
pairs.reserveCapacity(20)
```

Using `reserveCapacity(_:)` is an easy way to improve performance when you have an idea of how much data the dictionary needs to store.

Accessing values

As with arrays, there are several ways to access dictionary values.

Using subscripting

Dictionaries support subscripting to access values. Unlike arrays, you don't access a value by its index but rather by its key. For example, if you want to get Anna's score, you would type:

```
namesAndScores = ["Anna": 2, "Brian": 2, "Craig": 8, "Donna": 6]
// Restore the values

print(namesAndScores["Anna"])
// > Optional(2)
```

Notice that the return type is an optional. The dictionary will check if there's a pair with the key `Anna`, and if there is, return its value. If the dictionary doesn't find the key, it will return `nil`.

```
namesAndScores["Greg"] // nil
```

With arrays, out-of-bounds subscript access causes a runtime error, but dictionaries are different since their results are wrapped in an optional.

Subscript access using optionals is really powerful. You can find out if a specific player is in the game without having to iterate over all the keys, as you must do when you use an array.

Using properties and methods

Dictionaries, like arrays, conform to Swift's `Collection` protocol. Because of that, they share many of the same properties. For example, both arrays and dictionaries have `isEmpty` and `count` properties:

```
namesAndScores.isEmpty  //  false
namesAndScores.count    //  4
```

> **Note:** If you just want to know whether a dictionary has elements or not, it is always better to use the `isEmpty` property. A dictionary needs to loop through all of the values to compute the count. `isEmpty`, by contrast, always runs in constant time no matter how many values there are.

Modifying dictionaries

It's easy enough to create dictionaries and access their contents — but what about modifying them?

Adding pairs

Bob wants to join the game.

Bob

Take a look at his details before you let him join:

```
var bobData = [
  "name": "Bob",
  "profession": "Card Player",
  "country": "USA"
]
```

This dictionary is of type `[String: String]`, and it's mutable because it's assigned to a variable. Imagine you received more information about Bob and you wanted to add it to the dictionary. This is how you'd do it:

```
bobData.updateValue("CA", forKey: "state")
```

There's even a shorter way to add pairs, using subscripting:

```
bobData["city"] = "San Francisco"
```

Bob's a professional card player. So far, he sounds like a good addition to your roster.

Mini-exercise

Write a function that prints a given player's city and state.

Updating values

It appears that in the past, Bob was caught cheating when playing cards. He's not just a professional — he's a card shark! He asks you to change his name and profession so no one will recognize him.

Because Bob seems eager to change his ways, you agree. First, you change his name from Bob to Bobby:

```
bobData.updateValue("Bobby", forKey: "name") // Bob
```

You saw this method above when you read about adding pairs. Why does it return the string `Bob`? `updateValue(_:forKey:)` replaces the value of the given key with the new value and returns the old value. If the key doesn't exist, this method will add a new pair and return `nil`.

As with adding, you can do this with less code by using subscripting:

```
bobData["profession"] = "Mailman"
```

Like `updateValue(_:forKey:)`, this code updates the value for this key or, if the key doesn't exist, creates a new pair.

Removing pairs

Bob — er, sorry — *Bobby*, still doesn't feel safe, and he wants you to remove all information about his whereabouts:

```
bobData.removeValue(forKey: "state")
```

This method will remove the key `state` and its associated value from the dictionary. As you might expect, there's a shorter way to do this using subscripting:

```
bobData["city"] = nil
```

Assigning `nil` as a key's associated value removes the pair from the dictionary.

> **Note:** If you are using a dictionary that has values that are optional types, `dictionary[key] = nil` still removes the key completely. If you want keep the key and set the value to `nil` you must use the `updateValue` method.

Iterating through dictionaries

The `for-in` loop also works when you want to iterate over a dictionary. But since the items in a dictionary are pairs, you need to use a tuple:

```
for (player, score) in namesAndScores {
  print("\(player) - \(score)")
}
// > Craig - 8
// > Anna - 2
// > Donna - 6
// > Brian - 2
```

It's also possible to iterate over just the keys:

```
for player in namesAndScores.keys {
  print("\(player), ", terminator: "") // no newline
}
print("") // print one final newline
// > Craig, Anna, Donna, Brian,
```

You can iterate over just the values in the same manner with the `values` property of the dictionary.

Running time for dictionary operations

In order to be able to examine how dictionaries work, you need to understand what **hashing** is and how it works. Hashing is the process of transforming a value — `String`, `Int`, `Double`, `Bool`, etc — to a numeric value, known as the *hash value*. This value can then be used to quickly lookup the values in a *hash table*.

Swift dictionaries have a type requirement for keys. Keys must be **Hashable** or you will get a compiler error.

Fortunately, in Swift, all basic types are already `Hashable` and have a `hashValue` integer property. Here's an example:

```
print("some string".hashValue)
// > -497521651836391849
print(1.hashValue)
// > 1
print(false.hashValue)
// > 0
```

The hash value has to be deterministic — meaning that a given value must *always* return the same hash value. No matter how many times you calculate the hash value for `some string`, it will always give the same value. You should never save a hash value, however, as there is no guarantee it will be the same from run-to-run of your program.

Here's the performance of various dictionary operations. This great performance hinges on having a good hashing function that avoids value collisions. If you have a poor hashing function, all of the operations below degenerate to linear time, or $O(n)$ performance. Fortunately, the built-in types have great, general purpose `hashValue` implementations.

Accessing elements: Getting the value for a key is a constant time operation, or $O(1)$.

Inserting elements: To insert an element, the dictionary needs to calculate the hash value of the key and then store data based on that hash. These are all $O(1)$ operations.

Deleting elements: Again, the dictionary needs to calculate the hash value to know exactly where to find the element, and then remove it. This is also an $O(1)$ operation.

Searching for an element: As mentioned above, accessing an element has constant running time, so the complexity for searching is also $O(1)$.

While all of these running times compare favorably to arrays, remember that you lose order information when using dictionaries.

Key points

- A **dictionary** is an unordered collection of key-value pairs.
- The **keys** of a dictionary are all of the same type, and the **values** are all of the same type.
- Use **subscripting** to get values and to add, update or remove pairs.
- If a key is not in a dictionary, lookup returns `nil`.
- The key of a dictionary must be a type that conforms to the **`Hashable`** protocol.
- Basic Swift types such as `String`, `Int`, `Double` are `Hashable` out of the box.

Sets

A set is an unordered collection of unique values of the same type. This can be extremely useful when you want to ensure that an item doesn't appear more than once in your collection, and when the order of your items isn't important.

Creating sets

You can declare a set explicitly by writing `Set` followed by the type inside angle brackets:

```
let setOne: Set<Int>
```

Set literals

Sets don't have their own literals. You use **array literals** to create a set with initial values. Consider this example:

```
let someArray = [1, 2, 3, 1]
```

This is an array. So how would you use array literals to create a set? Like this:

```
var someSet: Set<Int> = [1, 2, 3, 1]
```

You have to explicitly declare the variable as a `Set`.

To see the most important features of a set in action, let's print the set you just created:

```
print(someSet)
// > [2, 3, 1]
```

First, you can see there's no specific ordering. Second, although you created the set with two instances of the value `1`, that value only appears once. Remember, a set's values must be unique.

Accessing elements

You can use `contains(_:)` to check for the existence of a specific element:

```
print(someSet.contains(1))
// > true
print(someSet.contains(4))
// > false
```

You can also use the `first` and `last` properties, which return one of the elements in the set. However, because sets are unordered, you won't know exactly which item you'll get.

Adding and removing elements

You can use `insert(_:)` to add elements to a set. If the element already exists, the method does nothing.

```
someSet.insert(5)
```

You can remove the element from the set like this:

```
let removedElement = someSet.remove(1)
print(removedElement!)
// > 1
```

`remove(_:)` returns the removed element if it's in the set, or `nil` otherwise.

Running time for set operations

Sets have a very similar implementations to those of dictionaries, and they also require the elements to be hashable. The running time of all the operations is identical to those of dictionaries.

Key points

- **Sets** are unordered collections of unique values of the same type.
- Sets are most useful when you need to know whether something is included in the collection or not.

Where to go from here?

Now that you've learned about the three collection types in Swift, you should have a good idea of what they can do and when you should use them. You'll see them come up as you continue on in the book.

The next chapter of the book covers **collection iteration with closures**. These let you iterate over the collection types you've learned in a less explicit and more readable manner than loops.

Before you move on, check out the following challenges to test your collection knowledge.

Challenges

1. Which of the following are valid statements?

```
1. let array1 = [Int]()
2. let array2 = []
3. let array3: [String] = []
```

For the next five statements, `array4` has been declared as:

```
let array4 = [1, 2, 3]
```

```
4. print(array4[0])
5. print(array4[5])
6. array4[1...2]
7. array4[0] = 4
8. array4.append(4)
```

For the final five statements, `array5` has been declared as:

```
var array5 = [1, 2, 3]
```

```
9. array5[0] = array5[1]
10. array5[0...1] = [4, 5]
11. array5[0] = "Six"
12. array5 += 6
13. for item in array5 { print(item) }
```

2. Write a function that removes the first occurrence of a given integer from an array of integers. This is the signature of the function:

```
func removingOnce(_ item: Int, from array: [Int]) -> [Int]
```

3. Write a function that removes all occurrences of a given integer from an array of integers. This is the signature of the function:

```
func removing(_ item: Int, from array: [Int]) -> [Int]
```

4. Arrays have a `reversed()` method that returns an array holding the same elements as the original array, in reverse order. Write a function that does the same thing, without using `reversed()`. This is the signature of the function:

```
func reversed(_ array: [Int]) -> [Int]
```

5. The function below returns a random number between 0 and the given argument:

```
import Foundation
func randomFromZero(to number: Int) -> Int {
  return Int(arc4random_uniform(UInt32(number)))
}
```

Use it to write a function that shuffles the elements of an array in random order. This is the signature of the function:

```
func randomized(_ array: [Int]) -> [Int]
```

6. Write a function that calculates the minimum and maximum value in an array of integers. Calculate these values yourself; don't use the methods `min` and `max`. Return `nil` if the given array is empty.

This is the signature of the function:

```
func minMax(of numbers: [Int]) -> (min: Int, max: Int)?
```

7. Which of the following are valid statements?

```
1. let dict1: [Int, Int] = [:]
2. let dict2 = [:]
```

```
3. let dict3: [Int: Int] = [:]
```

For the next four statements, use the following dictionary:

```
let dict4 = ["One": 1, "Two": 2, "Three": 3]
```

```
4. dict4[1]
5. dict4["One"]
6. dict4["Zero"] = 0
7. dict4[0] = "Zero"
```

For the next three statements, use the following dictionary:

```
var dict5 = ["NY": "New York", "CA": "California"]
```

```
8. dict5["NY"]
9. dict5["WA"] = "Washington"
10. dict5["CA"] = nil
```

8. Given a dictionary with two-letter state codes as keys, and the full state names as values, write a function that prints all the states with names longer than eight characters. For example, for the dictionary `["NY": "New York", "CA": "California"]`, the output would be `California`.

9. Write a function that combines two dictionaries into one. If a certain key appears in both dictionaries, ignore the pair from the first dictionary. This is the function's signature:

```
func merging(_ dict1: [String: String], with dict2: [String:
String]) -> [String: String]
```

10. Declare a function `occurrencesOfCharacters` that calculates which characters occur in a string, as well as how often each of these characters occur. Return the result as a dictionary. This is the function signature:

```
func occurrencesOfCharacters(in text: String) -> [Character:
Int]
```

Hint: `String` is a collection of characters that you can iterate over with a for statement.Bonus: To make your code shorter, dictionaries have a special subscript operator that let you add a default value if it is not found in the dictionary. For example, `dictionary["a", default: 0]` creates a 0 entry for the character "a" if it is not found instead of just returning `nil`.

11. Write a function that returns `true` if all of the values of a dictionary are unique. Use a set to test uniqueness. This is the function signature:

```
func isInvertible(_ dictionary: [String: Int]) -> Bool
```

12. Given the dictionary:

```
var nameTitleLookup: [String: String?] = ["Mary": "Engineer",
"Patrick": "Intern", "Ray": "Hacker"]
```

Set the value of the key `"Patrick"` to `nil` and completely remove the key and value for `"Ray"`.

Chapter 8: Collection Iteration with Closures

By Matt Galloway

The previous section taught you about functions. But Swift has another object you can use to break up code into reusable chunks: a **closure**. They become particularly useful when dealing with collections.

A closure is simply a function with no name; you can assign it to a variable and pass it around like any other value. This chapter shows you how convenient and useful closures can be.

Closure basics

Closures are so named because they have the ability to "close over" the variables and constants within the closure's own scope. This simply means that a closure can access, store and manipulate the value of any variable or constant from the surrounding context. Variables and constants used within the body of a closure are said to have been **captured** by the closure.

You may ask, "If closures are functions without names, then how do you use them?" To use a closure, you first have to assign it to a variable or constant.

Here's a declaration of a variable that can hold a closure:

```
var multiplyClosure: (Int, Int) -> Int
```

`multiplyClosure` takes two `Int` values and returns an `Int`. Notice that this is exactly the same as a variable declaration for a function. Like I said, a closure is simply a function without a name. The type of a closure is a function type.

You assign a closure to a variable like so:

```
multiplyClosure = { (a: Int, b: Int) -> Int in
  return a * b
}
```

This looks similar to a function declaration, but there's a subtle difference. There's the same parameter list, -> symbol and return type. But in the case of closures, these elements appear inside braces, and there is an `in` keyword after the return type.

With your closure variable defined, you can use it just as if it were a function, like so:

```
let result = multiplyClosure(4, 2)
```

As you'd expect, `result` equals 8. Again, though, there's a subtle difference.

Notice how the closure has no external names for the parameters. You can't set them like you can with functions.

Shorthand syntax

Compared to functions, closures are designed to be lightweight. There are many ways to shorten their syntax. First, if the closure consists of a single return statement, you can leave out the `return` keyword, like so:

```
multiplyClosure = { (a: Int, b: Int) -> Int in
  a * b
}
```

Next, you can use Swift's type inference to shorten the syntax even more by removing the type information:

```
multiplyClosure = { (a, b) in
  a * b
}
```

Remember, you already declared `multiplyClosure` as a closure taking two `Int`s and returning an `Int`, so you can let Swift infer these types for you.

And finally, you can even omit the parameter list if you want. Swift lets you refer to each parameter by number, starting at zero, like so:

```
multiplyClosure = {
  $0 * $1
}
```

The parameter list, return type and `in` keyword are all gone, and your new closure declaration is much shorter than the original. Numbered parameters like this should really only be used when the closure is short and sweet, like the one above.

If the parameter list is much longer it can be confusing to remember what each numbered parameter refers to. In these cases you should use the named syntax.

Consider the following code:

```
func operateOnNumbers(_ a: Int, _ b: Int,
                      operation: (Int, Int) -> Int) -> Int {
  let result = operation(a, b)
  print(result)
  return result
}
```

This declares a function named `operateOnNumbers`, which takes `Int` values as its first two parameters. The third parameter is named `operation` and is of a function type. `operateOnNumbers` itself returns an `Int`.

You can then use `operateOnNumbers` with a closure, like so:

```
let addClosure = { (a: Int, b: Int) in
  a + b
}
operateOnNumbers(4, 2, operation: addClosure)
```

Remember, closures are simply functions without names. So you shouldn't be surprised to learn that you can also pass in a function as the third parameter of `operateOnNumbers`, like so:

```
func addFunction(_ a: Int, _ b: Int) -> Int {
  return a + b
}
operateOnNumbers(4, 2, operation: addFunction)
```

`operateOnNumbers` is called the same way, whether the `operation` is a function or a closure.

The power of the closure syntax comes in handy again. You can define the closure inline with the `operateOnNumbers` function call, like this:

```
operateOnNumbers(4, 2, operation: { (a: Int, b: Int) -> Int in
  return a + b
})
```

There's no need to define the closure and assign it to a local variable or constant. You can simply declare the closure right where you pass it into the function as a parameter!

But recall that you can simplify the closure syntax to remove a lot of the boilerplate code. You can therefore reduce the above to the following:

```
operateOnNumbers(4, 2, operation: { $0 + $1 })
```

In fact, you can even go a step further. The + operator is just a function that takes two arguments and returns one result so you can write:

```
operateOnNumbers(4, 2, operation: +)
```

There's one more way you can simplify the syntax, but it can only be done when the closure is the final parameter passed to a function. In this case, you can move the closure outside of the function call:

```
operateOnNumbers(4, 2) {
  $0 + $1
}
```

This may look strange, but it's just the same as the previous code snippet, except you've removed the `operation` label and pulled the braces outside of the function call parameter list. This is called **trailing closure syntax**.

Closures with no return value

Until now, all the closures you've seen have taken one or more parameters and have returned values. But just like functions, closures aren't required to do these things. Here's how you declare a closure that takes no parameters and returns nothing:

```
let voidClosure: () -> Void = {
  print("Swift Apprentice is awesome!")
}
voidClosure()
```

The closure's type is `() -> Void`. The empty parentheses denote there are no parameters. You must declare a return type, so Swift knows you're declaring a closure. This is where `Void` comes in handy, and it means exactly what its name suggests: the closure returns nothing.

> **Note:** `Void` is actually just a typealias for `()`. This means you could have written `() -> Void` as `() -> ()`. A function's parameter list however must always be surrounded by parentheses, so `Void -> ()` or `Void -> Void` are invalid.

Capturing from the enclosing scope

Finally, let's return to the defining characteristic of a closure: it can access the variables and constants from within its own scope.

> **Note:** Recall that scope defines the range in which an entity (variable, constant, etc) is accessible. You saw a new scope introduced with `if`-statements. Closures also introduce a new scope and inherit all entities visible to the scope in which it is defined.

For example, take the following closure:

```
var counter = 0
let incrementCounter = {
  counter += 1
}
```

`incrementCounter` is rather simple: It increments the `counter` variable. The `counter` variable is defined outside of the closure. The closure is able to access the variable because the closure is defined in the same scope as the variable. The closure is said to **capture** the `counter` variable. Any changes it makes to the variable are visible both inside and outside the closure.

Let's say you call the closure five times, like so:

```
incrementCounter()
incrementCounter()
incrementCounter()
incrementCounter()
incrementCounter()
```

After these five calls, `counter` will equal 5.

The fact that closures can be used to capture variables from the enclosing scope can be extremely useful. For example, you could write the following function:

```
func countingClosure() -> () -> Int {
  var counter = 0
  let incrementCounter: () -> Int = {
    counter += 1
    return counter
  }
  return incrementCounter
}
```

This function takes no parameters and returns a closure. The closure it returns takes no parameters and returns an `Int`.

The closure returned from this function will increment its internal counter each time it is called. Each time you call this function you get a different counter.

For example, this could be used like so:

```
let counter1 = countingClosure()
let counter2 = countingClosure()

counter1() // 1
counter2() // 1
counter1() // 2
counter1() // 3
counter2() // 2
```

The two counters created by the function are mutually exclusive and count independently. Neat!

Custom sorting with closures

Closures come in handy when you start looking deeper at collections. In Chapter 7, you used array's `sort` method to sort an array. By specifying a closure, you can customize how things are sorted. You call `sorted()` to get a sorted version of the array as so:

```
let names = ["ZZZZZZ", "BB", "A", "CCCC", "EEEEE"]
names.sorted()
// ["A", "BB", "CCCC", "EEEEE", "ZZZZZZ"]
```

By specifying a custom closure, you can change the details of how the array is sorted. Specify a trailing closure like so:

```
names.sorted {
  $0.count > $1.count
}
// ["ZZZZZZ", "EEEEE", "CCCC", "BB", "A"]
```

Now the array is sorted by the length of the string with longer strings coming first.

Iterating over collections with closures

In Swift, collections implement some very handy features often associated with **functional programming**. These features come in the shape of functions that you can apply to a collection to perform an operation on it.

Operations include things like transforming each element or filtering out certain elements.

All of these functions make use of closures, as you will see now.

The first of these functions lets you loop over the elements in a collection and perform an operation like so:

```
let values = [1, 2, 3, 4, 5, 6]
values.forEach {
  print("\($0): \($0*$0)")
}
```

This loops through each item in the collection printing the value and its square.

Another function allows you to filter out certain elements, like so:

```
var prices = [1.5, 10, 4.99, 2.30, 8.19]

let largePrices = prices.filter {
  return $0 > 5
}
```

Here, you create an array of `Double` to represent the prices of items in a shop. To filter out the prices which are greater than $5, you use the `filter` function. This function looks like so:

```
func filter(_ isIncluded: (Element) -> Bool) -> [Element]
```

This means that `filter` takes a single parameter, which is a closure (or function) that takes an `Element` and returns a `Bool`. The `filter` function then returns an array of `Element`s. In this context, `Element` refers to the type of items in the array. In the example above, `Double`s.

The closure's job is to return `true` or `false` depending on whether or not the value should be kept or not. The array returned from `filter` will contain all elements for which the closure returned `true`.

In your example, `largePrices` will contain:

```
(10, 8.19)
```

Note: The array that is returned from `filter` (and all of these functions) is a new array. The original is not modified at all.

However, there is more!

Imagine you're having a sale and want to discount all items to 90% of their original price. There's a handy function named `map` which can achieve this:

```
let salePrices = prices.map {
  return $0 * 0.9
}
```

The `map` function will take a closure, execute it on each item in the array and return a new array containing each result with the order maintained. In this case, `salePrices` will contain:

```
[1.35, 9, 4.491, 2.07, 7.371]
```

The `map` function can also be used to change the type. You can do that like so:

```
let userInput = ["0", "11", "haha", "42"]

let numbers1 = userInput.map {
  Int($0)
}
```

This takes some strings that the user input and turns them into an array of `Int?`. They need to be optional because the conversion from `String` to `Int` might fail.

If you want to filter out the invalid (missing) values, you can use `flatMap()` like so:

let numbers2 = userInput.flatMap {Int($0)}

This is almost the same as `map` except it creates an array of `Int` and tosses out the missing values.

Another handy function is called `reduce`. This function takes a starting value and a closure. The closure takes two values: the current value and an element from the array.

The closure returns the next value that should be passed into the closure as the current value parameter.

This could be used with the `prices` array to calculate the total, like so:

```
let sum = prices.reduce(0) {
  return $0 + $1
}
```

The initial value is 0. Then the closure calculates the sum of the current value plus the current iteration's value. Thus you calculate the total of all the values in the array. In this case, `sum` will be:

```
26.98
```

Now that you've seen `filter`, `map` and `reduce`, hopefully it's becoming clear how powerful these functions can be, especially thanks to the syntax of closures. In just a few lines of code, you have calculated quite complex values from the collection.

These functions can also be used with dictionaries. Imagine you represent the stock in your shop by a dictionary mapping the price to number of items at that price. You could use that to calculate the total value of your stock like so:

```
let stock = [1.5: 5, 10: 2, 4.99: 20, 2.30: 5, 8.19: 30]
let stockSum = stock.reduce(0) {
  return $0 + $1.key * Double($1.value)
}
```

In this case, the second parameter to the `reduce` function is a named tuple containing the `key` and `value` from the dictionary elements. A type conversion of the value is required to perform the calculation.

Here, the result is:

```
384.5
```

There's also another form of reduce that is useful when the result you're reducing your collection into is an array or dictionary. It's called `reduce(into:_:)`. You use it like so:

```
let farmAnimals = ["🐎": 5, "🐄": 10, "🐑": 50, "🐶": 1]
let allAnimals = farmAnimals.reduce(into: []) {
  (result, this: (key: String, value: Int)) in
  for _ in 0 ..< this.value {
```

```
    result.append(this.key)
  }
}
```

It works in exactly the same way as the other version, except that you don't return something from the closure. Instead, each iteration you are given a mutable value to do with what you want. In this way, there is only ever one array in this example that is created and appended to. This makes it more performant and therefore more desirable to use.

There are also a few different functions which can be helpful when you need to chop up an array. The first function is called `dropFirst`, which works like so:

```
let removeFirst = prices.dropFirst()
let removeFirstTwo = prices.dropFirst(2)
```

The `dropFirst` function takes a single parameter which defaults to 1 and returns an array with the required number of elements removed from the front. In this case the results will be as follows:

```
removeFirst = [10, 4.99, 2.30, 8.19]
removeFirstTwo = [4.99, 2.30, 8.19]
```

Just like `dropFirst`, there also exists `dropLast` which removes elements from the end of the array. It works like this:

```
let removeLast = prices.dropLast()
let removeLastTwo = prices.dropLast(2)
```

The results of these are as you would expect, as follows:

```
removeLast = [1.5, 10, 4.99, 2.30]
removeLastTwo = [1.5, 10, 4.99]
```

And finally, you can select just the first or last elements of an array as shown below:

```
let firstTwo = prices.prefix(2)
let lastTwo = prices.suffix(2)
```

Here, `prefix` returns the required number of elements from the front of the array, and `suffix` returns the required number of elements from the back of the array. The results of this function are:

```
firstTwo = [1.5, 10]
lastTwo = [2.30, 8.19]
```

That wraps up collection iteration with closures!

Mini-exercises

1. Create a constant array called `names` which contains some names as strings. Any names will do — make sure there's more than three. Now use `reduce` to create a string which is the concatenation of each name in the array.
2. Using the same `names` array, first filter the array to contain only names which have more than four characters in them, and then create the same concatenation of names as in the above exercise. (Hint: you can chain these operations together.)
3. Create a constant dictionary called `namesAndAges` which contains some names as strings mapped to ages as integers. Now use `filter` to create a dictionary containing only people under the age of 18.
4. Using the same `namesAndAges` dictionary, filter out the adults (those 18 or older) and then use `map` to convert to an array containing just the names (i.e. drop the ages).

Key points

- **Closures** are functions without names. They can be assigned to variables and passed as parameters to functions.
- Closures have **shorthand syntax** that makes them a lot easier to use than other functions.
- A closure can **capture** the variables and constants from its surrounding context.
- A closure can be used to direct how a collection is sorted.
- There exists a handy set of functions on collections which can be used to iterate over the collection and transform the collection. Transforms include mapping each element to a new value, filtering out certain values and reducing the collection down to a single value.

Where to go from here?

Closures and functions are the fundamental types for storing your code into reusable pieces. Aside from declaring them and calling them, you've also seen how useful they are when passing them around as parameters to *other* functions and closures.

Why not stick around and find out if you've really learned this stuff? Check out the challenges below to test your knowledge before moving on.

Challenges

Challenge 1: Repeating yourself

Your first challenge is to write a function that will run a given closure a given number of times.

Declare the function like so:

```
func repeatTask(times: Int, task: () -> Void)
```

The function should run the `task` closure, `times` number of times.

Use this function to print `"Swift Apprentice is a great book!"` 10 times.

Challenge 2: Closure sums

In this challenge, you're going to write a function that you can reuse to create different mathematical sums.

Declare the function like so:

```
func mathSum(length: Int, series: (Int) -> Int) -> Int
```

The first parameter, `length`, defines the number of values to sum. The second parameter, `series`, is a closure that can be used to generate a series of values. `series` should have a parameter that is the position of the value in the series and return the value at that position.

`mathSum` should calculate `length` number of values, starting at position 1, and return their sum.

Use the function to find the sum of the first 10 square numbers, which equals 385. Then use the function to find the sum of the first 10 Fibonacci numbers, which equals 143. For the Fibonacci numbers, you can use the function you wrote in the functions chapter — or grab it from the solutions if you're unsure your solution is correct.

Challenge 3: Functional ratings

In this final challenge, you will have a list of app names with associated ratings they've been given. Note — these are all fictional apps!

Create the data dictionary like so:

```
let appRatings = [
  "Calendar Pro": [1, 5, 5, 4, 2, 1, 5, 4],
  "The Messenger": [5, 4, 2, 5, 4, 1, 1, 2],
  "Socialise": [2, 1, 2, 2, 1, 2, 4, 2]
]
```

First, create a dictionary called `averageRatings` which will contain a mapping of app names to average ratings. Use `forEach` to iterate through the `appRatings` dictionary, then use `reduce` to calculate the average rating and store this rating in the `averageRatings` dictionary.

Finally, use `filter` and `map` chained together to get a list of the app names whose average rating is greater than 3.

Chapter 9: Strings

By Matt Galloway

So far you have briefly seen what the type `String` has to offer for representing text. Text is an extremely common data type: people's names; their addresses; the words of a book. All of these are examples of text that an app might need to handle. It's worth having a deeper understanding of how `String` works and what it can do.

This chapter deepens your knowledge of strings in general, and more specifically how strings work in Swift. Swift is one of the few language that handles Unicode characters correctly while maintaining maximum predictable performance.

Strings as collections

In Chapter 2 you learned the basics of what a string is, and you learned what character sets and code points are. To recap, they define the mapping numbers to the character it represents. It's now time to look further into the `String` type.

It's pretty easy to conceptualize a string as a collection of characters. Because strings are collections, you can do things like this:

```
let string = "Matt"
for char in string {
  print(char)
}
```

This will print out every character of `Matt` individually. Simple, eh?

You can also use other collection operations, such as:

```
let stringLength = string.count
```

This will give you the length of the string.

Now imagine you want to get the fourth character in the string. You may think to do something like this:

```
let fourthChar = string[3]
```

However, if you did this you would receive the following error message:

```
'subscript' is unavailable: cannot subscript String with an Int,
see the documentation comment for discussion
```

Why is that? It's time to take a detour further into how strings work by introducing what a **grapheme cluster** is.

Grapheme clusters

As you know, a string is made up of a collection of Unicode characters. Until now, you have considered one code point to precisely equal one character, and vice versa. However the term "character" is fairly loose.

It may come as a surprise, but there are two ways to represent some characters. One example is the é in `café`, which is an `e` with an acute accent. You can represent this character with either a single character or with two.

The single character to represent this is code point 233. The two-character case is an `e` on its own followed by an acute accent **combining character**, which is a special character that modifies the previous character.

So you can represent the `e` with an acute accent by either of these means:

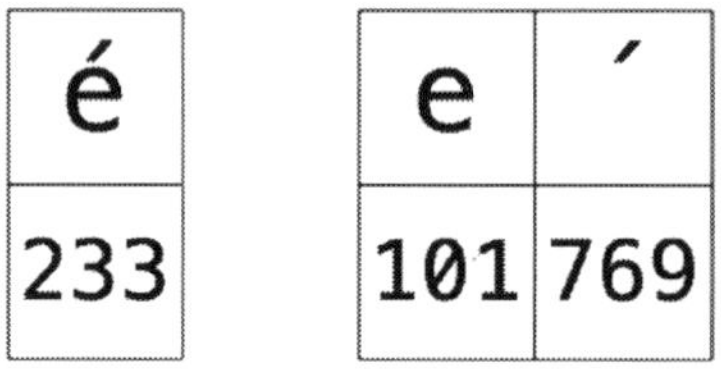

The combination of these two characters in the second diagram forms what is known as a **grapheme cluster** defined by the Unicode standard. When you think of a character, you're actually probably thinking of a grapheme cluster. Grapheme clusters are represented by the Swift type `Character`.

Another example of combining characters are the special characters used to change the skin color of certain emojis.

👍	🏽
128077	127997

👍🏽

Here, the thumbs up emoji is followed by a skin tone combining character. On platforms that support it, including iOS and macOS, the rendered emoji is a single thumbs up character with the skin tone applied.

Let's now take a look at what this means for strings when they are used as collections. Consider the following code:

```
let cafeNormal = "café"
let cafeCombining = "cafe\u{0301}"

cafeNormal.count      // 4
cafeCombining.count   // 4
```

Both of these counts turn out to equal 4. This is because Swift considers a string as a collection of grapheme clusters. The astute reader will also notice that this means that finding out the length of a string takes linear time, because you need to go through all characters to determine how many grapheme clusters there are. You cannot simply know from looking at how big the string is in memory.

> **Note:** In the code above, the acute accent combining character is written using the Unicode shorthand, which is `\u` followed by the code point in hexadecimal, in braces. You can use this shorthand to write any Unicode character. I had to use it here for the combining character because there's no way to type this character on my keyboard!

However there is a way to obtain access to the underlying Unicode code points in the string. You do this through the `unicodeScalars` **view** on the string. This view is also a collection itself. So you can do the following:

```
cafeNormal.unicodeScalars.count     // 4
cafeCombining.unicodeScalars.count  // 5
```

As you can see, in this case you are seeing the difference in the counts as you'd expect.

You can iterate through this Unicode scalars view like so:

```
for codePoint in cafeCombining.unicodeScalars {
  print(codePoint.value)
}
```

This will print the following list of numbers, as expected:

```
99
97
102
101
769
```

Indexing strings

As you saw earlier, indexing into a string to get a certain character (err, I mean grapheme cluster) is not as simple as using an integer subscript. This is because Swift wants you to be aware of what's going on under the hood and so makes the syntax a little more verbose.

You have to operate on the specific string index type in order to index into strings. For example, you obtain the index that represents the start of the string like so:

```
let firstIndex = cafeCombining.startIndex
```

If you option-click on `firstIndex` in a playground you will notice that it is of type `String.Index` and is not an integer.

You can then use this value to obtain the `Character` (grapheme cluster) at that index, like so:

```
let firstChar = cafeCombining[firstIndex]
```

In this case, `firstChar` will of course be "c". The type of this value is **Character** which is a grapheme cluster.

Similarly, you can obtain the last grapheme cluster like so:

```
let lastIndex = cafeCombining.endIndex
let lastChar = cafeCombining[lastIndex]
```

But if you do this you'll get a fatal error:

```
fatal error: Can't form a Character from an empty String
```

This is because the `endIndex` is actually 1 past the end of the string. So to obtain the last character you need to do this:

```
let lastIndex = cafeCombining.index(before:
cafeCombining.endIndex)
let lastChar = cafeCombining[lastIndex]
```

Here you're obtaining the index just before the end index and then obtaining the character at that index. Alternatively you could offset from the first character like so:

```
let fourthIndex = cafeCombining.index(cafeCombining.startIndex,
offsetBy: 3)
let fourthChar = cafeCombining[fourthIndex]
```

In this case, `fourthChar` is `é` as expected.

But as you know, the `é` in that case is actually made up of multiple code points. You can access these code points on the `Character` type in the same way as you can on `String`, through the `unicodeScalars` view. So you can do this:

```
fourthChar.unicodeScalars.count // 2
fourthChar.unicodeScalars.forEach { codePoint in
  print(codePoint.value)
}
```

This time you're using the `forEach` function to iterate through the Unicode scalars view. The count is 2 and as expected, the loop prints out:

```
101
769
```

Equality with combining characters

Combining characters make equality of strings a little trickier. For example, consider the word **café** written once using the single é character, and once using the combining character, like so:

c	a	f	é
99	97	102	233

c	a	f	e	´
99	97	102	101	769

These two strings are of course logically equal. When they are printed onscreen, they use the same **glyph** and look exactly the same. But they are represented inside the computer in different ways. Many programming languages would consider these strings to be unequal, because those languages work by comparing the code points one by one. Swift, however, considers these strings to be equal by default. Let's see that in action.

```
let equal = cafeNormal == cafeCombining
```

In this case, `equal` is `true`, because the two strings are logically the same.

String comparison in Swift uses a technique known as **canonicalization**. Say that three times fast! Before checking equality, Swift canonicalizes both strings, which means they're converted to use the same special character representation.

It doesn't matter which way Swift does the canonicalization — using the single character or using the combining character — as long as both strings get converted to the same style. Once the canonicalization is complete, Swift can compare individual characters to check for equality.

The same canonicalization comes into play when considering how many characters are in a certain string, which you saw earlier where `café` using the single `é` character and `café` using the `e` plus combining accent character had the same length.

Strings as bi-directional collections

Sometimes you want to reverse a string. Often this is so you can iterate through it backwards. Fortunately, Swift has a rather simple way to do this, through a method called `reversed()` like so:

```
let name = "Matt"
let backwardsName = name.reversed()
```

But what is the type of `backwardsName`? If you said `String`, then you would be wrong. It is actually a `ReversedCollection<String>`. This is a rather clever optimization that Swift makes. Instead of it being a concrete `String`, it is actually a **reversed collection**. This is a thin wrapper around any collection which allows you to use the collection as if it were the other way round, without incurring any more memory usage.

You can then access the `Characters` in the backwards string just as you would any other string, like so:

```
let secondCharIndex =
backwardsName.index(backwardsName.startIndex, offsetBy: 1)
let secondChar = backwardsName[secondCharIndex] // "t"
```

But what if you actually want a string? Well you can do that by initializing a `String` from the reversed collection, like so:

```
let backwardsNameString = String(backwardsName)
```

This will create a new `String` from the reversed collection. But when you do this, you end up making a reversed copy of the original string with its own memory storage. So if you don't actually need the whole reversed string then staying in the reversed collection domain will save memory space.

Substrings

Another thing that you often need to do when manipulating strings is to generate substrings. That is, pull out a part of the string into its own value. This can be done in Swift using a subscript that takes a range of indices.

For example, consider the following code:

```
let fullName = "Matt Galloway"
let spaceIndex = fullName.index(of: " ")!
let firstName = fullName[fullName.startIndex..<spaceIndex] //
"Matt"
```

This code finds the index that represents the first space (using a force unwrap here because you know one exists). Then it uses a range to find the grapheme clusters between the start index and the index of the space (not including the space).

Now is a good time to introduce a new type of range that you haven't seen before: the **open-ended range**. This type of range only takes one index and assumes the other is either the start or the end of the collection.

That last line of code can be rewritten as follows using an open-ended range:

```
let firstName = fullName[..<spaceIndex] // "Matt"
```

This time we omit the `fullName.startIndex` and Swift will infer that this is what you mean.

Similarly, you can also use a one-sided range to start at a certain index and go to the end of the collection, like so:

```
let lastName = fullName[fullName.index(after: spaceIndex)...] //
"Galloway"
```

There's something interesting to point out with substrings. If you look at their type, then you will see they are of type `Substring` rather than `String`. Just like with the reversed string, you can force this `Substring` into a `String` by doing the following:

```
let lastNameString = String(lastName)
```

The reason for this extra `Substring` type is a cunning optimization. A `Substring` shares the storage with its parent `String` that it was sliced from. This means that when you're in the process of slicing a string, you use no extra memory. Then, when you want the substring as a `String` you explicitly create a new string and the memory is copied into a new buffer for this new string.

The designers of Swift could have made this copy behavior by default. However, by having the separate type `Substring`, Swift makes it very explicit what is happening. The good news is that `String` and `Substring` share almost all of the same capabilities. You might not even realize which type you are using until you return or pass your `Substring` to another function that requires a `String`. In this case, you can simply initialize a new `String` from your `Substring` explicitly.

It is hopefully clear by now that Swift is very opinionated about strings, and very deliberate in the way it implements them. This is important because strings are complex beasts, but they are very frequently used. Therefore getting the API right for them is important.

Encoding

Up until now, this chapter hasn't talked about how strings are stored. You're going to look at that now.

Strings are made up of a collection of Unicode code points. These code points range from the number 0 up to 1114111 (or 0x10FFFF in hexadecimal). This means that the maximum number of bits you need to represent a code point is 21. However, if you are only ever using low code points, such as if your text contains only Latin characters, then you can get away with using only 8 bits per code point.

Numeric types in most programming languages come in sizes of addressable, powers-of-2 bits, such as 8-bits, 16-bits and 32-bits. This is because computers are made of billions of transistors that are either off or on; they just love powers of 2!

When choosing how to store strings, you could choose to store every individual code point in a 32-bit type, such as `UInt32`. So your `String` type would be backed by a `[UInt32]` (a `UInt32` array). Each of these `UInt32`s is what is known as a **code unit**. However, you would be wasting space because not all those bits are needed, especially if the string uses only low code points.

This choice of how to store strings is known as the string's **encoding**. This particular scheme described above is known as **UTF-32**. However, because it has inefficient memory usage it is very rarely used.

UTF-8

A much more common scheme is called **UTF-8**. This uses 8-bit code units instead. One reason for UTF-8's popularity is because it is fully compatible with the venerable, English-only, 7-bit ASCII encoding. But how do you store code points that need more than 8 bits?! Herein lies the magic of the encoding.

If the code point requires up to 7 bits, it is represented by simply one code unit and is identical to **ASCII**. But for code points above 7 bits, a scheme comes into play that uses up to 4 **code units** to represent the code point.

For code points of 8 to 11 bits, 2 code units are used. The first code unit's initial 3 bits are `110`. The remaining 5 bits are the first 5 bits of the code point. The second code unit's initial 2 bits are `10` and the remaining 6 bits are the remaining 6 bits of the code point.

For example, the code point `0x00BD` represents the ½ character. In binary this is `10111101`, and uses 8 bits. In UTF-8, this would comprise 2 code units of `11000010` and `10111101`.

To illustrate this, consider the following diagram:

1 1 0 1 0 0 1 0	1 0 1 1 1 1 0 1

Of course, code points higher than 11 bits are also supported. 12- to 16-bit code points use 3 UTF-8 code units, and 17- to 21-bit code points use 4 UTF-8 code units, according to the following scheme:

0 x x x x x x x			
1 1 0 x x x x x	1 0 x x x x x x		
1 1 1 0 x x x x	1 0 x x x x x x	1 0 x x x x x x	
1 1 1 1 0 x x x	1 0 x x x x x x	1 0 x x x x x x	1 0 x x x x x x

The "x"s are replaced with the bits from the code points.

In Swift, you can access the UTF-8 string encoding through the `utf8` view. For example, consider the following code:

```
let char = "\u{00bd}"
for i in char.utf8 {
  print(i)
}
```

The `utf8` view is a collection, just like the `unicodeScalars` view. Its values are the UTF-8 code units that make up the string. In this case, it's a single character, namely the one that we discussed above.

The above code will print the following:

```
194
189
```

If you pull out your calculator (or have a fantastic mental arithmetic mind) then you can validate that these are `11000010` and `10111101` respectively, as you expected!

Now consider a more complicated example which you'll refer back to later in this section. Take the following string:

```
+½⇨🙃
```

And iterate through the UTF-8 code units it contains:

```
let characters = "+\u{00bd}\u{21e8}\u{1f643}"
for i in characters.utf8 {
  print("\(i) : \(String(i, radix: 2))")
}
```

This time the `print` statement will print out both the decimal number and the number in binary. It prints the following (newlines added to split grapheme clusters):

```
43 : 101011

194 : 11000010
189 : 10111101

226 : 11100010
135 : 10000111
168 : 10101000

240 : 11110000
159 : 10011111
153 : 10011001
131 : 10000011
```

Feel free to verify that these are indeed correct. Notice that the first character used 1 code unit, the second used 2 code units, and so on.

UTF-8 is therefore much more compact than UTF-32. For this string, you used 10 bytes to store the 4 code points. In UTF-32 this would be 16 bytes (4 bytes per code unit, 1 code unit per code point, 4 code points).

There is a downside to UTF-8 though. To handle certain string operations you need to inspect every byte. For example, if you wanted to jump to the *n* th code point, you would need to inspect every byte until you have gone past *n*-1 code points. You cannot simply jump into the buffer because you don't know how far you have to jump.

UTF-16

There is another encoding that is useful to introduce, namely **UTF-16**. Yes, you guessed it. It uses 16-bit code units!

This means that code points that are up to 16 bits use 1 code unit. But how are code points of 17 to 21 bits represented? These use a scheme known as **surrogate pairs**. These are 2 UTF-16 code units that, when next to each other, represent a code point from the range above 16 bits.

There is a space within Unicode reserved for these surrogate pair code points. They are split into low and high surrogates. The high surrogates range from `0xD800` to `0xDBFF`, and the low surrogates range from `0xDC00` to `0xDFFF`. You may think that sounds the wrong way round, but the high and low here refers to the bits from the original code point that are represented by this surrogate.

Take the upside-down face emoji from the string you saw earlier. Its code point is `0x1F643`. To find out the surrogate pairs for this code point, you apply the following algorithm:

1. Subtract `0x10000` to give 0xF643, or `0000 1111 0110 0100 0011` in binary.
2. Split these 20 bits into two. This gives you `0000 1111 01` and `10 0100 0011`.
3. Take the first and add `0xD800` to it, to give `0xD83D`. This is your **high surrogate**.
4. Take the second and add `0xDC00` to it, to give `0xDE43`. This is your **low surrogate**.

So in UTF-16, that upside-down face emoji is represented by the code unit `0xD83D` followed by `0xDE43`. Neat!

Just as with UTF-8, Swift allows you to access the UTF-16 code units through the `utf16` view, like so:

```
for i in characters.utf16 {
  print("\(i) : \(String(i, radix: 2))")
}
```

In this case, the following is printed (again with newlines added to split grapheme clusters):

```
43 : 101011

189 : 10111101

8680 : 10000111101000

55357 : 1101100000111101
56899 : 1101111001000011
```

As you can see, the only code point that needs to use more than one code unit is the last one, which is your upside-down face emoji. And as expected, the values are correct!

So with UTF-16, your string this time uses 10 bytes (5 code units, 2 bytes per code unit). This turns out to be the same as UTF-8. In general, the memory usage with UTF-8 and UTF-16 will be different. For example, strings that are made up of code points of 7 bits or less will take up twice the space in UTF-16 as compared to UTF-8.

For a string made up of code points 7 bits or less, the string has to be entirely made up of those Latin characters contained in that range. Even the "£" sign is not in this range! So often the memory usage of UTF-16 and UTF-8 are comparable.

Swift string views make the `String` type encoding agnostic and is one of the only languages that does this. Internally it actually uses UTF-16. This is because it hits the sweet spot between memory usage and complexity of operations.

Converting indexes between encoding views

As you saw earlier, you use indexes to access grapheme clusters in a string. For example, using the same string from above, you can do the following:

```
let arrowIndex = characters.index(of: "\u{21e8}")!
characters[arrowIndex] // ⇨
```

Here, `arrowIndex` is of type `String.Index` and it is used to obtain the `Character` at that index.

You can convert this index into the index relating to the start of this grapheme cluster in the `unicodeScalars`, `utf8` and `utf16` views. You do that using the `samePosition(in:)` method on `String.Index`, like so:

```
if let unicodeScalarsIndex = arrowIndex.samePosition(in:
characters.unicodeScalars) {
  characters.unicodeScalars[unicodeScalarsIndex] // 8680
}

if let utf8Index = arrowIndex.samePosition(in: characters.utf8)
{
  characters.utf8[utf8Index] // 226
}

if let utf16Index = arrowIndex.samePosition(in:
characters.utf16) {
  characters.utf16[utf16Index] // 8680
}
```

`unicodeScalarsIndex` is of type `String.UnicodeScalarView.Index`. This grapheme cluster is represented by only one code point, so in the `unicodeScalars` view, the scalar returned is the one and only code point. If the `Character` were made up of two code points, such as the "e" and combining accent you saw earlier, the scalar returned in the code above would be just the "e".

Likewise, `utf8Index` is of type `String.UTF8View.Index` and the value at that index is the first UTF-8 code unit used to represent this code point. The same goes for the `utf16Index`, which is of type `String.UTF16View.Index`.

Key points

- Strings are collections of `Character` types.
- A `Character` is **grapheme cluster** and is made up of one or more **code points**.
- A **combining character** is a character which alters the previous character in some way.
- You use special (non-integer) indexes to subscript into the string to a certain grapheme cluster.
- Swift's use of **canonicalization** ensures that the comparison of strings accounts for combining characters.
- Slicing a string yields a substring with type `Substring`. This shares its storage with its parent `String`.
- You can convert from a `Substring` to a `String` by initializing a new `String` and passing the `Substring`.
- Swift `String` has a view called `unicodeScalars`, which is itself a collection of the individual Unicode code points that makes up the string.
- There are multiple ways to encode a string. UTF-8 and UTF-16 are the most popular.
- The individual parts of an encoding are called **code units**. UTF-8 uses 8-bit code units, and UTF-16 uses 16-bit code units.
- Swift's `String` has views called `utf8` and `utf16` which are collections allowing you to obtain the individual code units in the given encoding.

Where to go from here?

Strings are a fundamental part of any programming language, as text forms the bulk of the data that most programs will manipulate. In this chapter you have learned how many of the features of Swift's `String` type work.

In the coming chapters you will take a look at how to create your own types.

Challenges

Challenge 1

Write a function which take a string and prints out the count of each character in the string.

For bonus points, print them ordered by the count of each character.

For even more bonus points, print it as a nice histogram. You could use # characters to draw the bars.

Challenge 2

Write a function which tells you how many words there are in a string. Do it without splitting the string but rather iterating through the string yourself.

Challenge 3

Write a function which takes a string which looks like "Galloway, Matt" and returns one which looks like "Matt Galloway"; i.e. the string goes from `"<LAST_NAME>, <FIRST_NAME>"` to `"<FIRST_NAME> <LAST_NAME>"`.

Challenge 4

There exists a method on string named `components(separatedBy:)` that will split the string into chunks delimited by the given string and return an array containing the results.

Your challenge is to implement this yourself.

Hint: There exists a view on `String` named `indices` which lets you iterate through all the indices (of type `String.Index`) in the string. You will need to use this.

Challenge 5

Write a function which takes a string and returns a version of it with each individual word reversed.

For example, if the string is "My dog is called Rover" then the resulting string would be "yM god si dellac revoR".

Try to do it by iterating through the `indices` of the string until you find a space and then reversing what was before it. Build up the result string by continually doing that as you go through the string.

Hint: You'll need to do a similar thing to the previous challenge, but reverse the word each time. Can you explain why this is better in terms of memory usage than using the function you created in the previous challenge?

Section III: Building Your Own Types

You can create your own type by combining variables and functions into a new type definition. For example, integers and doubles might not be enough for your purposes, so you might need to create a type to store complex numbers. Or maybe storing first, middle and last names in three independent variables is getting difficult to manage, so you decide to create a `FullName` type.

When you create a new type, you give it a name; thus, these custom types are known as **named types**. Structures are a powerful tool for modeling real world concepts. You can encapsulate related concepts, properties and methods into a single, cohesive model.

- **Chapter 10, Structures**
- **Chapter 11, Properties**
- **Chapter 12, Methods**

Swift, in fact, includes four kinds of named types: structures, classes, enumerations and protocols. Now that you understand how structures work with methods and properties, you can see how the other named types use these same concepts, how they differ, and where you want to use each.

- **Chapter 13, Classes**
- **Chapter 14, Advanced Classes**
- **Chapter 15, Enumerations**
- **Chapter 16, Protocols**

Finally, you expand your knowledge of the type system by learning about generics: types and methods that take as input other types instead of just methods. Swift's key to safety, speed and expressiveness lies in the ability to utilize generic types.

- **Chapter 17, Generics**

Custom types make it possible to build large and complex things with the basic building blocks you've learned so far. It's time to take your Swift apprenticeship to the next level!

Chapter 10: Structures

By Ben Morrow

You've covered some fundamental building blocks of Swift. With variables, conditionals, strings, functions and collections, you're ready to conquer the world! Well, almost.

Most programs that perform complex tasks benefit from higher levels of abstraction. In addition to an `Int`, `String` or `Array`, most programs use new types specific to the domain of the task at hand. Keeping track of photos or contacts, for example, demands more than the simple types you've seen so far.

This chapter introduces **structures**, which are the first **named type** you will learn about. Structures are types that can store named properties and define their own behaviors. Like a `String`, `Int` or `Array`, you can define your own structures to create named types to use in your code. By the end of this chapter, you'll know how to define and use your own structures.

You'll begin your adventure into custom types with pizza.

Introducing structures

Imagine you live in a town called Pizzaville. As you might expect, Pizzaville is known for its amazing pizza. You own the most popular (and fastest!) pizza delivery restaurant in Pizzaville — "Swift Pizza".

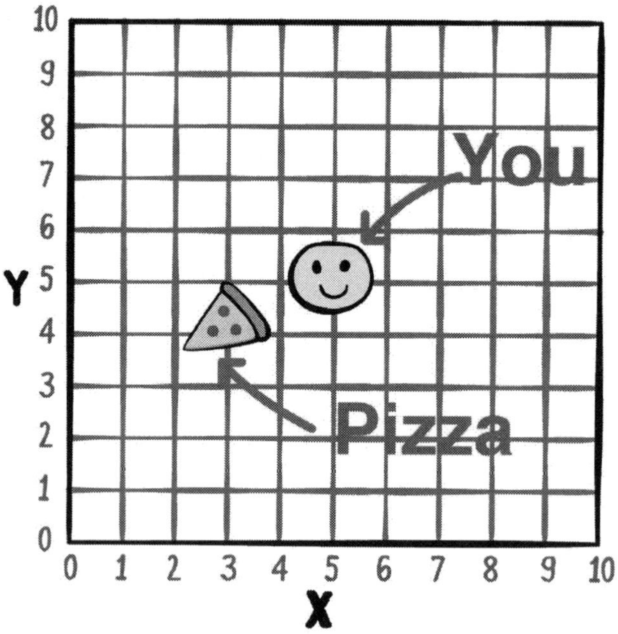

As the owner of a single restaurant, you still have a limited delivery area. You want to write a program that calculates if a potential customer is within range for your delivery drivers. The first version of your program might might look something like this:

```
let restaurantLocation = (2, 4)
let restaurantRange = 2.5

// Pythagorean Theorem 📐🎓
func distance(from source: (x: Int, y: Int), to target: (x: Int,
y: Int)) -> Double {
  let distanceX = Double(source.x - target.x)
  let distanceY = Double(source.y - target.y)
  return (distanceX * distanceX +
          distanceY * distanceY).squareRoot()
}

func isInDeliveryRange(location: (x: Int, y: Int)) -> Bool {
  let deliveryDistance = distance(from: location, to:
restaurantLocation)
  return deliveryDistance < restaurantRange
}
```

Simple enough, right? `distance(from:to:)` will calculate how far away you are from your pizza. `isInDeliveryRange(location:)` will return `true` only if you're not too far away.

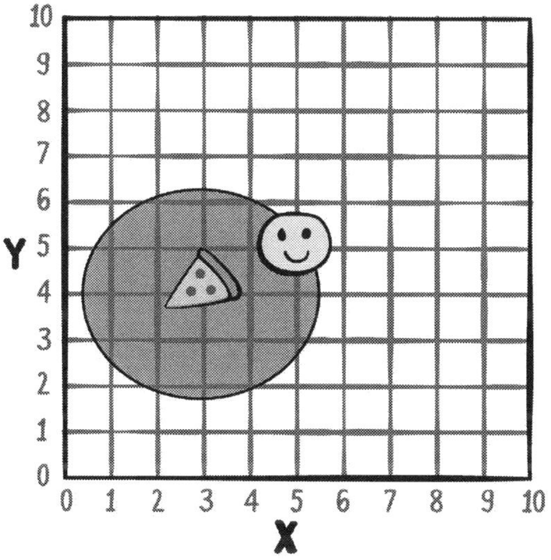

A successful pizza delivery business may eventually expand to include multiple locations, which adds a minor twist to the deliverable calculator. Replace your existing code with the following:

```
let restaurantLocation = (2, 4)
let restaurantRange = 2.5

let otherRestaurantLocation = (7, 8)
let otherRestaurantRange = 1.5

// Pythagorean Theorem 📐🎓
func distance(from source: (x: Int, y: Int), to target: (x: Int,
y: Int)) -> Double {
  let distanceX = Double(source.x - target.x)
  let distanceY = Double(source.y - target.y)
  return (distanceX * distanceX +
          distanceY * distanceY).squareRoot()
}

func isInDeliveryRange(location: (x: Int, y: Int)) -> Bool {
  let deliveryDistance =
    distance(from: location,
             to: restaurantLocation)

  let secondDeliveryDistance =
    distance(from: location,
             to: otherRestaurantLocation)

  return deliveryDistance < restaurantRange ||
         secondDeliveryDistance < otherRestaurantRange
}
```

`isInDeliveryRange(location:)` checks both locations to see if you can get your pizza from either one.

Eventually, the rising number of customers will force the business to expand, and soon it might grow to a total of 10 stores! Then what? Do you keep updating your function to check against all these sets of coordinates and ranges?

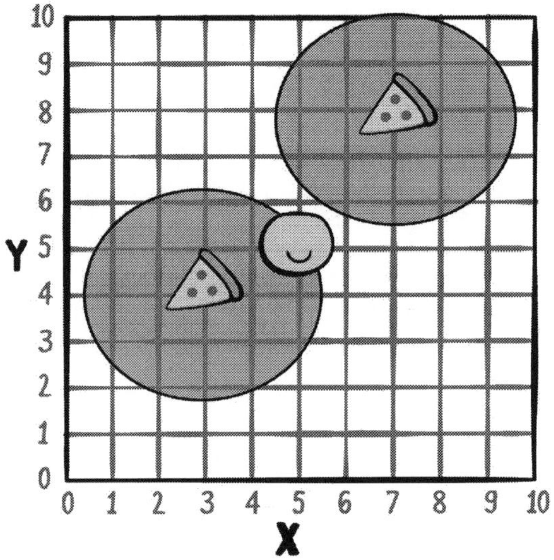

You might briefly consider creating an array of x/y coordinate tuples to keep track of your pizza restaurants, but that would be both difficult to read and maintain. Fortunately, Swift has additional tools to help you simplify the problem.

Your first structure

Structures are one of the named types in Swift that allow you to encapsulate related properties and behaviors. You can declare a new type, give it a name, and then use it in your code.

In the example of the pizza business, you've been using x/y coordinate tuples to represent locations.

As a first example of structures, promote locations from tuples to a structure type:

```
struct Location {
  let x: Int
  let y: Int
}
```

This block of code demonstrates the basic syntax for defining a structure. In this case, the code declares a type named `Location` that combines both x and y coordinates.

The basic syntax begins with the `struct` keyword followed by the name of the type and a pair of curly braces. Everything between the curly braces is a *member* of the struct.

In `Location`, both members, `x` and `y`, are **properties**. Properties are constants or variables that are declared as part of a type. Every instance of the type will have these properties. This means that in our example, every `Location` will have both an `x` and a `y` property.

You can instantiate a structure and store it in a constant or variable just like any other type you've worked with:

```
let storeLocation = Location(x: 2, y: 4)
```

To create the `Location` value, you use the name of the type along with a parameter list in parentheses. This parameter list provides a way to specify the values for the properties `x` and `y`. This is an example of an **initializer**.

Initializers enforce that all properties are set before you start using them. This is one of the key safety features of Swift. Accidentally using uninitialized variables is a big source of bugs in other languages. Another handy Swift feature is that you don't need to declare this initializer in the `Location` type. Swift automatically provides initializers for structures with all the properties in the parameter list.

You'll learn a lot more about initializers in Chapter 12, "Methods".

You may remember that there's also a range involved, and now that the pizza business is expanding, there may be different ranges associated with different restaurants. You can create another struct to represent the delivery area of a restaurant, like so:

```
struct DeliveryArea {
  let center: Location
  var radius: Double
}

var storeArea = DeliveryArea(center: storeLocation, radius: 4)
```

Now there's a new structure named `DeliveryArea` that contains a constant `center` property along with a variable `radius` property. As you can see, you can have a structure value inside a structure value; here, you use the `Location` type as the type of the `center` property of the `DeliveryArea` struct.

Mini-exercise

Write a structure that represents a pizza order. Include toppings, size and any other option you'd want for a pizza.

Accessing members

With your `DeliveryArea` defined and an instantiated value in hand, you may be wondering how you can *use* these values. Just as you have been doing with `Strings`, `Arrays`, and `Dictionaries`, you use **dot syntax** to access members:

```
print(storeArea.radius) // 4.0
```

You can even access *members of members* using dot syntax:

```
print(storeArea.center.x) // 2
```

Similar to how you can read values with dot syntax, you can also *assign* them. If the delivery radius of one pizza location becomes larger, you could assign the new value to the existing property:

```
storeArea.radius = 250
```

The semantics of constants and variables play a significant role in determining if a property can be assigned to. In this case, you can assign to `radius` because you declared it with `var`. On the other hand, you declared `center` with `let`, so you can't modify it. Your `DeliveryArea` struct allows a pizza restaurant's delivery range to be changed, but not its location!

In addition to choosing whether your properties should be variable or constants, you must also declare the structure itself as a variable if you want to be able to modify it after it is initialized:

```
let fixedArea = DeliveryArea(center: storeLocation, radius: 4)

// Error: Cannot assign to property
fixedArea.radius = 250
```

That code causes the compiler to emit an error. Change `fixedArea` from a `let` constant to a `var` variable to make it mutable.

Now you've learned how to control the mutability of the properties in your structure.

Mini-exercise

Rewrite `isInDeliveryRange` to use `Location` and `DeliveryArea`.

Introducing methods

Using some of the capabilities of structures, you could now make a pizza delivery range calculator that looks something like this:

```
let areas = [
  DeliveryArea(center: Location(x: 2, y: 4), radius: 2.5),
  DeliveryArea(center: Location(x: 9, y: 7), radius: 4.5)
]

func isInDeliveryRange(_ location: Location) -> Bool {
  for area in areas {
    let distanceToStore =
      distance(from: (area.center.x, area.center.y),
                 to: (location.x, location.y))

    if distanceToStore < area.radius {
      return true
    }
  }
  return false
}

let customerLocation1 = Location(x: 8, y: 1)
let customerLocation2 = Location(x: 5, y: 5)

print(isInDeliveryRange(customerLocation1)) // false
print(isInDeliveryRange(customerLocation2)) // true
```

In this example, there's an array `areas` and a function that uses that array to determine if a customer's location is within any of these areas.

Being in range is something you want to know about a particular restaurant. It'd be great if `DeliveryArea` could tell you if the restaurant could deliver to a location.

Much like a structure can have constants and variables, it can also define its *own* functions. In your playground, locate the implementation of `DeliveryArea`. Just before the closing curly brace, add the following code:

```
func contains(_ location: Location) -> Bool {
  let distanceFromCenter =
    distance(from: (center.x, center.y),
                   to: (location.x, location.y))

  return distanceFromCenter < radius
}
```

This defines a function `contains`, which is now a member of `DeliveryArea`. Functions that are members of types are called **methods**. Notice how `contains` uses the `center` and `radius` properties of the current location. This implicit access to properties and other members makes methods different from regular functions. You'll learn more about methods in Chapter 12.

Just like other members of structures, you can use dot syntax to access a method:

```
let area = DeliveryArea(center: Location(x: 5, y: 5), radius:
4.5)
let customerLocation = Location(x: 2, y: 2)
area.contains(customerLocation) // true
```

Mini-exercises

- Change `distance(from:to:)` to use `Locations` as parameters instead of x-y tuples.
- Change `contains(_:)` to call the new `distance(from:to:)` with `Locations`.
- Add a method `overlaps(with:)` on `DeliveryArea` that can tell you if the area overlaps with another area.

Structures as values

The term **value** has an important meaning when it comes to structures in Swift, and that's because structures create what are known as **value types**.

A value type is a type whose instances are *copied* on assignment.

```
var a = 5
var b = a
print(a) // 5
print(b) // 5

a = 10
print(a) // 10
print(b) // 5
```

This **copy-on-assignment** behavior means that when `a` is assigned to `b`, the value of `a` is copied into `b`. That's why it's important read = as "assign", not "is equal to" (which is what == is for).

How about the same principle, except with the `DeliveryArea` struct:

```
var area1 = DeliveryArea(center: Location(x: 2, y: 4), radius:
2.5)
var area2 = area1
print(area1.radius) // 2.5
print(area2.radius) // 2.5

area1.radius = 4
print(area1.radius) // 4.0
print(area2.radius) // 2.5
```

As with the previous example, `area2.radius` didn't pick up the new value set in `area1.radius`. This demonstrates the **value semantics** of working with structures. When you assign `area2` the value of `area1`, it gets an exact copy of this value. `area1` and `area2` are still completely independent!

Structures everywhere

You saw how the `Location` struct and a simple `Int` share the same copy-on-assignment behavior. This is because they are both value types, and both have value semantics.

You know structures represent values, so what exactly is an `Int` then? If you were to look at the definition of `Int` in the Swift library, you might be a bit surprised:

```
public struct Int : FixedWidthInteger, SignedInteger {
  // …
}
```

The `Int` type is *also* a structure. In fact, many of the standard Swift types are defined as structures, such as: `Double`, `String`, `Bool`, `Array` and `Dictionary`. As you will learn in future chapters, the value semantics of structs provide many other advantages over their reference type counterparts that make them ideal for representing core Swift types.

Conforming to a protocol

You may have noticed some unfamiliar parts to the `Int` definition from the Swift standard library above. The types `FixedWidthInteger` and `SignedInteger` appear right after the declaration of `Int`:

```
public struct Int : FixedWidthInteger, SignedInteger {
  // …
}
```

These types are known as *protocols*. By putting them after a colon when `Int` is declared, you are declaring that `Int` *conforms* to these protocols.

Protocols contain a set of requirements that conforming types **must** satisfy. A simple example from the standard library is `CustomStringConvertible`:

```
public protocol CustomStringConvertible {
  /// A textual representation of this instance.
  public var description: String { get }
}
```

This protocol contains one property requirement: `description`. This `description` is documented as "A textual representation of this instance."

If you were to modify `DeliveryArea` to conform to `CustomStringConvertible`, you would be required to add a `description` property with a "textual representation" of the instance. Try this now. Change `DeliveryArea` to:

```
struct DeliveryArea: CustomStringConvertible {
  let center: Location
  var radius: Double

  var description: String {
    return """
      Area with center: x: \(center.x) - y: \(center.y),
      radius: \(radius)
      """
  }

func contains(_ location: Location) -> Bool {
  let distanceFromCenter =
    distance(from: (center.x, center.y),
             to: (location.x, location.y))
  return distanceFromCenter < radius
  }
}
```

The value of the `description` property is based on the center and current radius. This is made possible by implementing it as a *computed* property.

You'll learn all about computed properties — and more — in the next chapter!

So what exactly does conforming to a protocol do? Because any type conforming to `CustomStringConvertible` must define `description`, you can call `description` on any instance of any type that conforms to `CustomStringConvertible`. The Swift standard library takes advantage of this with the `print()` function. That function will use `description` in the console instead of a rather noisy default description:

```
print(area1) // Area with center: x: 2 - y: 4, radius: 4.0
print(area2) // Area with center: x: 2 - y: 4, radius: 2.5
```

Any named type can use protocols to extend their behavior. In this case, you conformed your structure to a protocol defined in the Swift standard library. In Chapter 16, "Protocols", you will learn more about defining, using, and conforming to protocols.

Key points

- Structures are named types you can define and use in your code.
- Structures are **value types**, which means their values are copied on assignment.
- You use dot syntax to access the members of named types such as structures.
- Named types can have their own variables and functions, which are called properties and methods.
- Conforming to a protocol requires implementing the properties and methods required by that protocol.

Where to go from here?

Thanks to value semantics and copying, structures are *safe*, so you'll never need to worry about values being shared and possibly being changed behind your back by another piece of code.

Structures are also very *fast* compared to their reference alternatives, which you'll learn about in Chapter 13, "Classes".

Challenges

Challenge 1

Implement a "playable" version of Tic-Tac-Toe (OXO). The focus of this exercise is on using structures. Represent Xs with a global string constant "X" and Os with a global string contant "O". While X and O could be cleanly represented with an enumeration type, you will learn about those in Chapter 15, "Enumerations". For now, you can make the type called `BoardPiece` as an alias to `String` using `typealias`. The `BoardPiece` type can be used completely interchangeably with a `String`. While this doesn't afford much in the way of formal type safety, it does add to the readability and documentation of your code.

```
typealias BoardPiece = String
let X: BoardPiece = "X"
let O: BoardPiece = "O"
```

Challenge 2

Create a T-shirt structure that has size, color and material options. Provide methods to calculate the cost of a shirt based on its attributes.

Challenge 3

Write the engine for a Battleship-like game. If you aren't familiar with Battleship, see here: http://bit.ly/2xJEPLM

- Use an (x, y) coordinate system for your locations and model using a structure.
- Ships should also be modelled with structures. Record an origin, direction and length.
- Each ship should be able to report if a "shot" has resulted in a "hit".

Chapter 11: Properties

By Ben Morrow

In the last chapter, you learned that structures make you a more efficient programmer by grouping related properties and behaviors into structured types.

In the example below, the `Car` structure has two properties, both constants that store `String` values:

```
struct Car {
  let make: String
  let color: String
}
```

Values like these are called **properties**. The two properties of `Car` are both **stored properties**, which means they store actual string values for each instance of `Car`.

Some properties calculate values rather than store them; that means there's no actual memory allocated for them, but they get calculated on-the-fly each time you access them. Naturally, these are called **computed properties**.

In this chapter, you'll learn about both kinds of properties. You'll also learn some other neat tricks in dealing with properties, such as how to monitor changes in a property's value and delay initialization of a stored property.

Stored properties

As you may have guessed from the example in the introduction, you're already familiar with many of the features of stored properties. To review, imagine you're building an address book. The common unit you'll need is a `Contact`.

```
struct Contact {
  var fullName: String
  var emailAddress: String
}
```

You can use this structure over and over again, letting you build an array of contacts, each with a different value. The properties you want to store are an individual's full name and email address.

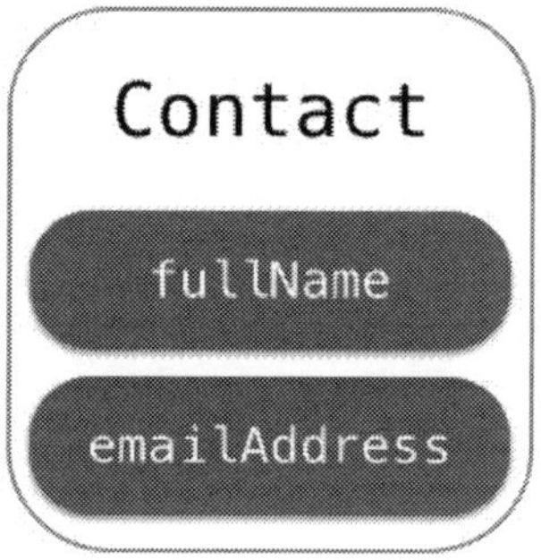

These are the properties of the `Contact` structure. You provide a data type for each, but opt not to assign a default value, because you plan to assign the value upon initialization. After all, the values will be different for each instance of `Contact`.

Remember that Swift automatically creates an initializer for you based on the properties you defined in your structure:

```
var person = Contact(fullName: "Grace Murray",
                     emailAddress: "grace@navy.mil")
```

You can access the individual properties using dot notation:

```
let name = person.fullName // Grace Murray
let email = person.emailAddress // grace@navy.mil
```

You can assign values to properties as long as they're defined as variables (and the instance is stored in a variable as well). When Grace married, she changed her last name:

```
person.fullName = "Grace Hopper"
let grace = person.fullName // Grace Hopper
```

If you'd like to prevent a value from changing, you can define a property as a constant instead using `let`.

```
struct Contact {
  var fullName: String
  let emailAddress: String
}

// Error: cannot assign to a constant
person.emailAddress = "grace@gmail.com"
```

Once you've initialized an instance of this structure, you can't change `emailAddress`.

Default values

If you can make a reasonable assumption about what the value of a property should be when the type is initialized, you can give that property a default value.

It doesn't make sense to create a default name or email address for a contact, but imagine there's a new property `type` to indicate what kind of contact it is:

```
struct Contact {
  var fullName: String
  let emailAddress: String
  var type = "Friend"
}
```

By assignment a value in the definition of `type`, you give this property a default value. Any contact created will automatically be a friend, unless you change the value of `type` to something like "Work" or "Family".

The downside is that the automatic initializer doesn't notice default values, so you'll still need to provide a value for each property unless you create your own custom initializer:

```
var person = Contact(fullName: "Grace Murray",
                     emailAddress: "grace@navy.mil",
                     type: "Friend")
```

You'll learn more about creating initializers in the next chapter.

Computed properties

Stored properties are certainly the most common, but there are also properties that are computed, which simply means they perform a calculation before returning a value.

While a stored property can be a constant or a variable, a computed property must be defined as a variable. Computed properties must also include a type, because the compiler needs to know what to expect as a return value.

The measurement for a TV is the perfect use case for a computed property. The industry definition of the screen size of a TV isn't the screen's height or width, but its diagonal measurement:

```
struct TV {
  var height: Double
  var width: Double

  // 1
  var diagonal: Int {
    // 2
    let result = (height * height + width *
width).squareRoot().rounded()
    // 3
    return Int(result)
  }
}
```

Let's go through this code one step at a time:

1. You use an `Int` type for your `diagonal` property. Although `height` and `width` are each a `Double`, TV sizes are usually advertised as nice, round numbers such as 50" rather than 49.52". Instead of the usual assignment operator = to assign a value as you would for a stored property, you use curly braces to enclose your computed property's calculation.
2. As you've seen before in this book, geometry can be handy; once you have the width and height, you can use the Pythagorean theorem to calculate the length of the diagonal. You use the `rounded` method to round the value with the standard rule: If it the decimal is 0.5 or above, it rounds up; otherwise it rounds down.
3. Now that you've got a properly rounded number, you return it as an `Int`. Had you converted `result` directly to `Int` without rounding first, the result would have been truncated, so 109.99 would have become 109.

Computed properties don't store any values; they simply return values based on calculations. From outside of the structure, a computed property can be accessed just like a stored property.

Test this with the TV size calculation:

```
var tv = TV(height: 53.93, width: 95.87)
let size = tv.diagonal // 110
```

You have a 110-inch TV. Let's say you decide you don't like the standard movie aspect ratio and would instead prefer a square screen. You cut off some of the screen width to make it equivalent to the height:

```
tv.width = tv.height
let diagonal = tv.diagonal // 76
```

Now you *only* have a 76-inch square screen. The computed property automatically provides the new value based on the new width.

Mini-exercise

Do you have a television or a computer monitor? Measure the height and width, plug it into a TV struct, and see if the diagonal measurement matches what you think it is.

Getter and setter

The computed property you wrote in the previous section is a called a **read-only computed property**. It has a block of code to compute the value of the property, called the **getter**.

It's also possible to create a **read-write computed property** with two blocks of code: a getter and a **setter**.

This setter works differently than you might expect. As the computed property has no place to store a value, the setter usually sets one or more related *stored* properties indirectly:

```
var diagonal: Int {
  // 1
  get {
    // 2
    let result = (height * height + width *
width).squareRoot().rounded()
    return Int(result)
  }
  set {
    // 3
    let ratioWidth = 16.0
    let ratioHeight = 9.0
    // 4
    let ratioDiagonal =
```

```
      (ratioWidth * ratioWidth + ratioHeight *
ratioHeight).squareRoot()
      height = Double(newValue) * ratioHeight / ratioDiagonal
      width = height * ratioWidth / ratioHeight
    }
}
```

Here's what's happening in this code:

1. Because you want to include a setter, you now have to be explicit about which calculations comprise the getter and which the setter, so you surround each code block with curly braces and precede it with either `get` or `set`. This isn't required for read-only computed properties, as their single code block is implicitly a getter.
2. You use the same code as before to get the computed value.
3. For a setter, you usually have to make some kind of assumption. In this case, you provide a reasonable default value for the screen ratio.
4. The formulas to calculate a height and width, given a diagonal and a ratio, are a bit deep. You could work them out with a bit of time, but I've done the dirty work for you and provided them here. The important parts to focus on are:

- The `newValue` constant lets you use whatever value was passed in during the assignment.
- Remember, the `newValue` is an `Int`, so to use it in a calculation with a `Double`, you must first convert it to a `Double`.
- Once you've done the calculations, you assign the height and width properties of the TV structure.

Now, in addition to setting the height and width directly, you can set them *indirectly* by setting the `diagonal` computed property. When you set this value, your setter will calculate and store the height and width.

Notice that there's no `return` statement in a setter — it only modifies the other stored properties. With the setter in place, you have a nice little screen size calculator:

```
tv.diagonal = 70
let height = tv.height // 34.32...
let width = tv.width // 61.01...
```

Now you can discover the biggest TV that will fit in your cabinet or on your shelf. :]

Type properties

In the previous section, you learned how to associate stored and computed properties with instances of a particular type. The properties on your instance of TV are separate from the properties on my instance of TV.

However, the type *itself* may also need properties that are common across all instances. These properties are called **type properties**.

Imagine you're building a game with many levels. Each level has a few attributes, or stored properties:

```
struct Level {
  let id: Int
  var boss: String
  var unlocked: Bool
}

let level1 = Level(id: 1, boss: "Chameleon", unlocked: true)
let level2 = Level(id: 2, boss: "Squid", unlocked: false)
let level3 = Level(id: 3, boss: "Chupacabra", unlocked: false)
let level4 = Level(id: 4, boss: "Yeti", unlocked: false)
```

You can use a type property to store the game's progress as the player unlocks each level. A type property is declared using `static`:

```
struct Level {
  static var highestLevel = 1
  let id: Int
  var boss: String
  var unlocked: Bool
}
```

Here, `highestLevel` is a property on `Level` itself rather than on the instances. That means you don't access this property on an instance:

```
// Error: you can't access a type property on an instance
let highestLevel = level3.highestLevel
```

Instead, you access it on the type itself:

```
let highestLevel = Level.highestLevel // 1
```

Using a type property means you can retrieve the same stored property value from anywhere in the code for your app or algorithm. The game's progress is accessible from any level or any other place in the game, like the main menu.

Property observers

For your `Level` implementation, it would be useful to automatically set the `highestLevel` when the player unlocks a new one. For that, you'll need a way to listen to property changes. Thankfully, there are a couple of **property observers** that get called before and after property changes.

A `willSet` observer is called when a property is about to be changed while a `didSet` observer is called after a property has been changed. Their syntax is similar to getters and setters:

```
struct Level {
  static var highestLevel = 1
  let id: Int
  var boss: String
  var unlocked: Bool {
    didSet {
      if unlocked && id > Level.highestLevel {
        Level.highestLevel = id
      }
    }
  }
}
```

Now, when the player unlocks a new level, it will update the `highestLevel` type property if the level is a new high. There are a couple of things to note here:

- You *can* access the value of `unlocked` from inside the `didSet` observer. Remember that `didSet` gets called *after* the value has been set.
- Even though you're inside an instance of the type, you still have to access type properties with the type name prefix. You are required to use the full name

`Level.highestLevel` rather than just `highestLevel` alone to indicate you're accessing a type property.

`willSet` and `didSet` observers are only available for stored properties. If you want to listen for changes to a computed property, simply add the relevant code to the property's setter.

Also, keep in mind that the `willSet` and `didSet` observers are *not* called when a property is set during initialization; they only get called when you assign a new value to a fully-initialized instance. That means property observers are only useful for variable properties, since constant properties are only set during initialization.

Limiting a variable

You can also use property observers to limit the value of a variable. Say you had a light bulb that could only support a maximum current flowing through its filament.

```
struct LightBulb {
  static let maxCurrent = 40
  var current = 0 {
    didSet {
      if current > LightBulb.maxCurrent {
        print("Current too high, falling back to previous
setting.")
        current = oldValue
      }
    }
  }
}
```

In this example, if the current flowing into the bulb exceeds the maximum value, it will revert to its last successful value. Notice there's a helpful `oldValue` constant available in `didSet` so you can access the previous value.

Give it a try:

```
var light = LightBulb()
light.current = 50
var current = light.current // 0
light.current = 40
current = light.current // 40
```

You try to set the light bulb to 50 amps, but the bulb rejected that input. Pretty cool!

> **Note:** Do not confuse property observers with getters and setters. A stored property can have a `didSet` and/or a `willSet` observer. A computed property has

a getter and optionally a setter. These, even though the syntax is similar, are completely different concepts!

Mini-exercise

In the light bulb example, the bulb goes back to a successful setting if the current gets too high. In real life, that wouldn't work. The bulb would burn out! Rewrite the structure so that the bulb turns off before the current burns it out. You'll need to use the `willSet` observer for this. This observer gets called *before* the value is changed. The value that is about to be set is available in the constant `newValue`. You can't change this `newValue`, and it will still be set, so you'll have to do more than just add a `willSet` observer. :]

Lazy properties

If you have a property that might take some time to calculate, you don't want to slow things down until you actually need the property. Say hello to the **lazy stored property**. This could be useful for such things as downloading a user's profile picture or making a serious calculation.

Look at this example of a `Circle` structure that uses pi in its circumference calculation:

```
struct Circle {
  lazy var pi = {
    return ((4.0 * atan(1.0 / 5.0)) - atan(1.0 / 239.0)) * 4.0
  }()
  var radius = 0.0
  var circumference: Double {
    mutating get {
      return pi * radius * 2
    }
  }
  init(radius: Double) {
    self.radius = radius
  }
}
```

Here, you're not trusting the value of pi available to you from the standard library; you want to calculate it yourself.

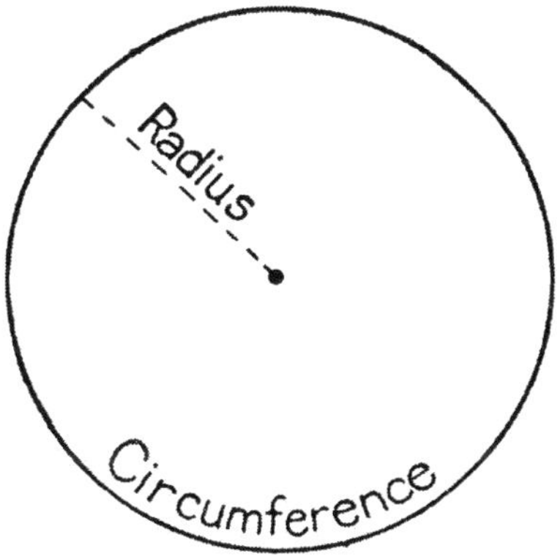

You can create a new `Circle` with its initializer, and the pi calculation won't run yet:

```
var circle = Circle(radius: 5) // got a circle, pi has not been
run
```

The calculation of `pi` waits patiently until you need it. Only when you ask for the circumference property is `pi` calculated and assigned a value.

```
let circumference = circle.circumference // 31.42
// also, pi now has a value
```

Since you've got eagle eyes, you've noticed that `pi` uses a `{ }()` pattern to calculate its value, even though it's a stored property. The trailing parentheses execute the code inside the closure curly braces immediately. But since `pi` is marked as `lazy`, this calculation is postponed until the first time you access the property.

For comparison, `circumference` is a computed property and therefore is calculated every time it's accessed. You expect the circumference's value to change if the radius changes. `pi`, as a lazy stored property, is only calculated the first time. That's great, because who wants to calculate the same thing over and over again?

The lazy property must be a variable, defined with `var`, instead of a constant defined with `let`. When you first initialize the structure, the property effectively has no value. Then when some part of your code requests the property, its value will be calculated. So even though the value only changes once, you still use `var`.

Here are two more advanced features of the code:

- Since the value of `pi` changes, the `circumference` getter must be marked as `mutating`. This changes the value of the structure.
- Since `pi` is a stored property of the structure, you need a custom initializer to use only the `radius`. Remember the automatic initializer of a structure includes all of the stored properties.

Don't worry about those advanced features too much for now. You'll learn more about both the `mutating` keyword and custom initializers in the next chapter. The important part to wrap your mind around is the how the `lazy` stored property works. The rest of the details are window dressing which you'll get more comfortable with in time.

Mini-exercises

Of course, you should absolutely trust the value of pi from the standard library. It's a type property, and you can access it as `Double.pi`. Given the `Circle` example above:

1. Remove the lazy stored property `pi`. Use the value of pi from the Swift standard library instead.
2. Remove the initializer. Since you only have one stored property, `radius`, you can rely on the automatically included initializer.

Key points

- **Properties** are variables and constants that are part of a named type.
- **Stored properties** allocate memory to store a value.
- **Computed properties** are calculated each time your code requests them and aren't stored as a value in memory.
- The **static** keyword marks a **type property** that's universal to all instances of a particular type.
- The **lazy** keyword prevents a value of a stored property from being calculated until your code uses it for the first time. You'll want to use **lazy initialization** when a property's initial value is computationally intensive or when you won't know the initial value of a property until after you've initialized the object.

Where to go from here?

You saw the basics of properties while learning about structures, and now you've seen the more advanced features they have to offer. You've already learned a bit about methods in the previous chapter and will learn even more about them in the next one!

Challenges

Challenge 1

Rewrite the IceCream structure below to use default values and lazy initialization:

```
struct IceCream {
  let name: String
  let ingredients: [String]
}
```

1. Use default values for the properties.
2. Lazily initialize the ingredients array.

Challenge 2

At the beginning of the chapter, you saw a Car structure. Dive into the inner workings of the car and rewrite the FuelTank structure below with property observer functionality:

```
struct FuelTank {
  var level: Double // decimal percentage between 0 and 1
}
```

1. Add a lowFuel stored property of Boolean type to the structure.
2. Flip the lowFuel Boolean when the level drops below 10%.
3. Ensure that when the tank fills back up, the lowFuel warning will turn off.
4. Set the level to a minimum of 0 or a maximum of 1 if it gets set above or below the expected values.
5. Add a FuelTank property to Car.

Chapter 12: Methods

By Ben Morrow

In the previous chapter, you learned about properties, which are constants and variables that are part of structures. **Methods**, as you've already seen, are merely functions that reside inside a structure.

In this chapter, you'll take a closer look at methods and initializers. As with properties, you'll begin to design more complex structures. The things you learn in this chapter will apply to methods across all named types, including classes and enumerations, which you'll see in later chapters.

Method refresher

Remember `Array.removeLast()`? It pops the last item off an instance of an array:

```
var numbers = [1, 2, 3]
numbers.removeLast()
numbers // [1, 2]
```

Methods like `removeLast()` help you control the data in the structure.

Comparing methods to computed properties

With computed properties, you saw in the last chapter that you could run code from inside a structure. That sounds a lot like a method. What's the difference? It really comes down to a matter of style, but there are a few helpful thoughts to help you decide. Properties hold values that you can get and set, while methods perform work. Sometimes this distinction gets fuzzy when a method's sole purpose is to return a single value.

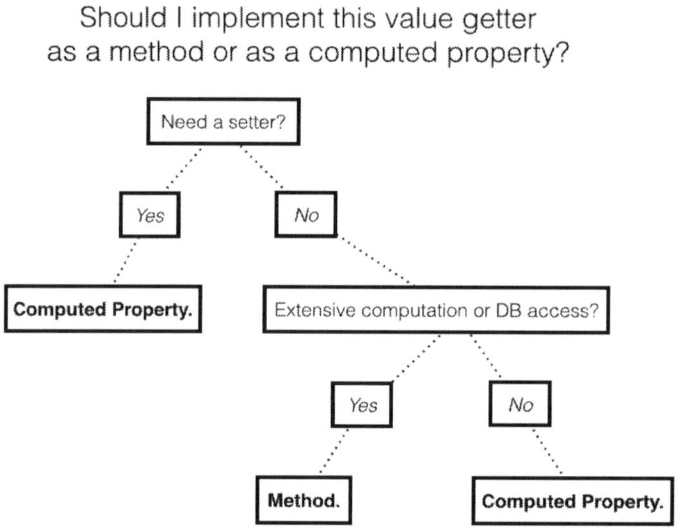

Ask yourself whether you want to be able to set a value as well as get the value. A computed property can have a setter component inside to write values. Another question to consider is whether the calculation requires extensive computation or reads from a database. Even for a simple value, a method helps you indicate to future developers that the call is expensive in time and computational resources. If the call is cheap (as in constant time O(1)), stick with a computed property.

Turning a function into a method

To explore methods and initializers, you will create a simple model for dates called `SimpleDate`. Be aware that Apple's Foundation library contains a robust, production-ready `Date` class that correctly handles all of the subtle intricacies of dealing with dates and times.

In the code below, how could you convert `monthsUntilWinterBreak(date:)` into a method?

```
let months = ["January", "February", "March",
              "April", "May", "June",
              "July", "August", "September",
              "October", "November", "December"]

struct SimpleDate {
  var month: String
}

func monthsUntilWinterBreak(from date: SimpleDate) -> Int {
  return months.index(of: "December")! - months.index(of:
date.month)!
}
```

> **Note:** If you live in the southern hemisphere, you can adjust the month for your winter break. :]

Making a method is as easy as moving the function inside the structure definition:

```
struct SimpleDate {
  var month: String

  func monthsUntilWinterBreak(from date: SimpleDate) -> Int {
    return months.index(of: "December")! - months.index(of:
date.month)!
  }
}
```

There's no identifying keyword for a method; it really is just a function inside a named type. You call methods on an instance using dot syntax just as you do for properties. And just like properties, as soon as you start typing a method name, Xcode will provide suggestions. You can select one with the Up and Down arrow keys on your keyboard, and you can autocomplete the call by pressing Tab:

```
let date = SimpleDate(month: "October")
date.monthsUntilWinterBreak(from: date) // 2
```

If you think about this code for a minute, you'll realize that the method's definition is awkward. There must be a way to access the content stored by the instance instead of passing the instance itself as a parameter to the method. It would be so much nicer to call this:

```
date.monthsUntilWinterBreak() // Error!
```

Introducing self

A structure definition is like a blueprint, whereas an instance is a real object. To access the value of an instance, you use the keyword **self** inside the structure. The Swift compiler passes it in to your method as secret parameter. The method definition transforms into this:

```
// 1
func monthsUntilWinterBreak() -> Int {
  // 2
  return months.index(of: "December")! - months.index(of:
self.month)!
}
```

Here's what changed:

1. Now there's no parameter in the method definition.
2. In the implementation, `self` replaces the old parameter name.

You can now call the method without passing a parameter:

```
date.monthsUntilWinterBreak() // 2
```

That's looking a lot cleaner! One more thing you can do to simplify the code is to remove `self.`:

`self` is your reference to the instance, but most of the time you don't need to use it because Swift understands your intent if you just use a variable name. While you can always use `self` to access the properties and methods of the current instance, most of the time you don't need to. In `monthsUntilWinterBreak()`, you can just say `month` instead of `self.month`:

```
return months.index(of: "December")! - months.index(of: month)!
```

Most programmers use `self` only when it is required, for example, to disambiguate between a local variable and a property with the same name. You'll get more practice using `self` a little later.

Mini-exercise

Since `monthsUntilWinterBreak()` returns a single value and there's not much calculation involved, transform the method into a computed property with a getter component.

Introducing initializers

You learned about initializers in the previous chapters, but let's look at them again with your newfound knowledge of methods.

Initializers are special methods you call to create a new instance. They omit the `func` keyword and even a name. Instead, they use `init`. An initializer can have parameters, but it doesn't have to.

Right now, when you create a new instance of the `SimpleDate` structure, you have to specify a value for the `month` property:

```
let date = SimpleDate(month: "January")
```

You might find it more efficient to have a handy no-parameter initializer. This would create a new `SimpleDate` instance with a reasonable default value:

```
let date = SimpleDate() // Error!
```

While the compiler gives you an error now, you can provide the no-parameter initializer. By implementing `init`, you can create the simplest path to initialization with default values.

```
struct SimpleDate {
  var month: String

  init() {
    month = "January"
  }

  func monthsUntilWinterBreak() -> Int {
    return months.index(of: "December")! - months.index(of:
month)!
  }
}
```

Here's what's happening in that code:

1. The `init()` definition requires neither the `func` keyword nor a name. You always use the name of the type to call an initializer.
2. Like a function, an initializer must have a parameter list, even if it is empty.
3. In the initializer, you assign values for all the stored properties of a structure.
4. An initializer never returns a value. Its task is simply to initialize a new instance.

Now you can use your simple initializer to create an instance:

```
let date = SimpleDate()
date.month // January
date.monthsUntilWinterBreak() // 11
```

You can test a change to the value in the initializer:

```
init() {
  month = "March"
}
```

The value of `monthsUntilWinterBreak()` will change accordingly:

```
let date = SimpleDate()
date.month // March
date.monthsUntilWinterBreak() // 9
```

As you think about the implementation here, a good user experience optimization would have the initializer use a default value based on today's date.

In the future, you'll be capable of retrieving the current date. Eventually you'll use the `Date` class from the Foundation library to work with dates. Before you get carried away with all the power that these libraries provide, let's continue implementing your own `SimpleDate` type from the ground up.

Initializers in structures

Initializers ensure all properties are set before the instance is ready to use:

```
struct SimpleDate {
  var month: String
  var day: Int

  init() {
    month = "January"
    day = 1
  }

  func monthsUntilWinterBreak() -> Int {
    return months.index(of: "December")! - months.index(of:
month)!
  }
}
```

If you tried to create an initializer without setting the `day` property, then the compiler would complain.

By creating even one custom initializer, you forgo the option to use the automatic **memberwise initializer**. Recall that the auto-generated memberwise initializer accepts all the properties in order as parameters, such as `init(month:day:)`, for the `SimpleDate` structure. When you write a custom initializer, the compiler scraps the one created automatically.

So this code won't work right now:

```
let valentinesDay = SimpleDate(month: "February", day: 14) //
Error!
```

Instead, you'll have to define your own initializer with parameters:

```
init(month: String, day: Int) {
  self.month = month
  self.day = day
}
```

In that code, you assign the incoming parameters to the properties of the structure. Notice how `self` is used to tell the compiler that you're referring to the property rather than the local parameter.

This wasn't necessary in the simple initializer:

```
init() {
  month = "January"
  day = 1
}
```

In that code, there aren't any parameters with the same names as the properties. Therefore, `self` isn't necessary for the compiler to understand you're referring to properties.

With the complex initializer in place, you can call the new initializer the same way you used to call the automatically generated initializer:

```
let valentinesDay = SimpleDate(month: "February", day: 14)
valentinesDay.month // February
valentinesDay.day // 14
```

Introducing mutating methods

Methods in structures cannot change the values of the instance without being marked as `mutating`. You can imagine a method in the `SimpleDate` structure that advances to the next day:

```
mutating func advance() {
  day += 1
}
```

> **Note:** The implementation above is a naive way of writing `advance()` because it doesn't account for what happens at the end of a month. In a challenge at the end of this chapter, you'll create a more the robust version.

The `mutating` keyword marks a method that changes a structure's value. Since a structure is a value type, the system copies it each time it's passed around an app. If a method changes the value of one of the properties, then the original instance and the copied instance will no longer be equivalent.

By marking a method as `mutating`, you're also telling the Swift compiler this method must not be called on constants. This is how Swift knows which methods to allow and which to reject at compile time. If you call a mutating method on a constant instance of a structure, the compiler will flag it as an error that must be corrected before you can run your program.

For mutating methods, Swift secretly passes in `self` just like it did for normal methods. But for mutating methods, the secret `self` gets marked as an `inout` parameter.

Type methods

Like type properties, you can use **type methods** to access data across all instances. You call type methods on the type itself, instead of on an instance. To define a type method, you prefix it with the `static` modifier.

Type methods are useful for things that are *about* a type in general, rather than something about specific instances.

For example, you could use type methods to group similar methods into a structure:

```
struct Math {
  // 1
  static func factorial(of number: Int) -> Int {
    // 2
    return (1...number).reduce(1, *)
  }
}
// 3
Math.factorial(of: 6) // 720
```

You might have custom calculations for things such as factorial. Instead of having a bunch of free-standing functions, you can group related functions together as type methods in a structure. The structure is said to act as a **namespace**.

Here's what's happening:

1. You use `static` to declare the type method, which accepts an integer and returns an integer.
2. The implementation uses a higher-order function called `reduce(_:_:)`. It effectively follows the formula for calculating a factorial: "The product of all the whole numbers from 1 to n". You could write this using a `for` loop, but the higher-order function expresses your intent in a cleaner way.
3. You call the type method on `Math`, rather than on an instance of the type.

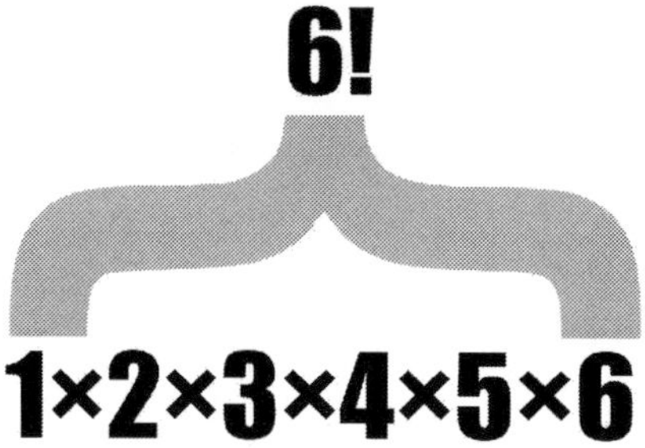

Type methods gathered into a structure will advantageously code complete in Xcode. In this example, you can see all the math utility methods available to you by typing `Math.`.

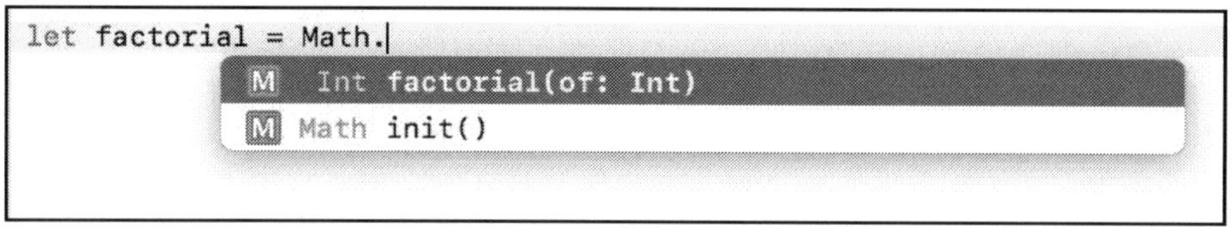

Mini-exercise

Add a type method to the `Math` structure that calculates the *n*-th triangle number. It will be very similar to the factorial formula, except instead of multiplying the numbers, you add them.

Adding to an existing structure with extensions

Sometimes you want to add functionality to a structure but don't want to muddy up the original definition. And sometimes you can't add the functionality because you don't have access to the source code. It is possible to *open* an existing structure (even one you do not have the source code for) and add methods, initializers and computed properties to it. This can be useful for code organization and is discussed in greater detail in Chapter 18. Doing so is as easy as using the keyword `extension`.

At the bottom of your playground, outside the definition of `Math`, add this type method named `primeFactors(of:)` using an extension:

```
extension Math {
  static func primeFactors(of value: Int) -> [Int] {
    // 1
```

```
    var remainingValue = value
    // 2
    var testFactor = 2
    var primes: [Int] = []
    // 3
    while testFactor * testFactor <= remainingValue {
      if remainingValue % testFactor == 0 {
        primes.append(testFactor)
        remainingValue /= testFactor
      }
      else {
        testFactor += 1
      }
    }
    if remainingValue > 1 {
      primes.append(remainingValue)
    }
    return primes
  }
}
```

This method finds the prime factors for a given number. For example, 81 returns `[3, 3, 3, 3]`. Here's what's happening in the code:

1. The `value` passed in as a parameter is assigned to the mutable variable, `remainingValue` so that it can be changed as the calculation runs.
2. The `testFactor` starts as two and will be divided into `remainingValue`.
3. The logic runs a loop until the `remainingValue` is exhausted. If it evenly divides, meaning there's no remainder, that value of the `testFactor` is set aside as a prime factor. If it doesn't evenly divide, `testFactor` is incremented for the next loop.

This algorithm is brute force, but does contain one optimization: the square of the `testFactor` should never be larger than the `remainingValue`. If it is, the `remainingValue` itself must be prime and it is added to the `primes` list.

You've now added a method to `Math` without changing its original definition. Verify that the extension works with this code:

```
Math.primeFactors(of: 81) // [3, 3, 3, 3]
```

Pretty slick! You're about to see how that can be powerful in practice.

Note: In an extension, you cannot add stored properties to an existing structure because that would change the size and memory layout of the structure and break existing code.

Keeping the compiler generated initializer using extensions

With your `SimpleDate` structure, you saw that as soon as you added your own `init()` the compiler generated memberwise initializer disappeared. It turns out that you can keep both if you add your own `init()` as an extension to `SimpleDate`:

```
struct SimpleDate {
  var month: String
  var day: Int

  func monthsUntilWinterBreak() -> Int {
    return months.index(of: "December")! - months.index(of:
month)!
  }

  mutating func advance() {
    day += 1
  }
}

extension SimpleDate {
  init() {
    month = "January"
    day = 1
  }
}
```

`init()` gets added to `SimpleDate` without sacrificing the automatically generated memberwise initializer. Hooray!

Key points

- **Methods** are behaviors that extend the functionality of a type.
- A method is a function defined inside of a named type.
- A method can access the value of an instance by using the keyword `self`.
- **Initializers** are methods that aid in the creation of a new instance.
- A **type method** adds behavior to a type instead of the instances of that type. To define a type method, you prefix it with the `static` modifier.
- You can open an existing structure and add methods, initializers and computed properties to it using an `extension`.
- By adding your own initializers in extensions, you can keep the compiler's initializer for a structure.

Where to go from here?

Methods and properties are the things that make up your types. Learning about them as you have these two chapters is important since you'll find them in all the named types — structures, classes, and enumerations.

You've tackled the basics with structures. Now you're ready to learn about the the next named type, **classes**, in the next chapter.

Challenges

1. Given the `Circle` structure below:

```
struct Circle {

  var radius = 0.0

  var area: Double {
    return .pi * radius * radius
  }

  init(radius: Double) {
    self.radius = radius
  }
}
```

Write a method that can change an instance's area by a growth factor. For example if you call `circle.grow(byFactor: 3)`, the area of the instance will triple.

Hint: Add a setter to `area`.

2. Here is a naïve way of writing `advance()` for the `SimpleDate` structure you saw earlier in the chapter:

```
let months = ["January", "February", "March",
              "April", "May", "June",
              "July", "August", "September",
              "October", "November", "December"]

struct SimpleDate {
 var month: String
 var day: Int

 mutating func advance() {
   day += 1
 }
```

```
}

var date = SimpleDate(month: "December", day: 31)
date.advance()
date.month // December; should be January!
date.day // 32; should be 1!
```

What happens when the function should go from the end of one month to the start of the next? Rewrite `advance()` to account for advancing from December 31st to January 1st.

3. Add type methods named `isEven` and `isOdd` to your `Math` namespace that return `true` if a number is even or odd respectively.
4. It turns out that `Int` is simply a struct. Add the computed properties `isEven` and `isOdd` to `Int` using an extension.

> **Note:** Generally, you want to be careful about what functionality you add to standard library types as it can cause confusion for readers.

5. Add the method `primeFactors()` to `Int`. Since this is an expensive operation, this is best left as an actual method.

Chapter 13: Classes

By Cosmin Pupăză

Structures introduced you to named types. In this chapter, you'll get acquainted with **classes**, which are much like structures — they are named types with properties and methods.

You'll learn classes are *reference* types, as opposed to *value* types, and have substantially different capabilities and benefits than their structure counterparts. While you'll often use structures in your apps to represent values, you'll generally use classes to represent *objects*.

What does *values* vs *objects* really mean, though?

Creating classes

Consider the following class definition in Swift:

```
class Person {
  var firstName: String
  var lastName: String

  init(firstName: String, lastName: String) {
    self.firstName = firstName
    self.lastName = lastName
  }

  var fullName: String {
    return "\(firstName) \(lastName)"
  }
}

let john = Person(firstName: "Johnny", lastName: "Appleseed")
```

That's simple enough! It may surprise you that the definition is almost identical to its struct counterpart. The keyword `class` is followed by the name of the class, and everything in the curly braces is a member of that class.

But you can also see some differences between a class and a struct: The class above defines an initializer that sets both `firstName` and `lastName` to initial values. Unlike a struct, a class doesn't provide a memberwise initializer automatically — which means you must provide it yourself if you need it.

If you forget to provide an initializer, the Swift compiler will flag that as an error:

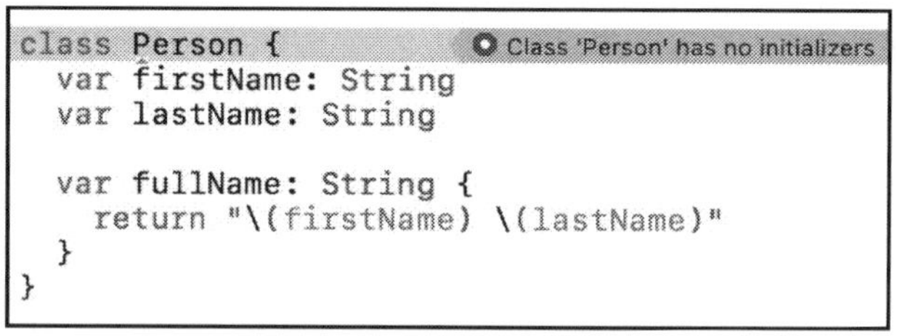

Default initialization aside, the initialization rules for classes and structs are very similar. Class initializers are functions marked `init`, and all stored properties must be assigned initial values before the end of `init`.

There is actually *much* more to class initialization than that, but you'll have to wait until the next chapter, "Advanced Classes", which will introduce you to the concept of **inheritance** and the effect it has on initialization rules. For now, you'll get comfortable with classes in Swift by working with basic class initializers.

Reference types

In Swift, an instance of a structure is an immutable value. An instance of a class, on the other hand, is a mutable object. Because classes are reference types, a variable of a class type does not store an actual instance, but a **reference** to a location in memory that stores the instance. If you were to create a `SimplePerson` class instance with only a name like this:

```
class SimplePerson {
  let name: String
  init(name: String) {
    self.name = name
  }
}

var var1 = SimplePerson(name: "John")
```

It would look something like this in memory:

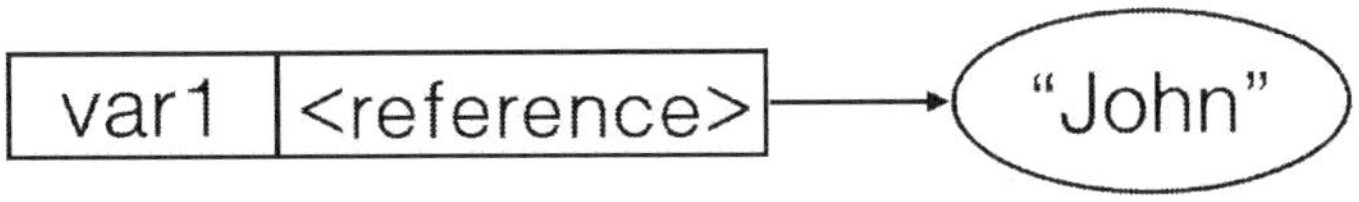

If you were to create a new variable `var2` and assign to it the value of `var1`:

```
var var2 = var1
```

Then the references inside both `var1` and `var2` would reference the same place in memory:

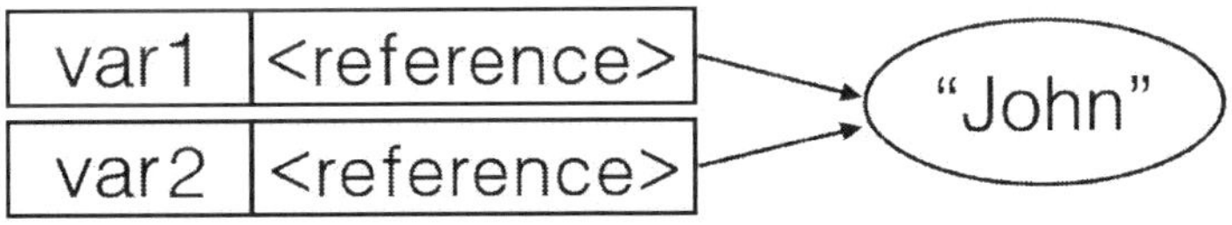

Conversely, a structure as a value type stores the actual value, providing direct access to it. Replace the `SimplePerson` class implementation with a struct like this:

```
struct SimplePerson {
  let name: String
}
```

In memory, the variable would not reference a place in memory but the value would instead belong to `var1` exclusively:

The assignment `var var2 = var1` would **copy** the *value* of `var1` in this case:

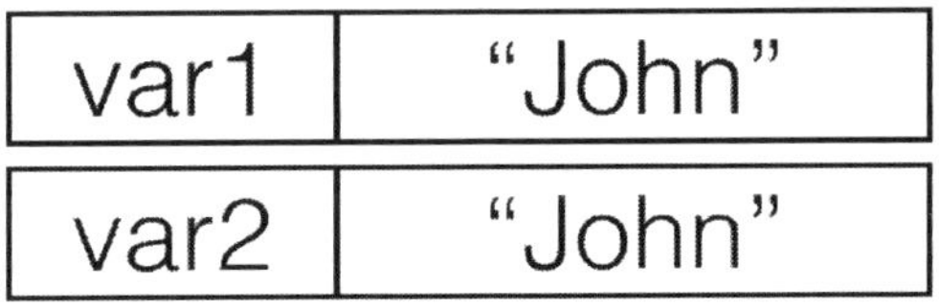

Value types and reference types each have their own distinct advantages — and disadvantages. Later in the chapter, you'll consider the question of which type to use in a given situation. For now, let's examine how classes and structs work under the hood.

While the below description doesn't apply to every situation (the Swift optimizer can be smart), it is a good first-order model to keep in mind.

The heap vs. the stack

When you create a reference type such as class, the system stores the actual instance in a region of memory known as the **heap**. Instances of a value type such as a struct resides in a region of memory called the **stack**, unless the value is part of a class instance, in which case the value is stored on the heap with the rest of the class instance.

Both the heap and the stack have essential roles in the execution of any program. A general understanding of what they are and how they work will help you visualize the functional differences between a class and a structure:

- The system uses the **stack** to store anything on the immediate thread of execution; it is tightly managed and optimized by the CPU. When a function creates a variable, the stack stores that variable and then destroys it when the function exits. Since the stack is so well organized, it's very efficient, and thus quite fast.
- The system uses the **heap** to store instances of reference types. The heap is generally a large pool of memory from which the system can request and dynamically allocate blocks of memory. Lifetime is flexible and dynamic. The heap doesn't automatically destroy its data like the stack does; additional work is required to do that. This makes creating and removing data on the heap a slower process, compared to on the stack.

Maybe you've already figured out how this relates to structs and classes. Take a look at the diagram below:

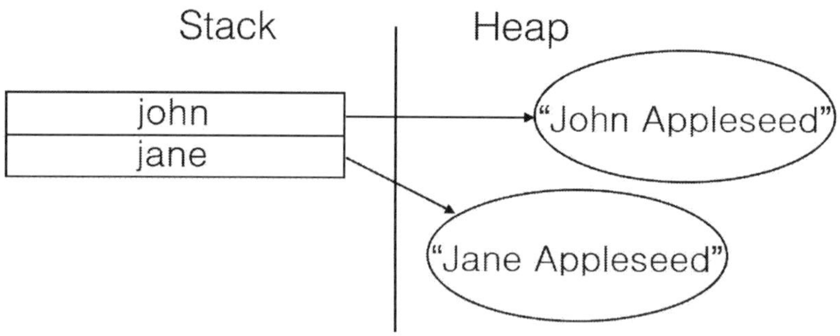

- When you create an instance of a class, your code requests a block of memory on the heap to store the instance itself; that's the first name and last name inside the instance on the right side of the diagram. It stores the *address* of that memory in your named variable on the stack; that's the *reference* stored on the left side of the diagram.

- When you create an instance of a struct (that is not part of an instance of a class), the instance itself is stored on the stack, and the heap is never involved.

This has only been a brief introduction to the dynamics of heaps and stacks, but you know enough at this point to understand the reference semantics you'll use to work with classes.

Working with references

In Chapter 10, "Structures", you saw the copy semantics involved when working with structures and other value types. Here's a little reminder, using the `Location` and `DeliveryArea` structures from that chapter:

```
struct Location {
  let x: Int
  let y: Int
}

struct DeliveryArea {
  var range: Double
  let center: Location
}

var area1 = DeliveryArea(range: 2.5,
                         center: Location(x: 2, y: 4))
var area2 = area1
print(area1.range) // 2.5
print(area2.range) // 2.5

area1.range = 4
print(area1.range) // 4.0
print(area2.range) // 2.5
```

When you assign the value of `area1` into `area2`, `area2` receives a *copy* of the `area1` value. That way when `area1.range` receives a new value of `4`, the number is only reflected in `area1` while `area2` still has the original value of `2.5`.

Since a class is a reference type, when you assign to a variable of a class type, the system does *not* copy the instance; only a reference is copied.

Contrast the previous code with the following code:

```
var homeOwner = john
john.firstName = "John" // John wants to use his short name!
john.firstName // "John"
homeOwner.firstName // "John"
```

As you can see, `john` and `homeOwner` truly have the same value!

This implied sharing among class instances results in a new way of thinking when passing things around. For instance, if the `john` object changes, then anything holding a reference to `john` will automatically see the update. If you were using a structure, you would have to update each copy individually, or it would still have the old value of "Johnny".

Mini-exercise

Change the value of `lastName` on `homeOwner`, then try reading `fullName` on both `john` and `homeOwner`. What do you observe?

Object identity

In the previous code sample, it's easy to see that `john` and `homeOwner` are pointing to the same object. The code is short and both references are named variables. What if you want to see if the value behind a variable *is* John?

You might think to check the value of `firstName`, but how would you know it's the John you're looking for and not an imposter? Or worse, what if John changed his name again?

In Swift, the === operator lets you check if the *identity* of one object is equal to the identity of another:

```
john === homeOwner // true
```

Just as the == operator checks if two *values* are equal, the === identity operator compares the memory address of two *references*. It tells you whether the value of the references are the same; that is, they point to the same block of data on the heap.

That means this === operator can tell the difference between the John you're looking for and an imposter-John.

```
let imposterJohn = Person(firstName: "Johnny", lastName:
"Appleseed")

john === homeOwner // true
john === imposterJohn // false
imposterJohn === homeOwner // false

// Assignment of existing variables changes the instances the
variables reference.
homeOwner = imposterJohn
john === homeOwner // false

homeOwner = john
john === homeOwner // true
```

This can be particularly useful when you cannot rely on regular equality (==) to compare and identify objects you care about:

```
// Create fake, imposter Johns. Use === to see if any of these
imposters are our real John.
var imposters = (0...100).map { _ in
  Person(firstName: "John", lastName: "Appleseed")
}

// Equality (==) is not effective when John cannot be identified
by his name alone
imposters.contains {
  $0.firstName == john.firstName && $0.lastName == john.lastName
} // true
```

By using the identity operator, you can verify that the *references* themselves are equal, and separate our real John from the crowd:

```
// Check to ensure the real John is not found among the
imposters.
imposters.contains {
  $0 === john
} // false

// Now hide the "real" John somewhere among the imposters.
imposters.insert(john, at: Int(arc4random_uniform(100)))

// John can now be found among the imposters.
imposters.contains {
  $0 === john
} // true

// Since `Person` is a reference type, you can use === to grab
the real John out of the list of imposters and modify the value.
// The original `john` variable will print the new last name!
if let indexOfJohn = imposters.index(where: { $0 === john }) {
  imposters[indexOfJohn].lastName = "Bananapeel"
}

john.fullName // John Bananapeel
```

Note: You have to import the `Foundation` framework in order to work with the `arc4random_uniform(_:)` function.

You may actually find that you won't use the identity operator === very much in your day-to-day Swift. What's important is to understand what it does, and what it demonstrates about the properties of reference types.

Mini-exercise

Write a function `memberOf(person: Person, group: [Person]) -> Bool` that will return `true` if `person` can be found inside `group`, and `false` if it can not.

Test it by creating two arrays of five `Person` objects for `group` and using `john` as the `person`. Put `john` in one of the arrays, but not in the other.

Methods and mutability

As you've read before, instances of classes are mutable objects whereas instances of structures are immutable values. The following example illustrates this difference:

```
struct Grade {
  let letter: String
  let points: Double
  let credits: Double
}

class Student {
  var firstName: String
  var lastName: String
  var grades: [Grade] = []

  init(firstName: String, lastName: String) {
    self.firstName = firstName
    self.lastName = lastName
  }

  func recordGrade(_ grade: Grade) {
    grades.append(grade)
  }
}

let jane = Student(firstName: "Jane", lastName: "Appleseed")
let history = Grade(letter: "B", points: 9.0, credits: 3.0)
var math = Grade(letter: "A", points: 16.0, credits: 4.0)

jane.recordGrade(history)
jane.recordGrade(math)
```

Note that `recordGrade(_:)` can mutate the array `grades` by adding more values to the end. Although this mutates the current object, the keyword `mutating` is not required.

If you had tried this with a struct, you'd have wound up with a build failure, because structures are immutable. Remember, when you change the value of a struct, instead of modifying the value, you're making a *new* value. The keyword `mutating` marks methods that replace the current value with a new one. With classes, this keyword is not used because the instance itself is mutable.

Mutability and constants

The previous example may have had you wondering how you were able to modify `jane` even though it was defined as a constant.

When you define a constant, the value of the constant cannot be changed. If you recall back to the discussion of value types vs reference types, it is important to remember that, with reference types, the value is a *reference*.

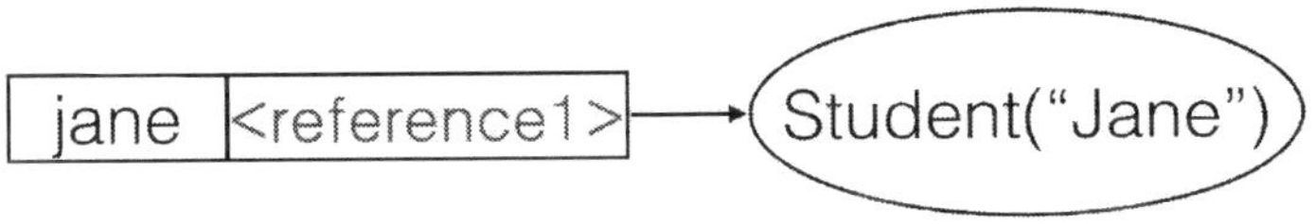

The value of "reference1" in red is the value stored in `jane`. This value is a reference and because `jane` is declared as a constant, this reference is constant. If you were to attempt to assign another student to `jane`, you would get a build error:

```
// Error: jane is a `let` constant
jane = Student(firstName: "John", lastName: "Appleseed")
```

If you declared `jane` as a variable instead, you would be able to assign to it another instance of `Student` on the heap:

```
var jane = Student(firstName: "Jane", lastName: "Appleseed")
jane = Student(firstName: "John", lastName: "Appleseed")
```

After the assignment of another `Student` to `jane`, the reference value behind `jane` would be updated to point to the new `Student` object.

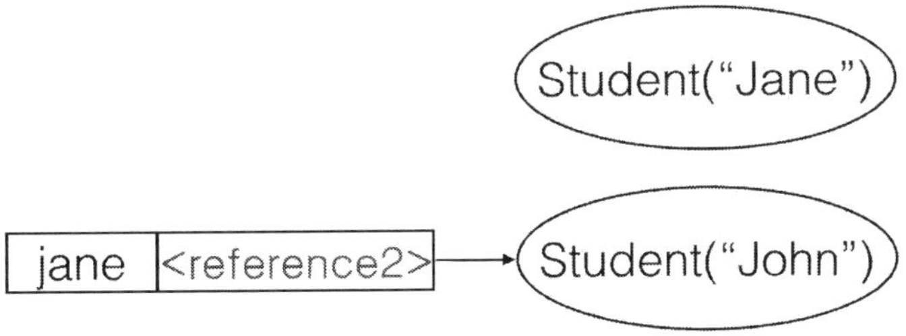

Since nothing would be referencing the original "Jane" object, its memory would be freed to use elsewhere. You'll learn more about this in Chapter 23, "Asynchronous Closures and Memory Management".

Any individual member of a class can be protected from modification through the use of constants, but because reference types are not *themselves* treated as values, they are not protected as a whole from mutation.

Mini-exercise

Add a computed property to `Student` that returns the student's Grade Point Average, or GPA. A GPA is defined as the number of points earned divided by the number of credits taken. For the example above, Jane earned (9 + 16 = 25) points while taking (3 + 4 = 7) credits, making her GPA (25 / 7 = 3.57).

> **Note:** Points in most American universities range from 4 per credit for an A, down to 1 point for a D (with an F being 0 points). For this exercise, you may of course use any scale that you want!

Understanding state and side effects

The referenced and mutable nature of classes leads to numerous programming possibilities, as well as many concerns. If you update a class instance with a new value, then every reference to that instance will also see the new value.

You can use this to your advantage. Perhaps you pass a `Student` instance to a sports team, a report card and a class roster. Imagine all of these entities need to know the student's grades, and because they all point to the same instance, they'll all see new grades as the instance records them.

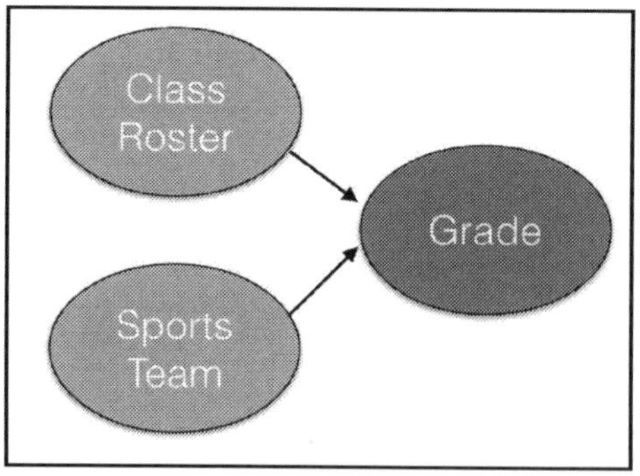

The result of this sharing is that class instances have **state**. Changes in state can sometimes be obvious, but often they're not.

To illustrate this, add a `credits` property to the `Student` class.

```
var credits = 0.0
```

and update `recordGrade(_:)` to use this new property:

```
func recordGrade(_ grade: Grade) {
  grades.append(grade)
  credits += grade.credits
}
```

In this slightly modified example of `Student`, `recordGrade(_:)` now adds the number of credits to the `credits` property. Calling `recordGrade(_:)` has the side effect of updating `credits`.

Now, observe how side effects can result in non-obvious behavior:

```
jane.credits // 7

// The teacher made a mistake; math has 5 credits
math = Grade(letter: "A", points: 20.0, credits: 5.0)
jane.recordGrade(math)

jane.credits // 12, not 8!
```

Whoever wrote the modified `Student` class did so somewhat naïvely by assuming that the same grade won't get recorded twice! Because class instances are mutable, you need to be careful about unexpected behavior around shared references.

While confusing in a small example such as this, mutability and state could be extremely jarring as classes grow in size and complexity. Situations like this would be much more common with a `Student` class that scales to 20 stored properties and has 10 methods.

Extending a class using an extension

As you saw with structs, classes can be *re-opened* using the `extension` keyword to add methods and computed properties. Add a `fullName` computed property to `Student`:

```
extension Student {
  var fullName: String {
    return "\(firstName) \(lastName)"
  }
}
```

Functionality can also be added to classes using *inheritance*. You can even add new stored properties to inheriting classes. You will explore this technique in detail in the next chapter.

When to use a class versus a struct

Now that you know the differences and similarities between a class and a struct, you may be wondering "How do I know which to use?"

Values vs. objects

While there are no hard and fast rules, one strategy is to think about value versus reference semantics and use structures as *values* and classes as *objects with identity*. An **object** is an instance of a reference type. Such instances have **identity**. This means that every object is unique and no two objects are considered equal just because they hold the same state. This is why you had to use === to see if objects are truly equal and not just containing the same state. This is in contrast to instances of value types, which *are* values and are by definition considered equal if they are the same value.

For example: A delivery range is a value and should be implemented as a struct, while a student is an object and should be implemented as a class. No two students should be considered equal just because they have the same name!

Speed

Speed considerations may also come into play, as structs rely on the faster stack while classes rely on the slower heap. If you will have *many* instances of a type created (hundreds to many thousands), or if these instances will only exist in memory for a very short time, then you should generally lean towards using a struct. If your instance will have a longer lifecycle in memory, or if you will create relatively few instances, then creating class instances on the heap generally won't create much overhead.

For instance, you may want to use a struct to calculate the total distance of a running route using many GPS-based waypoints, like the `Location` struct you used in Chapter 10, "Structures". Not only will you create many waypoints, but they will also be created and destroyed quickly as you modify the route.

You could also use a class for an object to store route history, as you'll only have one object for each user and you'd likely use the same history object for the user's lifetime.

Minimalist approach

Another approach is to use only what you need. If your data will never change or you need a simple data store, then use structures. If you need to update your data and you need it to contain logic to update its own state, then use classes. Often, it's best to begin with a struct. If later you need the added capabilities of a class, then convert the struct to a class.

Structures vs. classes recap

Structures

- Useful for representing values
- Implicit copying of values
- Becomes completely immutable when declared with `let`
- Fast memory allocation (stack)

Classes

- Useful for representing objects with identity
- Implicit sharing of objects
- Internals can remain mutable even when declared with `let`
- Slower memory allocation (heap)

Key points

- Like structures, **classes** are a named type that can have properties and methods.
- Classes use **references** that are shared on assignment.
- Class instances are called **objects**.
- Objects are **mutable**.
- Mutability introduces **state**, which adds complexity when managing your objects.
- Use classes when you want **reference semantics**; structures for **value semantics**.

Where to go from here?

Classes should feel familiar to you after having learned about structs. However, there are enough subtle differences around copying, sharing and mutability that it's important to keep them distinct in your head!

When deciding between a struct and a class, you've seen some of the factors to take into consideration — and there will be more things to consider in the very next chapter!

Challenges

Challenge 1: Movie lists — benefits of reference types

Imagine you're writing a movie-viewing application in Swift. Users can create lists of movies and share those lists with other users.

Create a `User` and a `List` class that uses reference semantics to help maintain lists between users.

- `User`: Has a method `addList(_:)` which adds the given list to a dictionary of `List` objects (using the `name` as a key), and `list(forName:) -> List?` which will return the `List` for the provided name.
- `List`: Contains a name and an array of movie titles. A `print` method will print all the movies in the list.
- Create `jane` and `john` users and have them create and share lists. Have both `jane` and `john` modify the same list and call `print` from both users. Are all the changes reflected?
- What happens when you implement the same with structs? What problems do you run into?

Challenge 2: T-Shirt store — class or struct?

Your challenge here is to build a set of objects to support a T-shirt store. Decide if each object should be a class or a struct, and why.

- `TShirt`: Represents a shirt style you can buy. Each `TShirt` has a size, color, price, and an optional image on the front.
- `User`: A registered user of the t-shirt store app. A user has a name, email, and a `ShoppingCart` (see below).
- `Address`: Represents a shipping address, containing the name, street, city, and zip code.
- `ShoppingCart`: Holds a current order, which is composed of an array of `TShirt` that the `User` wants to buy, as well as a method to calculate the total cost. Additionally, there is an `Address` that represents where the order will be shipped.

Bonus: After you've decided on whether to use a class or struct for each object, go ahead and implement them all!

Chapter 14: Advanced Classes

By Cosmin Pupăză

The previous chapter introduced you to the basics of defining and using classes in Swift. Classes are reference types and can be used to support traditional object-oriented programming.

Classes introduce inheritance, overriding, polymorphism and composition which makes them suited for this purpose. These extra features require special consideration for initialization, class hierarchies, and understanding the class lifecycle in memory.

This chapter will introduce you to the finer points of classes in Swift, and help you understand how you can create more complex classes.

Introducing inheritance

In the previous chapter, you saw a `Grade` struct and a pair of class examples: `Person` and `Student`.

```
struct Grade {
  var letter: Character
  var points: Double
  var credits: Double
}

class Person {
  var firstName: String
  var lastName: String

  init(firstName: String, lastName: String) {
    self.firstName = firstName
    self.lastName = lastName
```

```
  }
}

class Student {
  var firstName: String
  var lastName: String
  var grades: [Grade] = []

  init(firstName: String, lastName: String) {
    self.firstName = firstName
    self.lastName = lastName
  }

  func recordGrade(_ grade: Grade) {
    grades.append(grade)
  }
}
```

It's not difficult to see that there's an incredible amount of redundancy between `Person` and `Student`. Maybe you've also noticed that a `Student` *is* a `Person`!

This simple case demonstrates the idea behind class inheritance. Much like in the real world, where you can think of a student as a person, you can represent the same relationship in code by replacing the original `Student` class implementation with the following:

```
class Student: Person {
  var grades: [Grade] = []

  func recordGrade(_ grade: Grade) {
    grades.append(grade)
  }
}
```

In this modified example, the `Student` class now **inherits** from `Person`, indicated by a colon after the naming of `Student`, followed by the class from which `Student` inherits, which in this case is `Person`.

Through inheritance, `Student` automatically gets the properties and methods declared in the `Person` class. In code, it would be accurate to say that a `Student` *is-a* `Person`.

With much less duplication of code, you can now create `Student` objects that have all the properties and methods of a `Person`:

```
let john = Person(firstName: "Johnny", lastName: "Appleseed")
let jane = Student(firstName: "Jane", lastName: "Appleseed")

john.firstName // "John"
jane.firstName // "Jane"
```

Additionally, only the `Student` object will have all of the properties and methods defined in `Student`:

```
let history = Grade(letter: "B", points: 9.0, credits: 3.0)
jane.recordGrade(history)
// john.recordGrade(history) // john is not a student!
```

A class that inherits from another class is known as a **subclass** or a **derived class**, and the class from which it inherits is known as a **superclass** or a **base class**.

The rules for subclassing are fairly simple:

- A Swift class can inherit from only one other class, a concept known as **single inheritance**.
- There's no limit to the depth of subclassing, meaning you can subclass from a class that is *also* a subclass, like below:

```
class BandMember: Student {
  var minimumPracticeTime = 2
}

class OboePlayer: BandMember {
  // This is an example of an override, which we'll cover soon.
  override var minimumPracticeTime: Int {
    get {
      return super.minimumPracticeTime * 2
    }
    set {
      super.minimumPracticeTime = newValue / 2
    }
  }
}
```

A chain of subclasses is called a **class hierarchy**. In this example, the hierarchy would be `OboePlayer` -> `BandMember` -> `Student` -> `Person`. A class hierarchy is analogous to a family tree. Because of this analogy, a superclass is also called the **parent class** of its **child class**.

Polymorphism

The `Student/Person` relationship demonstrates a computer science concept known as **polymorphism**. In brief, polymorphism is a programming language's ability to treat an object differently based on context.

A `OboePlayer` is of course a `OboePlayer`, but it is also a `Person`. Because it derives from `Person`, you could use a `OboePlayer` object anywhere you'd use a `Person` object.

This example demonstrates how you can treat a `OboePlayer` as a `Person`:

```
func phonebookName(_ person: Person) -> String {
  return "\(person.lastName), \(person.firstName)"
}

let person = Person(firstName: "Johnny", lastName: "Appleseed")
let oboePlayer = OboePlayer(firstName: "Jane",
                            lastName: "Appleseed")

phonebookName(person) // Appleseed, Johnny
phonebookName(oboePlayer) // Appleseed, Jane
```

Because `OboePlayer` derives from `Person`, it is a valid input into the function `phonebookName(_:)`. More importantly, the function has no idea that the object passed in is anything *other* than a regular `Person`. It can only observe the elements of `OboePlayer` that are defined in the `Person` base class.

With the polymorphism characteristics provided by class inheritance, Swift is treating the object pointed to by `oboePlayer` differently based on the context. This can be particularly useful to you when you have diverging class hierarchies, but want to have code that operates on a common type or base class.

Runtime hierarchy checks

Now that you are coding with polymorphism, you will likely find situations where the specific type behind a variable can be different. For instance, you could define a variable `hallMonitor` as a `Student`:

```
var hallMonitor = Student(firstName: "Jill",
                          lastName: "Bananapeel")
```

But what if `hallMonitor` were a more derived type, such as an `OboePlayer`?

```
hallMonitor = oboePlayer
```

Because `hallMonitor` is defined as a `Student`, the compiler won't allow you to attempt calling properties or methods for a more derived type.

Fortunately, Swift provides the `as` operator to treat a property or a variable as another type:

- `as`: Cast to a specific type that is known at compile time to succeed, such as casting to a supertype.
- `as?`: An optional downcast (to a subtype). If the downcast fails, the result of the expression will be `nil`.

- `as!`: A forced downcast. If the downcast fails, the program will crash. Use this rarely, and only when you are certain the cast will never fail.

These can be used in various contexts to treat the `hallMonitor` as a `BandMember`, or the `oboePlayer` as a less-derived `Student`.

```
oboePlayer as Student
(oboePlayer as Student).minimumPracticeTime // ERROR: No longer
a band member!

hallMonitor as? BandMember
(hallMonitor as? BandMember)?.minimumPracticeTime // 4
(optional)

hallMonitor as! BandMember // Careful! Failure would lead to a
runtime crash.
(hallMonitor as! BandMember).minimumPracticeTime // 4 (force
unwrapped)
```

The optional downcast `as?` is particularly useful in `if let` or `guard` statements:

```
if let hallMonitor = hallMonitor as? BandMember {
  print("This hall monitor is a band member and practices
         at least \(hallMonitor.minimumPracticeTime)
         hours per week.")
}
```

You may be wondering under what contexts you would use the `as` operator by itself. Any object contains all the properties and methods of its parent class, so what use is casting it to something it already is?

Swift has a strong type system, and the interpretation of a specific type can have an effect on **static dispatch**, or the decision of which specific operation is selected at compile time.

Sound confusing? How about an example?

Assume you have two functions with identical names and parameter names for two different parameter types:

```
func afterClassActivity(for student: Student) -> String {
  return "Goes home!"
}

func afterClassActivity(for student: BandMember) -> String {
  return "Goes to practice!"
}
```

If you were to pass `oboePlayer` into `afterClassActivity(for:)`, which one of these implementations would get called? The answer lies in Swift's dispatch rules, which in this case will select the more specific version that takes in an `OboePlayer`.

If instead you were to cast `oboePlayer` to a `Student`, the `Student` version would be called:

```
afterClassActivity(for: oboePlayer) // Goes to practice!
afterClassActivity(for: oboePlayer as Student) // Goes home!
```

Inheritance, methods and overrides

Subclasses receive all properties and methods defined in their superclass, plus any additional properties and methods the subclass defines for itself. In that sense, subclasses are *additive*; for example, you've already seen that the `Student` class can add additional properties and methods for handling a student's grades. These properties and methods wouldn't be available to any `Person` class instances, but they *would* be available to `Student` subclasses.

Besides creating their own methods, subclasses can *override* methods defined in their superclass. Assume that student athletes become ineligible for the athletics program if they're failing three or more classes. That means you need to keep track of failing grades somehow.

```
class StudentAthlete: Student {
  var failedClasses: [Grade] = []

  override func recordGrade(_ grade: Grade) {
    super.recordGrade(grade)

    if grade.letter == "F" {
      failedClasses.append(grade)
    }
  }

  var isEligible: Bool {
    return failedClasses.count < 3
  }
}
```

In this example, the `StudentAthlete` class overrides `recordGrade(_:)` so it can keep track of any courses the student has failed. The `StudentAthlete` class then has its own computed property, `isEligible`, that uses this information to determine the athlete's eligibility.

When overriding a method, use the `override` keyword before the method declaration.

If your subclass were to have an identical method declaration as its superclass, but you omitted the `override` keyword, Swift would indicate a build error.

```
class StudentAthlete: Student {
  var failedClasses: [Grade] = []

  func recordGrade(_ grade: Grade) {   Overriding declaration requires an 'override' keyword
    super.recordGrade(grade)

    if grade.letter == "F" {
      failedClasses.append(grade)
    }
  }

  var isEligible: Bool {
    return failedClasses.count < 3
  }
}
```

This makes it very clear whether a method is an override of an existing one or not.

Introducing super

You may have also noticed the line `super.recordGrade(grade)` in the overridden method. The `super` keyword is similar to `self`, except it will invoke the method in the nearest implementing superclass. In the example of `recordGrade(_:)` in `StudentAthlete`, calling `super.recordGrade(grade)` will execute the method as defined in the `Student` class.

Remember how inheritance let you define `Person` with first name and last name properties and avoid repeating those properties in subclasses? Similarly, being able to call the superclass methods means you can write the code to record the grade once in `Student` and then call "up" to it as needed in subclasses.

Although it isn't always required, it's often important to call `super` when overriding a method in Swift. The `super` call is what will record the grade itself in the `grades` array, because that behavior isn't duplicated in `StudentAthlete`. Calling `super` is also a way of avoiding the need for duplicate code in `StudentAthlete` and `Student`.

When to call super

As you may notice, exactly *when* you call super can have an important effect on your overridden method.

Suppose you replace the overriden `recordGrade(_:)` method in the `StudentAthlete` class with the following version that recalculates the `failedClasses` each time a grade is recorded:

```
override func recordGrade(_ grade: Grade) {
  var newFailedClasses: [Grade] = []
  for grade in grades {
    if grade.letter == "F" {
      newFailedClasses.append(grade)
    }
```

```
    }
    failedClasses = newFailedClasses

    super.recordGrade(grade)
  }
```

This version of `recordGrade(_:)` uses the `grades` array to find the current list of failed classes. If you've spotted a bug in the code above, good job! Since you call `super` last, if the new `grade.letter` is an `F`, the code won't update `failedClasses` properly.

While it's not a hard rule, it's generally best practice to call the `super` version of a method first when overriding. That way, the superclass won't experience any side effects introduced by its subclass, and the subclass won't need to know the superclass's implementation details.

Preventing inheritance

Sometimes you'll want to disallow subclasses of a particular class. Swift provides the `final` keyword for you to guarantee a class will never get a subclass:

```
final class FinalStudent: Person {}
class FinalStudentAthlete: FinalStudent {} // Build error!
```

By marking the `FinalStudent` class `final`, you tell the compiler to prevent any classes from inheriting from `FinalStudent`. This can remind you — or others on your team! — that a class wasn't designed to have subclasses.

Additionally, you can mark individual *methods* as `final`, if you want to allow a class to have subclasses, but protect individual methods from being overridden:

```
class AnotherStudent: Person {
  final func recordGrade(_ grade: Grade) {}
}

class AnotherStudentAthlete: AnotherStudent {
  override func recordGrade(_ grade: Grade) {} // Build error!
}
```

There are benefits to initially marking any new class you write as `final`. This tells the compiler it doesn't need to look for any more subclasses, which can shorten compile time, and it also requires you to be very explicit when deciding to subclass a class previously marked `final`. You will learn more about controlling who can override a class in Chapter 18, "Access Control and Code Organization".

Inheritance and class initialization

The previous chapter briefly introduced you to class initializers, which are similar to their struct counterparts. With subclasses, there are a few more considerations with regard to how you set up instances.

> **Note**: In the chapter's playground I have renamed `Student` and `StudentAthlete` to `NewStudent` and `NewStudentAthlete` in order to keep both versions working side-by-side.

Modify the `StudentAthlete` class to add a list of sports an athlete plays:

```
class StudentAthlete: Student {
  var sports: [String]
  // original code
}
```

Because `sports` doesn't have an initial value, `StudentAthlete` must provide one in its own initializer:

```
class StudentAthlete: Student {
  var sports: [String]

  init(sports: [String]) {
    self.sports = sports
    // Build error - super.init isn't called before
    // returning from initializer
  }
  // original code
}
```

Uh-oh! The compiler complains that you didn't call `super.init` by the end of the initializer:

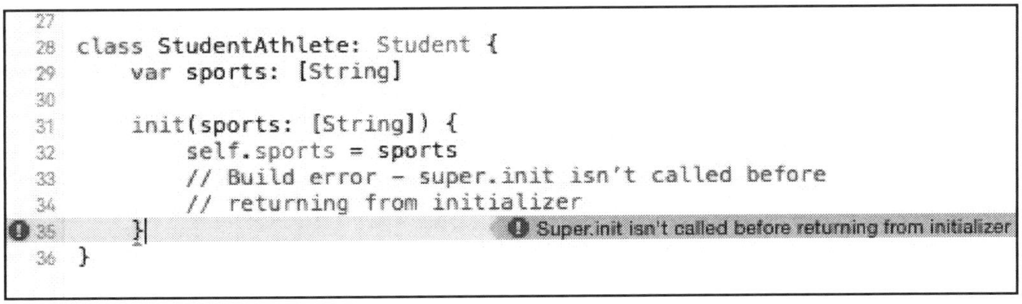

Initializers in subclasses are *required* to call `super.init` because without it, the superclass won't be able to provide initial states for all its stored properties — in this case, `firstName` and `lastName`.

Let's make the compiler happy:

```
class StudentAthlete: Student {
  var sports: [String]

  init(firstName: String, lastName: String, sports: [String]) {
    self.sports = sports
    super.init(firstName: firstName, lastName: lastName)
  }
  // original code
}
```

The initializer now calls the initializer of its superclass, and the build error is gone.

Notice that the initializer now takes in a `firstName` and a `lastName` to satisfy the requirements for calling the `Person` initializer.

You also call `super.init` *after* you initialize the `sports` property, which is an enforced rule.

Two-phase initialization

Because of Swift's requirement that all stored properties have initial values, initializers in subclasses must adhere to Swift's convention of **two-phase initialization**.

- **Phase one:** Initialize all of the stored properties in the class instance, from the bottom to the top of the class hierarchy. You can't use properties and methods until phase one is complete.
- **Phase two:** You can now use properties and methods, as well as initializations that require the use of `self`.

Without two-phase initialization, methods and operations on the class might interact with properties before they've been initialized.

The transition from phase one to phase two happens after you've initialized all stored properties in the base class of a class hierarchy.

In the scope of a subclass initializer, you can think of this as coming after the call to `super.init`.

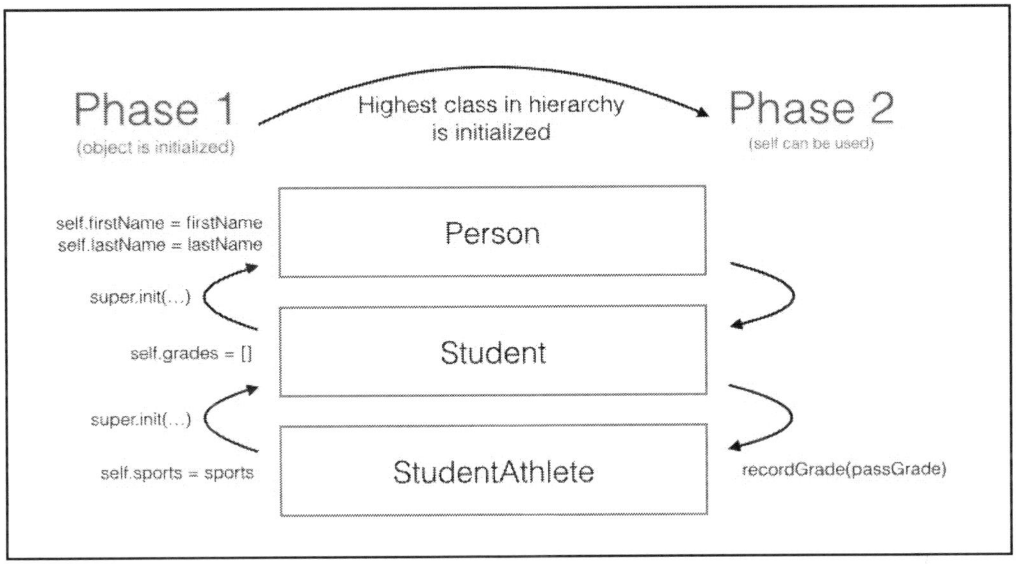

Here's the `StudentAthlete` class again, with athletes automatically getting a starter grade:

```
class StudentAthlete: Student {
  var sports: [String]

  init(firstName: String, lastName: String, sports: [String]) {
    // 1
    self.sports = sports
     // 2
    let passGrade = Grade(letter: "P", points: 0.0,
                          credits: 0.0)
     // 3
    super.init(firstName: firstName, lastName: lastName)
     // 4
    recordGrade(passGrade)
  }
  // original code
}
```

The above initializer shows two-phase initialization in action.

1. First, you initialize the `sports` property of `StudentAthlete`. This is part of the first phase of initialization and has to be done early, before you call the superclass initializer.

2. Although you can create local variables for things like grades, you can't call `recordGrade(_:)` yet because the object is still in the first phase.

3. You call `super.init`. When this returns, you know that you've also initialized every class in the hierarchy, because the same rules are applied at every level.
4. After `super.init` returns, the initializer is in phase 2, so you call `recordGrade(_:)`.

Mini-exercise

What's different in the two-phase initialization in the base class `Person`, as compared to the others?

Required and convenience initializers

You already know it's possible to have multiple initializers in a class, which means you could potentially call *any* of those initializers from a subclass.

Often, you'll find that your classes have various initializers that simply provide a "convenient" way to initialize an object:

```
class Student {
  let firstName: String
  let lastName: String
  var grades: [Grade] = []

  init(firstName: String, lastName: String) {
    self.firstName = firstName
    self.lastName = lastName
  }

  init(transfer: Student) {
    self.firstName = transfer.firstName
    self.lastName = transfer.lastName
  }

  func recordGrade(_ grade: Grade) {
    grades.append(grade)
  }
}
```

In this example, the `Student` class can be built with another `Student` object. Perhaps the student switched majors? Both initializers fully set the first and last names.

Subclasses of `Student` could potentially rely on the `Student`-based initializer when they make their call to `super.init`. Additionally, the subclasses might not even provide a method to initialize with first and last names. You might decide the first and last name-based initializer is important enough that you want it to be available to *all* subclasses.

Swift supports this through the language feature known as **required initializers**.

```
class Student {
  let firstName: String
  let lastName: String
  var grades: [Grade] = []

  required init(firstName: String, lastName: String) {
    self.firstName = firstName
    self.lastName = lastName
  }
  // original code
}
```

In the modified version of `Student` above, the first and last name-based initializer has been marked with the keyword `required`. This keyword will force all subclasses of `Student` to implement this initializer.

Now that there's a required initializer on `Student`, `StudentAthlete` *must* override and implement it too.

```
class StudentAthlete: Student {
  // Now required by the compiler!
  required init(firstName: String, lastName: String) {
    self.sports = []
    super.init(firstName: firstName, lastName: lastName)
  }
  // original code
}
```

Notice how the `override` keyword isn't required with required initializers. In its place, the `required` keyword must be used to make sure that any subclass of `StudentAthlete` still implements this required initializer.

You can also mark an initializer as a **convenience** initializer:

```
class Student {
  convenience init(transfer: Student) {
    self.init(firstName: transfer.firstName,
              lastName: transfer.lastName)
  }
  // original code
}
```

The compiler forces a `convenience` initializer to call a non-convenience initializer (directly or indirectly), instead of handling the initialization of stored properties itself. A non-convenience initializer is called a **designated** initializer and is subject to the rules of two-phase initialization. All initializers you've written in previous examples were in fact designated initializers.

You might want to mark an initializer as `convenience` if you only use that initializer as an easy way to initialize an object, but you still want it to leverage one of your designated initializers.

Here's a summary of the compiler rules for using designated and convenience initializers:

1. A designated initializer must call a designated initializer from its immediate superclass.
2. A convenience initializer must call another initializer from the same class.
3. A convenience initializer must ultimately call a designated initializer.

Mini-exercise

Create two more convenience initializers on `Student`. Which other initializers are you able to call?

When and why to subclass

This chapter has introduced you to class inheritance, along with the numerous programming techniques that subclassing enables.

But you might be asking, "When should I subclass?"

Rarely is there a right or wrong answer to that important question. Understanding the trade-offs can help you make the best decision for any particular case.

Using the `Student` and `StudentAthlete` classes as an example, you might decide you can simply put all of the characteristics of `StudentAthlete` into `Student`:

```
class Student: Person {
  var grades: [Grade]
  var sports: [Sport]
  // original code
}
```

In reality, this *could* solve all of the use cases for your needs. A `Student` that doesn't play sports would simply have an empty `sports` array, and you would avoid some of the added complexities of subclassing.

Single responsibility

In software development, the guideline known as the **single responsibility principle** states that any class should have a single concern. In `Student`/`StudentAthlete`, you might argue that it shouldn't be the `Student` class's job to encapsulate responsibilities that only make sense to student athletes.

Strong types

Subclassing creates an additional type. With Swift's type system, you can declare properties or behavior based on objects that are student athletes, not regular students:

```
class Team {
  var players: [StudentAthlete] = []

  var isEligible: Bool {
    for player in players {
      if !player.isEligible {
        return false
      }
    }
    return true
  }
}
```

A team has players who are student athletes. If you tried to add a regular `Student` object to the array of players, the type system wouldn't allow it. This can be useful as the compiler can help you enforce the logic and requirement of your system.

Shared base classes

You can subclass a shared base class multiple times by classes that have mutually exclusive behavior:

```
// A button that can be pressed.
class Button {
  func press() {}
}

// An image that can be rendered on a button
class Image {}

// A button that is composed entirely of an image.
class ImageButton: Button {
  var image: Image

  init(image: Image) {
    self.image = image
  }
}

// A button that renders as text.
class TextButton: Button {
```

```
  var text: String

  init(text: String) {
    self.text = text
  }
}
```

In this example, you can imagine numerous `Button` subclasses that share only the fact that they can be pressed. The `ImageButton` and `TextButton` classes likely have entirely different mechanisms to render the appearance of a button, so they might have to implement their own behavior when the button is pressed.

You can see here how storing `image` and `text` in the `Button` class — not to mention any other kind of button there might be — would quickly become impractical. It makes sense for `Button` to be concerned with the press behavior, and the subclasses to handle the actual look and feel of the button.

Extensibility

Sometimes you simply must subclass if you're extending the behavior of code you don't own. In the example above, it's possible `Button` is part of a framework you're using, and there's no way you can modify or extend the source code to fit your needs.

In that case, subclass `Button` so you can add your custom subclass and use it with code that's expecting an object of type `Button`. Using access control, discussed in detail in Chapter 18, "Access Control and Code Organization", the author of a class can designate if any of the members of a class can be overridden or not.

Identity

Finally, it's important to understand that classes and class hierarchies model what objects *are*. If your goal is to share behavior (what objects *can do*) between types, more often than not you should prefer protocols over subclassing. You'll learn about protocols in Chapter 16, "Protocols".

Understanding the class lifecycle

In the previous chapter, you learned that objects are created in memory and that they're stored on the heap. Objects on the heap are *not* automatically destroyed, because the heap is simply a giant pool of memory. Without the utility of the call stack, there's no automatic way for a process to know that a piece of memory will no longer be in use.

In Swift, the mechanism for deciding when to clean up unused objects on the heap is known as **reference counting**. In short, each object has a reference count that's incremented for each constant or variable with a reference to that object, and decremented each time a reference is removed.

> **Note:** You might see the reference count called a "retain count" in other books and online resources. They refer to the same thing!

When a reference count reaches zero, that means the object is now abandoned since nothing in the system holds a reference to it. When that happens, Swift will clean up the object.

Here's a demonstration of how the reference count changes for an object. Note that there's only one actual object created in this example; the one object just has many references to it.

```
var someone = Person(firstName: "Johnny", lastName: "Appleseed")
// Person object has a reference count of 1 (someone variable)

var anotherSomeone: Person? = someone
// Reference count 2 (someone, anotherSomeone)

var lotsOfPeople = [someone, someone, anotherSomeone, someone]
// Reference count 6 (someone, anotherSomeone, 4 references in
lotsOfPeople)

anotherSomeone = nil
// Reference count 5 (someone, 4 references in lotsOfPeople)

lotsOfPeople = []
// Reference count 1 (someone)

someone = Person(firstName: "Johnny", lastName: "Appleseed")
// Reference count 0 for the original Person object!
// Variable someone now references a new object
```

In this example, you don't have to do any work yourself to increase or decrease the object's reference count. That's because Swift has a feature known as **automatic reference counting** or **ARC**.

While some older languages require you to increment and decrement reference counts in *your* code, the Swift compiler adds these calls automatically at compile time.

> **Note:** If you use a low-level language like C, you're required to manually free memory you're no longer using yourself. Higher-level languages like Java and C# use something called **garbage collection**. In that case, the runtime of the language will search your process for references to objects, before cleaning up those that are no longer in use. Garbage collection, while more powerful than ARC, comes with a memory utilization and performance cost that Apple decided wasn't acceptable for mobile devices or a general systems language.

Deinitialization

When an object's reference count reaches zero, Swift removes the object from memory and marks that memory as free.

A **deinitializer** is a special method on classes that runs when an object's reference count reaches zero, but before Swift removes the object from memory.

Modify class `Person` as follows:

```
class Person {
  // original code
  deinit {
    print("\(firstName) \(lastName) is being removed
          from memory!")
  }
}
```

Much like `init` is a special method in class initialization, `deinit` is a special method that handles deinitialization. Unlike `init`, `deinit` isn't required and is automatically invoked by Swift. You also aren't required to override it or call `super` within it. Swift will make sure to call each class deinitializer.

If you add this deinitializer, you'll see the message `Johnny Appleseed is being removed from memory!` in the debug area after running the previous example.

What you do in an deinitializer is up to you. Often you'll use it to clean up other resources, save state to a disk or execute any other logic you might want when an object goes out of scope.

Mini-exercises

Modify the `Student` class to have the ability to record the student's name to a list of graduates. Add the name of the student to the list when the object is deallocated.

Retain cycles and weak references

Because classes in Swift rely on reference counting to remove them from memory, it's important to understand the concept of a **retain cycle**.

Add a field representing a classmate — for example, a lab partner — and a deinitializer to class `Student` like this:

```
class Student: Person {
  var partner: Student?
  // original code
  deinit {
    print("\(firstName) is being deallocated!")
  }
}

var alice: Student? = Student(firstName: "Alice",
                              lastName: "Appleseed")
var bob: Student? = Student(firstName: "Bob",
                            lastName: "Appleseed")

alice?.partner = bob
bob?.partner = alice
```

Now suppose both `alice` and `bob` drop out of school:

```
alice = nil
bob = nil
```

If you run this in your playground, you'll notice that you don't see the message `Alice/Bob is being deallocated!`, and Swift doesn't call `deinit`. Why is that?

Alice and Bob each have a reference to *each other*, so the reference count never reaches zero! To make things worse, by assigning `nil` to `alice` and `bob`, there are no more references to the initial objects. This is a classic case of a retain cycle, which leads to a software bug known as a **memory leak**.

With a memory leak, memory isn't freed up even though its practical lifecycle has ended. Retain cycles are the most common cause of memory leaks.

Fortunately, there's a way that the `Student` object can reference another `Student` without being prone to retain cycles, and that's by making the reference **weak**:

```
class Student: Person {
  weak var partner: Student?
  // original code
}
```

This simple modification marks the `partner` variable as `weak`, which means the reference in this variable will not take part in reference counting. When a reference isn't weak, it's called a **strong reference**, which is the default in Swift. Weak references must be declared as optional types so that when the object that they are referencing is released, it automatically becomes `nil`.

Key points

- **Class inheritance** is one of the most important features of classes and enables **polymorphism**.
- Swift classes use **two-phase initialization** as a safety measure to ensure all stored properties are initialized before they are used.
- **Subclassing** is a powerful tool, but it's good to know when to subclass. Subclass when you want to extend an object and could benefit from an "is-a" relationship between subclass and superclass, but be mindful of the inherited state and deep class hierarchies.
- Class instances have their own lifecycles which are controlled by their **reference counts**.
- **Automatic reference counting**, or **ARC**, handles reference counting for you automatically, but it's important to watch out for **retain cycles**.

Where to go from here?

Classes and structs are the most common types you'll use to model things in your apps, from students to grades to people to teams. As you've seen, classes are more complex, and support things such as reference semantics and inheritance.

In the next chapter, you'll learn about the third type available to you: enumerations.

Challenges

1. Create three simple classes called `A`, `B`, and `C` where `C` inherits from `B` and `B` inherits from `A`. In each class initializer, call `print("I'm <X>!")` both before and after `super.init()`. Create an instance of `C` called `c`. What order do you see each `print()` called in?

2. Implement `deinit` for each class. Create your instance `c` inside of a `do { }` scope which will cause the reference count to go to zero when it exits the scope. Which order are the classes deinitialized in?

3. Cast the instance of type `C` to an instance of type `A`. Which casting operation do you use and why?

4. Create a subclass of `StudentAthlete` called `StudentBaseballPlayer` and include properties for `position`, `number`, and `battingAverage`. What are the benefits and drawbacks of subclassing `StudentAthlete` in this scenario?

5. Fix the following classes so there isn't a memory leak when you add an order:

```
class Customer {
  let name: String
  var orders: [Order] = []

  init(name: String) {
    self.name = name
  }

  func add(_ order: Order) {
    order.customer = self
    orders.append(order)
  }
}

class Order {
  let product: String
  var customer: Customer?

  init(product: String) {
    self.product = product
  }
}
```

Chapter 15: Enumerations

By Ben Morrow

One day in your life as a developer, you'll realize you're being held captive by your laptop. Determined to break from convention, you decide to set off on a long trek by foot. Of course, you need a map of the terrain you'll encounter. Since it's the 21st century, and you're fluent in Swift, you apply yourself to one final project: a custom map app.

As you code away, you think it would be swell if you could represent the cardinal directions as variables: north, south, east, west. But what's the best way to do this in code?

You could represent each value as an integer, like so:

- North: `1`
- South: `2`
- East: `3`
- West: `4`

You can see how this could quickly get confusing if you or your users happen to think of the directions in a different order. "What does 3 mean again?" To alleviate that, you might represent the values as strings, like so:

- North: `"north"`
- South: `"south"`
- East: `"east"`
- West: `"west"`

The trouble with strings, though, is that the value can be any string. What would your app do if it received `"up"` instead of `"north"`? Furthermore, when you're composing code, it's easy to miss a typo like `"nrth"`.

Wouldn't it be great if there were a way to create a group of related values? If you find yourself headed in this... *direction*, you'll want to use an **enumeration**.

An enumeration is a list of related values that define a common type and let you work with values in a type-safe way. The compiler will catch your mistake if your code expects a `Direction` and you try to pass in a float like `10.7` or a misspelled direction like `"Souuth"`.

Besides cardinal directions, other good examples of related values are colors (black, red, blue), card suits (hearts, spades, clubs, diamonds) and roles (administrator, editor, reader).

Enumerations in Swift are more powerful than they are in other languages such as C or Objective-C. They share features with the structure and class types you learned about in the previous chapters. An enumeration can have methods and computed properties, all while acting as a convenient state machine.

In this chapter, you'll learn how enumerations work and when they're useful. As a bonus, you'll finally discover what an optional is under the hood. Hint: They are implemented with enumerations!

Your first enumeration

Your challenge: construct a function that will determine the school semester based on the month. One way to solve this would be to use an array of strings and match them msemesters with a `switch` statement:

```
let months = ["January", "February", "March", "April", "May",
              "June", "July", "August", "September", "October",
              "November", "December"]

func semester(for month: String) -> String {
  switch month {
  case "August", "September", "October", "November", "December":
    return "Autumn"
  case "January", "February", "March", "April", "May":
    return "Spring"
```

```
    default:
      return "Not in the school year"
    }
}

semester(for: "April") // Spring
```

Running this code in a playground, you can see that the function correctly returns `"Spring"`. But as I mentioned in the introduction, you could easily mistype a string. A better way to tackle this would be with an enumeration.

Declaring an enumeration

To declare an enumeration, you list out all the possible member values as `case` clauses:

```
enum Month {
  case january
  case february
  case march
  case april
  case may
  case june
  case july
  case august
  case september
  case october
  case november
  case december
}
```

This code creates a new enumeration called `Month` with 12 possible member values. The commonly accepted best practice is to start each member value with a lower case first letter, just like a property.

You can simplify the code a bit by collapsing the `case` clauses down to one line, with each value separated by a comma:

```
enum Month {
  case january, february, march, april, may, june, july, august,
  september, october, november, december
}
```

That looks snazzy and simple. So far, so good.

Deciphering an enumeration in a function

You can rewrite the function that determines the semester so that it uses enumeration values instead of string-matching.

```
func semester(for month: Month) -> String {
  switch month {
  case Month.august, Month.september, Month.october,
       Month.november, Month.december:
    return "Autumn"
  case Month.january, Month.february, Month.march, Month.april,
       Month.may:
    return "Spring"
  default:
    return "Not in the school year"
  }
}
```

Since Swift is strongly-typed and uses type inference, you can simplify `semester(for:)` by removing the enumeration name in places where the compiler already knows the type. Keep the dot prefix, but lose the enumeration name, as shown below for the cases inside the `switch` statement:

```
func semester(for month: Month) -> String {
  switch month {
  case .august, .september, .october, .november, .december:
    return "Autumn"
  case .january, .february, .march, .april, .may:
    return "Spring"
  default:
    return "Not in the school year"
  }
}
```

Also recall that `switch` statements must be exhaustive with their cases. The compiler will warn you if they aren't. When your case patterns are `String` elements, you need a `default` case because it's impossible to create cases to match every possible `String` value. However, enumerations have a limited set of values you can match against. So if you have cases for each member value of the enumeration, you can safely remove the `default` case of the `switch` statement:

```
func semester(for month: Month) -> String {
  switch month {
  case .august, .september, .october, .november, .december:
    return "Autumn"
  case .january, .february, .march, .april, .may:
    return "Spring"
  case .june, .july:
    return "Summer"
  }
}
```

That's much more readable. There is another huge benefit to getting rid of the `default`. If in a future update someone added `.undecember` or `.duodecember` to the Month enumeration, the compiler would automatically flag this and any other `switch` statement as being non-exhaustive, allowing you to handle this specific case.

You can test this function in a playground like so:

```
var month = Month.april
semester(for: month) // "Spring"

month = .september
semester(for: month) // "Autumn"
```

The variable declaration for `month` uses the full enumeration type and value. In the second assignment, you can use the shorthand `.september`, since the compiler already knows the type. Finally, you pass both months to `semester(for:)`, where a `switch` statement returns the strings `"Spring"` and `"Autumn"` respectively.

Mini-exercise

Wouldn't it be nice to request the semester from an instance like `month.semester` instead of using the function?

Add a `semester` computed property to the `month` enumeration so that you can run this code:

```
let semester = month.semester // "Autumn"
```

Code completion prevents typos

Another advantage of using enumerations instead of strings is that you'll never have a typo in your member values. Xcode provides code completion:

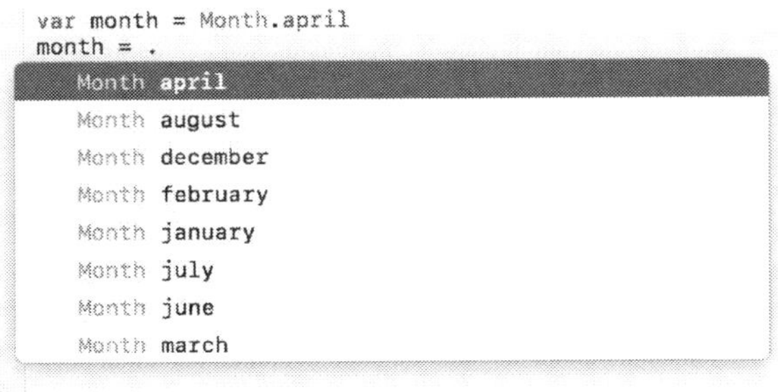

And if you do misspell an enumeration value, the compiler will complain with an error, so you won't get too far down the line without recognizing your mistake:

Raw values

Unlike enumeration values in C, Swift `enum` values are *not* backed by integers as a default. That means `january` is *itself* the value.

But you can associate a raw value with each enumeration case simply by declaring the raw value in the enumeration declaration:

```
enum Month: Int {
```

Swift enumerations are flexible: you can specify other raw value types like `String`, `Float` or `Character`. As in C, if you use integers and don't specify values as you've done here, Swift will automatically assign the values 0, 1, 2 and up.

In this case, it would be better if January had the raw value of `1` rather than `0`. To specify your own raw values, use the = assignment operator:

```
enum Month: Int {
  case january = 1, february = 2, march = 3, april = 4, may = 5,
  june = 6, july = 7, august = 8, september = 9,
  october = 10, november = 11, december = 12
}
```

This code assigns an integer value to each enumeration case.

There's another handy shortcut here: the compiler will automatically increment the values if you provide the first one and leave out the rest:

```
enum Month: Int {
  case january = 1, february, march, april, may, june, july,
  august, september, october, november, december
}
```

You can use the enumeration values alone and never refer to the raw values if you don't want to. But the raw values will be there behind the scenes if you ever do need them!

Accessing the raw value

Enumeration instances with raw values have a handy `rawValue` property. With the raw values in place, your enumeration has a sense of order and you can calculate the number of months left until winter break:

```
func monthsUntilWinterBreak(from month: Month) -> Int {
  return Month.december.rawValue - month.rawValue
}
monthsUntilWinterBreak(from: .april) // 8
```

Initializing with the raw value

You can use the raw value to instantiate an enumeration value with an initializer. You can use `init(rawValue:)` to do this, but if you try to use the value afterward, you'll get an error:

```
let fifthMonth = Month(rawValue: 5)
monthsUntilWinterBreak(from: fifthMonth) // Error: not unwrapped
```

There's no guarantee that the raw value you submitted exists in the enumeration, so the initializer returns an optional. Enumeration initializers with the `rawValue:` parameter are **failable initializers**, meaning if things go wrong, the initializer will return `nil`.

If you're using these raw value initializers in your own projects, remember that they return optionals. If you're unsure if the raw value is correct, you'll need to either check for `nil` or use optional binding. In this case, the value 5 must be correct so it's appropriate to force unwrap the optional:

```
let fifthMonth = Month(rawValue: 5)!
monthsUntilWinterBreak(from: fifthMonth) // 7
```

That's better! Now there's no error, and `monthsUntilWinterBreak(from:)` returns 7 as expected.

Mini-exercise

Make `monthsUntilWinterBreak` a computed property of the `Month` enumeration, so that you can execute the following code:

```
let monthsLeft = fifthMonth.monthsUntilWinterBreak // 7
```

String raw values

Similar to the handy trick of incrementing an `Int` raw value, if you specify a raw value type of `String` you'll get another automatic conversion. Let's pretend you're building a news app that has tabs for each section. Each section has an icon. Icons are a good chance to deploy enumerations because by their nature, they are a limited set:

```
// 1
enum Icon: String {
  case music
  case sports
  case weather

  var filename: String {
    // 2
    return "\(rawValue).png"
  }
}
let icon = Icon.weather
icon.filename // weather.png
```

Here's what's happening in this code:

1. The enumeration sports a `String` raw value type.
2. Calling `rawValue` inside the enumeration definition is equivalent to calling `self.rawValue`. Since the raw value is a string, you can use it to build a file name.

Note you didn't have to specify a `String` for each member value. If you set the raw value type of the enumeration to `String` and don't specify any raw values yourself, the compiler will use the enumeration case names as raw values. The `filename` computed property will generate an image asset name for you. You can now fetch and display images for the tab icons in your app.

Next, let's jump back to working with number raw values and learn how to use enumerations for banking.

Unordered raw values

Integer raw values don't have to be in an incremental order. Coins are a good use case:

```
enum Coin: Int {
  case penny = 1
  case nickel = 5
  case dime = 10
  case quarter = 25
}
```

You can instantiate values of this type and access their raw values as usual:

```
let coin = Coin.quarter
coin.rawValue // 25
```

Mini-exercise

Create an array called `coinPurse` that contains coins. Add an assortment of pennies, nickels, dimes and quarters to it.

Associated values

Associated values take Swift enumerations to the next level in expressive power. They let you associate a custom value (or values) with each enumeration case.

Here are some unique qualities of associated values:

1. Each enumeration case has zero or more associated values.
2. The associated values for each enumeration case have their own data type.
3. You can define associated values with label names like you would for named function parameters.

An enumeration can have raw values or associated values, but not both.

In the last mini-exercise, you defined a coin purse. Let's say you took your money to the bank and deposited it. You could then go to an ATM and withdraw your money:

```
var balance = 100

func withdraw(amount: Int) {
  balance -= amount
}
```

The ATM will never let you withdraw more than you put in, so it needs a way to let you know whether the transaction was successful. You can implement this as an enumeration with associated values:

```
enum WithdrawalResult {
  case success(newBalance: Int)
  case error(message: String)
}
```

Each case has a required value to go along with it. For the success case, the associated `Int` will hold the new balance; for the error case, the associated `String` will have some kind of error message.

Then you can rewrite the `withdraw` function to use the enumeration cases:

```
func withdraw(amount: Int) -> WithdrawalResult {
  if amount <= balance {
    balance -= amount
    return .success(newBalance: balance)
  } else {
    return .error(message: "Not enough money!")
  }
}
```

Now you can perform a withdrawal and handle the result:

```
let result = withdraw(amount: 99)

switch result {
case .success(let newBalance):
  print("Your new balance is: \(newBalance)")
case .error(let message):
  print(message)
}
```

Notice how you used `let` bindings to read the associated values. Associated values aren't properties you can access freely, so you'll need bindings like these to read them. Remember that the newly bound constants `newBalance` and `message` are local to the `switch` cases. They aren't required to have the same name as the associated values, although it's common practice to do so.

You'll see `"Your new balance is: 1"` printed out in the debug console.

Many real-world contexts function by accessing associated values in an enumeration. For example, internet servers often use enumerations to differentiate between types of requests:

```
enum HTTPMethod {
  case get
  case post(body: String)
}
```

In the bank account example, you had multiple values you wanted to check for in the enumeration. In places where you only have one, you could instead use pattern matching in an `if case` or `guard case` statement. Here's how that works:

```
let request = HTTPMethod.post(body: "Hi there")
```

```
guard case .post(let body) = request else {
  fatalError("No message was posted")
}
print(body)
```

In this code, `guard case` checks to see if `request` contains the `post` enumeration case and if so, reads and binds the associated value.

You'll also see enumerations used in error handling. The bank account example had multiple cases, but just one generic error case with an associated string. In Chapter 21, "Error Handling" you'll see how to set up an enumeration with multiple cases to cover individual error conditions.

Enumeration as state machine

An enumeration is an example of a state machine, meaning it can only ever be a single enumeration value at a time, never more. The friendly traffic light illustrates this concept well:

```
enum TrafficLight {
  case red, yellow, green
}
let trafficLight = TrafficLight.red
```

A working traffic light will never be red and green simultaneously. You can observe this state machine behavior in other modern devices that follow a predetermined sequence of actions in response to a sequence of events. Examples of state machines include:

- Vending machines that dispense soda when the customer deposits the proper amount of money
- Elevators that drop riders off at upper floors before going down
- Combination locks that require combination numbers in the proper order

To operate as expected, these devices depend on an enumeration's guarantee that it will only ever be in one state at a time.

Mini-exercise

A household light switch is another example of a state machine. Create an enumeration for a light that can switch `.on` and `.off`.

Case-less enumerations

In Chapter 12, “Methods” you learned how to create a namespace for a group of related type methods. The example in that chapter looked like this:

```
struct Math {
  static func factorial(of number: Int) -> Int {
    return (1...number).reduce(1, *)
  }
}
let factorial = Math.factorial(of: 6) // 720
```

One thing you may not have realized at the time is that you could create an instance of `Math`, like so:

```
let math = Math()
```

The `math` instance doesn’t serve any purpose since it is completely empty; it doesn’t have any stored properties. In cases like this, the better design is actually to transform `Math` from a structure to an enumeration:

```
enum Math {
  static func factorial(of number: Int) -> Int {
    return (1...number).reduce(1, *)
  }
}
let factorial = Math.factorial(of: 6) // 720
```

Now if you try to make an instance, the compiler will give you an error:

```
let math = Math() // ERROR: No accessible initializers
```

Enumerations with no cases are sometimes referred to as **uninhabited types** or **bottom types**.

As you learned at the beginning of this chapter, enumerations are quite powerful. They can do most everything a structure can, including having custom initializers, computed properties and methods. In order to create an instance of an enumeration though, you have to assign a member value as the state. If there are no member values, then you won’t be able to create an instance.

That works perfectly for you in this case (pun intended). There’s no reason to have an instance of `Math`. You should make the design decision that there will *never* be an instance of the type. This will prevent future developers from accidentally creating an instance and help enforce its use as you intended. So in summary, choose a case-less enumeration when it would be confusing if a valueless instance existed.

Mini-exercise

Euler's number is useful in calculations for statistical bell curves and compound growth rates. Add the constant *e*, 2.7183, to your `Math` namespace. Then you can figure out how much money you'll have if you invest $25,000 at 7% continuous interest for 20 years:

```
let nestegg = 25000 * pow(Math.e, 0.07 * 20) // $101,380.95
```

> **Note:** In everyday life, you should use `M_E` from the Foundation library for the value of *e*. The `Math` namespace here is just for practice.

Optionals

Since you've made it through the lesson on enumerations, the time has come to let you in on a little secret. There's a Swift language feature that has been using enumerations right under your nose all along: optionals! In this section, you'll explore their underlying mechanism.

Optionals act like containers that have either something or nothing inside:

```
var age: Int?
age = 17
age = nil
```

Optionals are really enumerations with two cases:

1. `.none` means there's no value.
2. `.some` means there is a value, which is attached to the enumeration case as an associated value.

You can extract the associated value from an optional with a `switch` statement, as you've already seen:

```
switch age {
case .none:
  print("No value")
case .some(let value):
  print("Got a value: \(value)")
}
```

You'll see the `"No value"` message printed out in the debug console.

Although optionals are really enumerations under the hood, Swift hides the implementation details with things like optional binding, the ? and ! operators, and keywords such as `nil`.

```
let optionalNil: Int? = .none
optionalNil == nil    // true
optionalNil == .none  // true
```

If you try this in a playground, you'll see that `nil` and `.none` are equivalent.

In Chapter 17, "Generics" you'll learn a bit more about the underlying mechanism for optionals, including how to write your own code to function in the same manner as optionals.

Now that you know how optionals work, the next time you need a value container, you'll have the right tool for the job.

Key points

- An **enumeration** is a list of mutually exclusive cases that define a common type.
- Enumerations provide a type-safe alternative to old-fashioned integer values.
- You can use enumerations to handle responses, store state and encapsulate values.
- **Uninhabited enumerations** can be used as namespaces and prevent the creation of instances.

Where to go from here?

In this chapter, you learned how to make enumerations dance. Using enumerations makes your code much more readable than the alternative of integer values. Xcode makes this even easier by providing code completion and the Swift compiler guards against typos.

As you develop apps in Swift, you'll have many opportunities to use enumerations. Their inherent safety characteristics, such as strong typing and exhaustive case handler checking, will make your code more robust and less prone to errors.

Challenges

Challenge 1: Adding raw values

Taking the coin example from earlier in the chapter, begin with the following array of coins:

```
enum Coin: Int {
  case penny = 1
  case nickel = 5
  case dime = 10
  case quarter = 25
}

let coinPurse: [Coin] =
[.penny, .quarter, .nickel, .dime, .penny, .dime, .quarter]
```

Write a function where you can pass in the array of coins, add up the value and return the number of cents.

Challenge 2: Computing with raw values

Taking the example from earlier in the chapter, begin with the `Month` enumeration:

```
enum Month: Int {
  case january = 1, february, march, april, may, june, july,
       august, september, october, november, december
}
```

Write a computed property to calculate the number of months until summer.

Hint: You'll need to account for a negative value if summer has already passed in the current year. To do that, imagine looping back around for the next full year.

Challenge 3: Pattern matching enumeration values

Taking the map example from earlier in the chapter, begin with the `Direction` enumeration:

```
enum Direction {
  case north
  case south
  case east
  case west
}
```

Imagine starting a new level in a video game. The character makes a series of movements in the game. Calculate the position of the character on a top-down level map after making a set of movements:

```
let movements: [Direction] = [.north, .north, .west, .south,
  .west, .south, .south, .east, .east, .south, .east]
```

Hint: Use a tuple for the location:

```
var location = (x: 0, y: 0)
```

Chapter 16: Protocols

By Janie Clayton

In this book, you've learned about the three named types: structs, classes and enums. There's one more named type to learn about: the **protocol**.

Unlike the other named types, protocols don't define anything you instantiate directly. Instead, they define an interface or blueprint that actual concrete types **conform** to. With a protocol, you define a common set of properties and behaviors that concrete types go and implement.

In this chapter, you'll learn about protocols and see why they're central to programming in Swift.

Introducing protocols

You define a protocol much as you do any other named type. Enter the following into a playground:

```
protocol Vehicle {
  func accelerate()
  func stop()
}
```

The keyword `protocol` is followed by the name of the protocol, followed by the curly braces with the members of the protocol inside. The big difference you'll notice is that the protocol *doesn't contain any implementation.*

That means you can't instantiate a `Vehicle` directly:

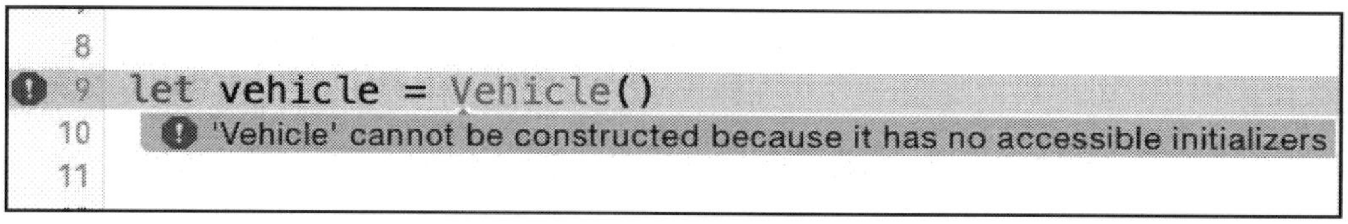

Instead, you use protocols to enforce methods and properties on *other* types. What you've defined here is something like the *idea* of a vehicle — it's something that can accelerate and stop.

Protocol syntax

A protocol can be **adopted** by a class, struct, or enum — and when another type adopts a protocol, it's required to implement the methods and properties defined in the protocol. Once a type implements all members of a protocol, the type is said to **conform** to the protocol.

Here's how you declare protocol conformance for your type. In the playground, define a new class that will conform to `Vehicle`:

```
class Unicycle: Vehicle {
  var peddling = false

  func accelerate() {
    peddling = true
  }

  func stop() {
    peddling = false
  }
}
```

You follow the name of the named type with a semicolon and the name of the protocol you want to conform to. This syntax might look familiar, since it's the same syntax you use to make a class inherit from another class. In this example, `Unicycle` conforms to the `Vehicle` protocol.

Note that it *looks* like class inheritance but it isn't; structs and enumerations can also conform to protocols with this syntax.

If you were to remove the definition of `stop()` from the class `Unicycle` above, Swift would display an error since `Unicycle` wouldn't have fully conformed to the `Vehicle` protocol.

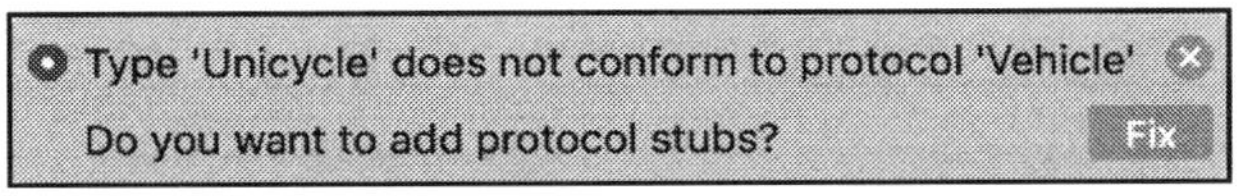

You'll come back to the details of implementing protocols in a bit, but first you'll see what's possible when defining protocols.

Methods in protocols

In the `Vehicle` protocol above, you define a pair of methods, `accelerate()` and `stop()`, that all types conforming to `Vehicle` must implement.

You define methods on protocols much like you would on any class, struct or enum with parameters and return values:

```
enum Direction {
  case left
  case right
}

protocol DirectionalVehicle {
  func accelerate()
  func stop()
  func turn(_ direction: Direction)
  func description() -> String
}
```

There are a few differences to note. You don't, and in fact cannot, define any *implementation* for the methods. This is to help you enforce a strict separation of interface and code, as the protocol by itself makes no assumption about the implementation details of any type that conforms to the protocol.

Also, methods defined in protocols can't contain default parameters:

```
protocol OptionalDirectionVehicle {
  // Build error!
  func turn(_ direction: Direction = .left)
}
```

To provide `direction` as an optional argument, you'd define both versions of the method explicitly:

```
protocol OptionalDirectionVehicle {
  func turn()
  func turn(_ direction: Direction)
}
```

You would then define both versions of `turn()` in any conforming type.

Properties in protocols

You can also define properties in a protocol:

```
protocol VehicleProperties {
  var weight: Int { get }
  var name: String { get set }
}
```

When defining properties in a protocol, you must explicitly mark them as `get` or `get set`, somewhat similar to the way you declare computed properties. However, much like methods, you don't include any *implementation* for properties. Are you starting to see a pattern here? :]

The fact that you must mark `get` and `set` on properties shows that a protocol doesn't know about a property's implementation, which means it makes no assumption about the property's *storage*. You can implement these property requirements as computed properties *or* as regular variables. All the protocol requires is that the property is either readable, if it has only a `get` requirement, or readable and writable, if it has both a `get` and a `set` requirement.

Even if the property has only a `get` requirement, you're still allowed to implement it as a stored property or a read-write computed property, as the requirements in the protocol are only minimum requirements. Your conforming type must have *at least* the functionality required by the protocol.

Initializers in protocols

While protocols themselves can't be initialized, they can declare initializers that conforming types should have:

```
protocol Account {
  var value: Double { get set }
  init(initialAmount: Double)
  init?(transferAccount: Account)
}
```

In the `Account` protocol above, you define two initializers as part of the protocol. This behaves much as you might expect, in that any type that conforms to `Account` is required to have these initializers.

If you conform to a protocol with required initializers using a class type, those initializers must use the `required` keyword:

```
class BitcoinAccount: Account {
  var value: Double
  required init(initialAmount: Double) {
    value = initialAmount
  }
  required init?(transferAccount: Account) {
    guard transferAccount.value > 0.0 else {
      return nil
    }
    value = transferAccount.value
  }
}

var accountType: Account.Type = BitcoinAccount.self
let account = accountType.init(initialAmount: 30.00)
let transferAccount = accountType.init(transferAccount:
account)!
```

Protocol inheritance

The `Vehicle` protocol contains a set of methods that could apply to any type of vehicle, such as a bike, a car, a snowmobile or even an airplane!

You may wish to define a protocol that contains all the qualities of a `Vehicle`, but that is also specific to vehicles with wheels. For this, you can have protocols that inherit from other protocols, much like you can have classes that inherit from other classes:

```
protocol WheeledVehicle: Vehicle {
  var numberOfWheels: Int { get }
  var wheelSize: Double { get set }
}
```

Now any type you mark as conforming to the `WheeledVehicle` protocol will have all the members defined within the braces, in addition to all of the members of `Vehicle`. As with subclassing, any type you mark as a `WheeledVehicle` will have an `is-a` relationship with the protocol `Vehicle`.

Mini-exercises

1. Create a protocol `Area` that defines a read-only property `area` of type `Double`.
2. Implement `Area` with structs representing `Square`, `Triangle`, and `Circle`.
3. Add a circle, a square, and a triangle to an array. Convert the array of shapes to an array of areas using `map`.

Implementing protocols

As you've already seen, when you declare your type as conforming to a protocol, you must implement *all* the requirements declared in the protocol:

```
class Bike: Vehicle {
  var peddling = false
  var brakesApplied = false

  func accelerate() {
    peddling = true
    brakesApplied = false
  }

  func stop() {
    peddling = false
    brakesApplied = true
  }
}
```

The class `Bike` implements all the methods defined in `Vehicle`. If `accelerate()` or `stop()` weren't defined, you'd receive a build error.

Defining a protocol guarantees any type that conforms to the protocol will have *all* the members you've defined in the protocol.

Implementing properties

Recall that properties in protocols come with a `get` and possibly a `set` requirement and that a conforming type must conform to *at least* these requirements.

Upgrade `Bike` to a `WheeledVehicle`:

```
class Bike: WheeledVehicle {

  let numberOfWheels = 2
  var wheelSize = 16.0

  var peddling = false
  var brakesApplied = false

  func accelerate() {
    peddling = true
    brakesApplied = false
  }

  func stop() {
    peddling = false
    brakesApplied = true
  }
}
```

The `numberOfWheels` constant fulfills the `get` requirement. The `wheelSize` variable fulfills both `get` and `set` requirements.

Protocols don't care how you implement their requirements, as long as you implement them. Your choices for implementing a `get` requirement are:

- A constant stored property
- A variable stored property
- A read-only computed property
- A read-write computed property

Your choices for implementing both a `get` and a `set` property are limited to a variable stored property or a read-write computed property.

Associated types in protocols

You can also add an **associated type** as a protocol member. When using `associatedtype` in a protocol, you're simply stating there *is* a type used in this protocol, without specifying what type this should be. It's up to the protocol adopter to decide what the exact type should be.

This lets you give arbitrary names to types without specifying exactly which type it will eventually be:

```
protocol WeightCalculatable {
  associatedtype WeightType
  var weight: WeightType { get }
}
```

This delegates the decision of the type of `weight` to the concrete implementation.

You can see how this works in the two examples below:

```
class HeavyThing: WeightCalculatable {
  // This heavy thing only needs integer accuracy
  typealias WeightType = Int

  var weight: Int {
    return 100
  }
}

class LightThing: WeightCalculatable {
  // This light thing needs decimal places
  typealias WeightType = Double

  var weight: Double {
    return 0.0025
  }
}
```

In these examples, you use `typealias` to be explicit about the associated type. This usually isn't required, as the compiler can often infer the type. In the previous examples, the type of `weight` makes it clear what the associated type should be, so you can remove `typealias`.

You may have noticed that the contract of `WeightCalculatable` now changes depending on the choice of associated type in the adopting type. Note that this prevents you from using the protocol as a simple variable type, because the compiler doesn't know what `WeightType` will be ahead of time.

```
// Build error!
// protocol 'WeightCalculatable' can only be used as a generic
// constraint because it has Self or associated type
requirements.
let weightedThing: WeightCalculatable = LightThing()
```

You'll learn all about **generic constraints** in the next chapter.

Implementing multiple protocols

A class can only inherit from a single class — this is the property of "single inheritance". In contrast, a class can adopt as many protocols as you'd like!

Suppose instead of creating a `WheeledVehicle` protocol that inherits from `Vehicle`, you made `Wheeled` its own protocol.

```
protocol Wheeled {
  var numberOfWheels: Int { get }
  var wheelSize: Double { get set }
}

class Bike: Vehicle, Wheeled {
  // Implement both Vehicle and Wheeled
}
```

Protocols support "multiple conformance", so you can apply any number of protocols to types you define. In the example above, the `Bike` class now has to implement all members defined in the `Vehicle` and `Wheeled` protocols.

Protocol Composition

In the previous section you learned how to implement multiple protocols. Sometimes you need a function to take a data type that must conform to multiple protocols. That is where **protocol composition** comes in. Imagine you need a function that needs access to the `Vehicle` protocol's `stop()` function and the `Wheeled` protocol's `numberOfWheels` property. You can do this using the & composition operator.

```
func roundAndRound(transportation: Vehicle & Wheeled) {
    transportation.stop()
    print("The brakes are being applied to \
(transportation.numberOfWheels) wheels.")
}

roundAndRound(transportation: Bike())
// The brakes are being applied to 2 wheels.
```

Extensions and protocol conformance

You can also adopt protocols using extensions. This lets you add protocol conformances to types you don't necessarily own. Consider the simple example below which adds a custom protocol to `String`:

```
protocol Reflective {
  var typeName: String { get }
}

extension String: Reflective {
  var typeName: String {
    return "I'm a String"
  }
}

let title = "Swift Apprentice!"
title.typeName // I'm a String
```

Even though `String` is part of the standard library, you're still able to make `String` adopt and conform to the `Reflective` protocol.

Another advantage of using extensions is that you can nicely group together the protocol adoption with the requisite methods and properties, instead of having a pile of protocols cluttering up your type definition.

The following code breaks out the adoption of `Vehicle` into an extension on `AnotherBike`:

```
class AnotherBike: Wheeled {
  var peddling = false
  let numberOfWheels = 2
  var wheelSize = 16.0
}

extension AnotherBike: Vehicle {
  func accelerate() {
    peddling = true
  }

  func stop() {
    peddling = false
  }
}
```

This extension pairs `accelerate` and `stop` with `Vehicle`. If you were to remove the `Vehicle` protocol from `AnotherBike`, you could simply delete the extension that adopts this protocol entirely.

A caveat: you can't declare *stored* properties in extensions. You can still declare stored properties in the original type declaration and satisfy protocol conformance to any protocol adopted in an extension, but completely implementing protocols in extensions isn't always possible due to the limits of extensions.

Requiring reference semantics

Protocols can be adopted by both value types (structs and enums) and reference types (classes), so you might wonder if protocols have reference or value semantics.

The truth is... it depends! If you have an instance of a class or struct assigned to a variable of a protocol type, it will express value or reference semantics that match the type it was defined as.

To illustrate, take the simple example of a `Named` protocol below, implemented as a struct and a class:

```
protocol Named {
  var name: String { get set }
}

class ClassyName: Named {
  var name: String
  init(name: String) {
    self.name = name
  }
}

struct StructyName: Named {
  var name: String
}
```

If you were to assign a `Named` variable an instance of a reference type, you would see the behavior of reference semantics:

```
var named: Named = ClassyName(name: "Classy")
var copy = named

named.name = "Still Classy"
named.name // Still Classy
copy.name // Still Classy
```

Likewise, if you assign an instance of a value type, you would see the behavior of value semantics:

```
named = StructyName(name: "Structy")
copy = named
```

```
named.name = "Still Structy?"
named.name // Still Structy?
copy.name // Structy
```

The situation isn't always this clear. You'll notice that, most of the time, Swift will favor value semantics over reference semantics. If you're designing a protocol to be adopted exclusively by classes, it's best to request that Swift uses reference semantics when using this protocol as a type.

```
protocol Named: class {
  var name: String { get set }
}
```

By using the `class` constraint above, you indicate that only classes may adopt this protocol. This makes it clear that Swift should use reference semantics.

Protocols: more than bags of syntax

As you have seen, protocols let you specify many syntax requirements for conforming types. However, they can't (and never will) be able to let you specify every conceivable requirement that the compiler can check. For example, a protocol may need to specify complexity requirements (O(1) vs O(n)) for an operation. It can do this only by stating it in comments. It is important for you to understand all of the requirements that a protocol makes to correctly conform.

Protocols in the standard library

The Swift standard library uses protocols extensively in ways that may surprise you. Understanding the roles protocols play in Swift can help you write clean, decoupled "Swifty" code.

Equatable

Some of the simplest code compares two integers with the == operator:

```
let a = 5
let b = 5

a == b // true
```

You can do the same thing with strings:

```
let swiftA = "Swift"
```

```
let swiftB = "Swift"

swiftA == swiftB // true
```

But you can't use == on *any* type. Suppose you wrote a struct that represents a team's record and wanted to determine if two records were equal:

```
struct Record {
  var wins: Int
  var losses: Int
}

let recordA = Record(wins: 10, losses: 5)
let recordB = Record(wins: 10, losses: 5)

recordA == recordB // Build error!
```

You can't apply the == operator to the struct you just defined. But the use of the equality operator isn't simply "magic" reserved for standard Swift types like `Int` and `String`; they're structs, just like `Record`. This means you can extend the use of this operator to your own code!

Both `Int` and `String` conform to the `Equatable` protocol from the the standard library that defines a single static method:

```
protocol Equatable {
  static func ==(lhs: Self, rhs: Self) -> Bool
}
```

You can apply this protocol to `Record` like so:

```
extension Record: Equatable {
  static func ==(lhs: Record, rhs: Record) -> Bool {
    return lhs.wins == rhs.wins &&
           lhs.losses == rhs.losses
  }
}
```

Here, you're defining (or *overloading*) the == operator for comparing two `Record` instances. In this case, two records are equal if they have the same number of wins and losses.

Now, you're able to use the == operator to compare two `Record` types, just like you can with `String` or `Int`:

```
recordA == recordB // true
```

Comparable

A subprotocol of `Equatable` is `Comparable`:

```
protocol Comparable: Equatable {
  static func <(lhs: Self, rhs: Self) -> Bool
  static func <=(lhs: Self, rhs: Self) -> Bool
  static func >=(lhs: Self, rhs: Self) -> Bool
  static func >(lhs: Self, rhs: Self) -> Bool
}
```

In addition to the equality operator ==, `Comparable` requires you to overload the comparison operators <, <=, > and >= for your type. In practice, you'll usually only provide <, as the standard library can implement <=, > and >= for you, using your implementations of == and <.

Make `Record` adopt `Comparable` as shown below:

```
extension Record: Comparable {
  static func <(lhs: Record, rhs: Record) -> Bool {
    if lhs.wins == rhs.wins {
      return lhs.losses > rhs.losses
    }
    return lhs.wins < rhs.wins
  }
}
```

This implementation of < considers one record lesser than another record if the first record either has fewer wins than the second record, or an equal number of wins but a greater number of losses.

"Free" functions

While == and < are useful in their own right, the Swift library provides you with many "free" functions and methods for types that conform to `Equatable` and `Comparable`.

For any collection you define that contains a `Comparable` type, such as an `Array`, you have access to methods such as `sort()` that are part of the standard library:

```
let teamA = Record(wins: 14, losses: 11)
let teamB = Record(wins: 23, losses: 8)
let teamC = Record(wins: 23, losses: 9)
var leagueRecords = [teamA, teamB, teamC]

leagueRecords.sort()
// {wins 14, losses 11}
// {wins 23, losses 9}
// {wins 23, losses 8}
```

Since you've given `Record` the ability to compare two values, the standard library has all the information it needs to sort an array of `Record`s!

As you can see, implementing `Comparable` and `Equatable` gives you quite an arsenal of tools:

```
leagueRecords.max() // {wins 23, losses 8}
leagueRecords.min() // {wins 14, losses 11}
leagueRecords.starts(with: [teamA, teamC]) // true
leagueRecords.contains(teamA) // true
```

Other useful protocols

While learning the *entire* Swift standard library isn't vital to your success as a Swift developer, there are a few other important protocols you'll find useful in almost any project.

Hashable

The `Hashable` protocol, a subprotocol of `Equatable`, is a requirement for any type you want to use as a key to a `Dictionary`.

```
protocol Hashable : Equatable {
  var hashValue: Int { get }
}
```

Hash values help you quickly find elements in a collection. In order for this to work, values that are considered equal by == must also have the same hash value. Because the number of hash values is limited, there's a finite probability that non-equal values can have the same hash.

The mathematics behind hash values are quite complex, but the important thing to keep in mind is that equal values *must* have equal hash values. Most Swift types adopt `Hashable`, so you can usually rely on hash values of properties to build your hash value.

For example:

```
class Student {
  let email: String
  var firstName: String
  var lastName: String

  init(email: String, firstName: String, lastName: String) {
    self.email = email
    self.firstName = firstName
    self.lastName = lastName
  }
```

```
}

extension Student: Equatable {
  static func ==(lhs: Student, rhs: Student) -> Bool {
    return lhs.email == rhs.email
  }
}

extension Student: Hashable {
  var hashValue: Int {
    return email.hashValue
  }
}
```

You assign students an email address when they enroll and use this to uniquely identify the student. Student objects are considered equal (meaning they describe the same student) if they have the same email address. Therefore, the hash value for a `Student` must be based on the student's email address. Since `String` conforms to `Hashable`, you can simply return the hash value of `email` instead of calculating a hash yourself.

You can now use the `Student` type as the key in a `Dictionary`:

```
let john = Student(email: "johnny.appleseed@apple.com",
firstName: "Johnny", lastName: "Appleseed")
let lockerMap = [john: "14B"]
```

CustomStringConvertible

The very handy `CustomStringConvertible` protocol helps you log and debug instances.

When you call `print()` on an instance such as a `Student`, Swift prints a vague description:

```
print(john)
// Student
```

As if you didn't already know that! The `CustomStringConvertible` protocol has only a `description` property requirement. This property customizes how the instance appears in `print()` statements and in the debugger:

```
protocol CustomStringConvertible {
  var description: String { get }
}
```

By adopting `CustomStringConvertible` on the `Student` type, you can provide a more readable representation.

```
extension Student: CustomStringConvertible {
  var description: String {
    return "\(firstName) \(lastName)"
  }
}
print(john)
// Johnny Appleseed
```

`CustomDebugStringConvertible` is similar to `CustomStringConvertible`: It behaves exactly like `CustomStringConvertible` except it also defines a `debugDescription`. Use `CustomDebugStringConvertible` along with `debugPrint()` to print to the output only in debug configurations.

Key points

- Protocols define a contract that classes, structs and enums can **adopt**.
- By adopting a protocol, a type is required to **conform** to the protocol by implementing all methods and properties of the protocol.
- A type can adopt any number of protocols, which allows for a quasi-multiple inheritance not permitted through subclassing.
- You can use extensions for protocol adoption and conformance.
- The Swift standard library uses protocols extensively. You can use many of them, such as `Equatable` and `Hashable`, on your own named types.

Where to go from here?

Protocols help you decouple interface from implementation. Since protocols are types themselves, you can still declare an array of `Vehicle` instances. The array could then contain bicycles, trucks, or cars. In addition, bicycles could be enumerations and trucks could be classes! But every `Vehicle` has a particular set of properties and methods you know you must implement.

In the next chapter, you'll see how protocols are used to constrain and implement generic code. Also, in Chapter 25, you'll learn about protocol-oriented programming and see how to use protocols as alternatives to object-oriented techniques and inheritance when building your types.

Challenges

Pet shop tasks

Create a collection of protocols for tasks at a pet shop that has dogs, cats, fish and birds.

The pet shop duties can be broken down into these tasks:

- All pets need to be fed.
- Pets that can fly need to be caged.
- Pets that can swim need to be put in a tank.
- Pets that walk need exercise.
- Tanks and cages need to occasionally be cleaned.

1. Create classes or structs for each animal and adopt the appropriate protocols. Feel free to simply use a `print()` statement for the method implementations.
2. Create homogeneous arrays for animals that need to be fed, caged, cleaned, walked, and tanked. Add the appropriate animals to these arrays. The arrays should be declared using the protocol as the element type, for example `var caged: [Cageable]`
3. Write a loop that will perform the proper tasks (such as feed, cage, walk) on each element of each array.

Chapter 17: Generics

By Alexis Gallagher

The truth is, you already know about generics. Every time you use a Swift array, you're using generics. This might even give the impression that generics are *about* collections, but that impression is both incorrect and misleading.

In this chapter, you'll learn about the fundamentals of what generics *are*. This will give you a solid foundation for understanding how to write your own generic code. Finally, you'll loop back to look at generic types in the Swift standard library — arrays, dictionaries and optionals — using this new perspective.

Introducing generics

To get started, you'll consider how you might model pets and their keepers. You could do this using different values for each or you could do this by using different types for each. You'll see that by using types, instead of values, the Swift **type checker** can reason about your code *at compile time*. Not only do you need to do less at runtime resulting in faster code, but you can catch problems that were not possible using just values.

Values defined by other values

Suppose you're running a pet shop that sells only dogs and cats, and you want to use a Swift playground to model that business. To start, you define a type, `PetKind`, that can hold two possible values corresponding to the two kinds of pets that you sell:

```
enum PetKind {
  case cat
  case dog
}
```

So far, so good. Now suppose you want to model not just the animals but also the employees, the pet keepers who look after the pets. Your employees are highly specialized. Some keepers only look after cats, and others only dogs.

So you define a `KeeperKind` type, as follows:

```
struct KeeperKind {
  var keeperOf: PetKind
}
```

Then you can initialize a `catKeeper` and `dogKeeper` in the following way:

```
let catKeeper = KeeperKind(keeperOf: .cat)
let dogKeeper = KeeperKind(keeperOf: .dog)
```

There are two points to note about how you're modeling your shop.

First, you're representing the different kinds of pets and keepers by *varying the values of types*. There's only one type for pet kinds — `PetKind` — and one type for keeper kinds — `KeeperKind`. Different kinds of pets are represented only by distinct values of the `PetKind` type, just as different kinds of keepers are represented by distinct values of the `KeeperKind` type.

Second, *one range of possible values determines another range of possible values*. Specifically, the range of possible `KeeperKind` values mirrors the range of possible `PetKind` values.

If your store started selling birds, you'd simply add a `.bird` member to the `PetKind` enumeration, and you'd immediately be able to initialize a value describing a bird keeper, `KeeperKind(keeperOf: .bird)`. And if you started selling a hundred different kinds of pets, you'd immediately be able to represent a hundred different kinds of keepers.

In contrast, you could have defined a second unrelated enumeration instead of `KeeperKind`:

```
enum EnumKeeperKind {
  case catKeeper
  case dogKeeper
}
```

In this case, nothing would enforce this relationship except your diligence in always updating one type to mirror the other. If you added `PetKind.snake` but forgot to add `EnumKeeperKind.snakeKeeper`, then things would get out of whack.

But with `KeeperKind`, you explicitly established the relationship via a property of type `PetKind`. Every possible `PetKind` value implies a corresponding `KeeperKind` value. Or you could say, the set of possible `PetKind` values defines the set of possible `KeeperKind` values.

To summarize, you can depict the relationship like so:

PetKind values	KeeperKind values
.cat	KeeperKind(keeperOf:.cat)
.dog	KeeperKind(keeperOf:.dog)
.etc	.etc

Types defined by other types

The model above fundamentally works by varying the *values of types*. Now consider another way to model the pet-to-keeper system — by varying *the types themselves*.

Suppose that instead of defining a single type `PetKind` that represents all kinds of pets, you chose to define a distinct type for every kind of pet you sell. This is quite a plausible choice if you're working in an object-oriented style, where you model the pets' behaviors with different methods for each pet. Then you'd have the following:

```
class Cat {}
class Dog {}
```

Now how do you represent the corresponding kinds of keepers? You could simply write the following:

```
class KeeperForCats {}
class KeeperForDogs {}
```

But that's no good. This approach has *exactly* the same problem as manually defining a parallel enum of `KeeperKind` values — it relies on you to enforce the required domain relationship of one kind of keeper for every kind of pet.

What you'd really like is a way to *declare* a relationship just like the one you established for values. You'd like to declare that every possible pet type implies the existence of a corresponding keeper type, a correspondence that you'd depict like so:

Pet types	Keeper types
Cat	Keeper (of Cat...)
Dog	Keeper (of Dog...)
etc.	etc.

You'd like to establish that for every possible pet type, there is defined a corresponding Keeper type. But you don't want to do this manually. You want a way to *automatically* define a set of new types for all the keepers.

This, it turns out, is exactly what generics are for!

Anatomy of generic types

Generics provide a mechanism for using one set of types to define a new set of types.

In your example, you can define a **generic type** for keepers, like so:

```
class Keeper<Animal> {}
```

This definition immediately defines all the corresponding keeper types, as desired:

Pet types	Keeper types
Cat	Keeper<Cat>
Dog	Keeper<Dog>

You can verify these types are real by creating values of them, specifying the entire type in the initializer:

```
var aCatKeeper = Keeper<Cat>()
```

What's going on here? First, `Keeper` is the name of a generic type.

But you might say that a generic type isn't really a type at all. It's more like a recipe for making real types, or **concrete types**. One sign of this is the error you get if you try to instantiate it in isolation:

```
var aKeeper = Keeper()  // compile-time error!
```

The compiler complains here because it doesn't know what kind of keeper you want. That `Animal` in angle brackets is the **type parameter** that specifies the type for the kind of animal you're keeping.

Once you provide the required type parameter, as in `Keeper<Cat>`, the generic `Keeper` becomes a new concrete type. `Keeper<Cat>` is different from `Keeper<Dog>`, even though they started from the same generic type. These resulting concrete types are called **specializations** of the generic type.

To summarize the mechanics, in order to define a generic type like `Keeper<Animal>` you only need to choose the name of the generic type and of the type parameter. The name of the type parameter should clarify the relationship between the type parameter and the generic type. You'll encounter names like `T` (short for Type) from time to time, but these names should be avoided when the type parameter has a clear role such as `Animal`.

In one stroke, the generic type `Keeper<Animal>` defines a *family* of new types. Those are all the specializations of `Keeper<Animal>` implied by all possible concrete types that one could substitute for the type parameter `Animal`.

Notice that the type `Keeper` doesn't currently store anything at all, or even use the type `Animal` in any way. Essentially, generics are a way to systematically define sets of types.

Using type parameters

Usually, though, you'll want to *do* something with type parameters.

Suppose you want to keep better track of individuals. First, you enrich your type definitions to include identifiers, such as names. This lets every value represent the identity of an individual animal or keeper:

```
class Cat {
  var name: String

  init(name: String) {
    self.name = name
  }
}

class Dog {
  var name: String

  init(name: String) {
    self.name = name
  }
}

class Keeper<Animal> {
  var name: String

  init(name: String) {
    self.name = name
  }
}
```

You also want to track which keeper looks after which animals. Suppose every keeper is responsible for one animal in the morning and another in the afternoon. You can express this by adding properties for the morning and afternoon animals. But what type should those properties have?

Clearly, if a particular keeper only manages dogs, then the properties must only hold dogs. And if cats, then cats. In general, if it's a keeper of `Animal`, then the morning and afternoon animal properties should be of type `Animal`.

To express this, you merely need to *use* the type parameter that previously only distinguished the nature of your keeper types:

```
class Keeper<Animal> {
  var name: String
  var morningCare: Animal
  var afternoonCare: Animal

  init(name: String, morningCare: Animal, afternoonCare: Animal)
{
    self.name = name
    self.morningCare = morningCare
    self.afternoonCare = afternoonCare
  }
}
```

By using `Animal` in the body of the generic type definition above, you can express that the morning and afternoon animals must be the kind of animal the keeper knows best.

Just as function parameters become constants to use within the function body, you can use type parameters such as `Animal` throughout your type definitions. You can use the type parameter anywhere in the definition of `Keeper<Animal>` for stored properties as well as for computed properties, method signatures or nested types.

Now when you instantiate a `Keeper`, Swift will make sure, at compile time, that the morning and afternoon types are the same:

```
let jason = Keeper(name: "Jason",
                   morningCare: Cat(name: "Whiskers"),
                   afternoonCare: Cat(name: "Sleepy"))
```

Here, the keeper Jason manages the cat Whiskers in the morning and the cat Sleepy in the afternoon. The type of `jason` is `Keeper<Cat>`. Note that you did not have to specify a value for the type parameter. Because you used instances of `Cat` as the values for `morningCare` and `afternoonCare`, Swift knows the type of `jason` should be `Keeper<Cat>`.

Mini-exercises

- Try instantiating another `Keeper`, but this time for dogs.
- What do you think would happen if you tried to instantiate a `Keeper` with a dog in the morning and a cat in the afternoon?

- What happens if you try to instantiate a `Keeper`, but for strings?

Type constraints

In your definition of `Keeper`, the identifier `Animal` serves as a type parameter, which is a named placeholder for some actual type that will be supplied later.

This is much like the parameter `cat` in a simple function like `func feed(cat: Cat) { /* open can, etc... */ }`. But when defining a function, you can't simply pass any argument to the function. You can only pass values of type `Cat`.

At present, you could offer any type at all as the kept `Animal`, even something nonsensically unlike an animal, like a `String` or `Int`.

This is no good. What you'd like is something analogous to a function, something where you can restrict what kinds of types are allowed to fill the type parameter. In Swift, you do this with *type constraints*.

There are two kinds of constraints. The simplest kind of type constraint looks like this:

```
class Keeper<Animal: Pet> {
  /* definition body as before */
}
```

The identifier `Pet` must name a type or a protocol. The new expression within the type parameter brackets, `Animal: Pet`, specifies the requirement that whatever type is offered to be `Animal` must meet the requirement of either being a subclass of `Pet` or of implementing the `Pet` protocol.

For instance, you can enforce these restrictions by using the revised `Keeper` definition above, and also redefine `Cat` and other animals to implement a `Pet` or **retro-actively model** conformance to the protocol using an `extension`.

```
protocol Pet {
  var name: String { get }  // all pets respond to a name
}
extension Cat: Pet {}
extension Dog: Pet {}
```

This works because `Cat` and `Dog` already implement a `name` stored property. Next, create some arrays of cats and dogs like so:

```
let cats = ["Miss Gray", "Whiskers"].map { Cat(name: $0) }
let dogs = ["Sparky", "Rusty", "Astro"].map { Dog(name: $0) }
let pets: [Pet] = [Cat(name: "Mittens"), Dog(name: "Yeller")]
```

Notice that `cats`, `dogs`, and `pets` all have different types. If you Option-click on each one, you can see the types are `[Cat]`, `[Dog]`, and `[Pet]` respectively.

The `cats` and `dogs` arrays are said to be **homogeneous** because the elements have the same type. The constant `pets` is **heterogeneous** because it is a mix of dog and cat types.

By constraining a type, you can operate on it. For example, since you now know that pets respond to `name`, you can write a set of generic functions that herd pets.

Write four different flavors of a `herd` functions like so:

```
// 1
func herd(_ pets: [Pet]) {
  pets.forEach {
    print("Come \($0.name)!")
  }
}

// 2
func herd<Animal: Pet>(_ pets: [Animal]) {
  pets.forEach {
    print("Here \($0.name)!")
  }
}

// 3
func herd<Animal: Dog>(_ dogs: [Animal]) {
  dogs.forEach {
    print("Here \($0.name)! Come here!")
  }
}
```

1. This method handles a array of type `Pet` that can mix `Dog` and `Cat` elements.
2. This method handles arrays of any kind of `Pet` but they all need to be of a single type. The angle brackets after the function name let you specify the generic type to be used in the function.
3. Handles dogs and only dogs (or subtypes of dogs).

Swift binds the function call to the most specific types it can. So:

```
herd(pets) // Calls 1
herd(cats) // Calls 2
herd(dogs) // Calls 3
```

The second kind of type constraint involves making explicit assertions that a type parameter, or its associated type, must equal another parameter or one of its conforming types. By combining many type parameters and sets of requirements relating their associated types, one can define a complex relationships on top of generic types.

To demostrate this, suppose you want to add an extension to arrays of Cats that adds the method meow(). Element is the associated type of an Array. You can require that Element be of type (or subtype of) Cat:

```
extension Array where Element: Cat {
  func meow() {
    forEach { print("\($0.name) says meow!") }
  }
}
```

Now you can call the meow method:

```
cats.meow()
```

On the other hand, this will not work with dogs:

```
dogs.meow() // error: 'Dog' is not a subtype of 'Cat'
```

These mistakes may seem obvious here, but type constraints can prevent you from making subtle mistakes at compile time.

Arrays

While the original Keeper type illustrates that generic type doesn't need to store anything or use its type parameter, the most common example of a generic type does both. This is, of course, the Array type.

The need for generic arrays was part of the original motivation to invent generic types. Since so many programs need arrays which are homogeneous, generic arrays make all that code safer. Once the compiler infers (or is told) the type of an array's elements at one point in the code, it can spot any deviations at other points in the code before the program ever runs.

You've been using Array all along, but only with a syntactic sugar: [Element] instead of Array<Element>. Consider an array declared like so:

```
let animalAges: [Int] = [2,5,7,9]
```

This is equivalent to the following:

```
let animalAges: Array<Int> = [2,5,7,9]
```

Array<Element> and [Element] are exactly interchangeable. So you could even call an array's default initializer by writing [Int]() instead of Array<Int>().

Since Swift arrays simply allow indexed access to a sequence of elements, they impose no requirements on their `Element` type. But this isn't always the case.

Dictionaries

Swift generics allow for multiple type parameters and for complex sets of restrictions on them. These let you use generic types and protocols with associated types to model complex algorithms and data structures. A `Dictionary` is a straightforward example of this.

`Dictionary` has two type parameters in the comma-separated generic parameter list that falls between the angle brackets, as you can see in its declaration:

```
struct Dictionary<Key: Hashable, Value> // etc..
```

`Key` and `Value` represent the types of the dictionary's keys and values. But the annotation on `Key`, `Key : Hashable`, says more. Everything after that colon is a **type constraint**. A type constraint indicates a required supertype, and/or a required protocol or list of protocols, for any type that will serve as the argument for that type parameter.

For instance, the type constraint for `Dictionary` requires that any type serving as the key for the dictionary be hashable, because the dictionary is a hash map and must hash its keys to enable fast lookup.

To instantiate types such as `Dictionary` with multiple type parameters, simply provide a comma-separated type argument list:

```
let intNames: Dictionary<Int, String> = [42: "forty-two"]
```

As with arrays, dictionaries get some special treatment in Swift since they're built-in and rather common. You've already seen the shorthand notation `[Key: Value]`, and you can also use type inference:

```
let intNames2: [Int: String] = [42: "forty-two", 7: "seven"]
let intNames3 = [42: "forty-two", 7: "seven"]
```

Optionals

Finally, no discussion of generics would be complete without mentioning optionals. Optionals are implemented as enumerations, but they're also just another generic type, which you could have defined yourself.

Suppose you were writing an app that let a user enter her birthdate in a form, but didn't require it. You might find it handy to define an enum type, as follows:

```
enum OptionalDate {
  case none
  case some(Date)
}
```

Similarly, if another form allowed but didn't require the user to enter her last name, you might define the following type:

```
enum OptionalString {
  case none
  case some(String)
}
```

Then you could capture all the information a user did or did not enter into a struct with properties of those types:

```
struct FormResults {
  // other properties here
  var birthday: OptionalDate
  var lastName: OptionalString
}
```

And if you found yourself doing this repeatedly for new types of data the user might not provide, then at some point you'd want to generalize this into a generic type that represented the concept of "a value of a certain type that might be present". Therefore, you'd write the following:

```
enum Optional<Wrapped> {
  case none
  case some(Wrapped)
}
```

At this point, you would have reproduced Swift's own `Optional<Wrapped>` type, since this is quite close to the definition in the Swift standard library! It turns out, `Optional<Wrapped>` is close to being a plain old generic type, like one you could write yourself.

Why "close"? It would *only* be a plain old generic type if you interacted with optionals only by writing out their full types, like so:

```
var birthdate: Optional<Date> = .none
if birthdate == .none {
  // no birthdate
}
```

But, of course, it's more common and conventional to write something like this:

```
var birthdate: Date? = nil
if birthdate == nil {
  // no birthdate
}
```

In fact, those two code blocks say exactly the same thing. The second relies on special language support for optionals: the `Wrapped?` shorthand syntax for specifying the optional type `Optional<Wrapped>`, and `nil`, which can stand for the `.none` value of an `Optional<Wrapped>` specialized on any type.

As with arrays and dictionaries, optionals get a privileged place in the language with this syntax to make using them more concise. But all of these features provide more convenient ways to access the underlying type, which is simply a generic enumeration type.

Generic function parameters

So far, you've looked at definitions of generic types in functions, classes, structures, and enumerations. With the exception of `Dictionary`, all of these had a single generic parameter.

The generic **type parameter list** comes after the type name or function name. You can then use the generic parameters in the rest of the definition.

This function takes two arguments and swaps their order:

```
func swapped<T, U>(_ x: T, _ y: U) -> (U, T) {
  return (y, x)
}

swapped(33, "Jay")  // returns ("Jay", 33)
```

A generic function definition demonstrates a confusing aspect about the syntax: having both type parameters and function parameters. You have both the generic parameter list of type parameters `<T, U>`, and the list of function parameters `(_ x: T, _ y: U)`.

Think of the type parameters as arguments *for the compiler*, which it uses to define one possible function. Just as your generic `Keeper` type meant the compiler could make dog keepers and cat keepers and any other kind of keeper, the compiler can now make a non-generic specialized `swapped` function for any two types for you to use.

Key points

- Generics express systematic variation at the level of types via **type parameters** that range over possible concrete type values.
- Generics are like functions *for the compiler*. They are evaluated at compile time and result in new types which are specializations of the generic type.
- A generic type is not a real type on its own, but more like a recipe, program, or template for defining new types.
- Generics are everywhere in Swift: in optionals, arrays, dictionaries, other collection structures, and more.

Where to go from here?

In Swift, generics are everywhere! Every Swift array and every optional is a generic. Every time you write `nil`, you're using a generic. Even the most basic operators like + and == are all defined with generics.

It's fair to say it's impossible to write Swift without using generics. But because generics are integrated so gracefully into the language, it's surprisingly easy to write Swift without really understanding what generics are. Understanding generics is important when digging into the standard library or writing your own generic code.

A next step for deeper investigation is to explore how Swift uses generics in the standard library. In particular, there is much to learn in examining how the collections types make deft use of generics, protocols, associated types, and rich type constraints to provide powerful abstractions — without unnecessarily locking you into specific types.

Remember that generics are fundamentally a mechanism for allowing systematic variation at the level of types, as opposed to values. They let you write code that defines an infinite or a carefully circumscribed set of types or functions in one expression. But this isn't magic. To understand how generics do this, it helps to think of them as functions that are run not by your program, but by the compiler when it builds your program.

If you simply squint a little as you keep this perspective in mind, all the regular ways you think about parameters, variables, constraints and evaluation apply directly to generics.

Challenges

Challenge: Building a collection

Consider the pet and keeper example from earlier in the chapter:

```
class Cat {
  var name: String

  init(name: String) {
    self.name = name
  }
}

class Dog {
  var name: String

  init(name: String) {
    self.name = name
  }
}

class Keeper<Animal> {
  var name: String
  var morningCare: Animal
  var afternoonCare: Animal

  init(name: String, morningCare: Animal, afternoonCare: Animal)
{
    self.name = name
    self.morningCare = morningCare
    self.afternoonCare = afternoonCare
  }
}
```

Imagine that instead of looking after only two animals, every keeper looks after a changing number of animals throughout the day. It could be one, two, or ten animals per keeper instead of just morning and afternoon ones. You'd have to do things like the following:

```
let christine = Keeper<Cat>(name: "Christine")

christine.lookAfter(someCat)
christine.lookAfter(anotherCat)
```

You'd want to be able to access the count of all of animals for a keeper like `christine.countAnimals` and to access the 51st animal via a zero-based index like `christine.animalAtIndex(50)`.

Of course, you're describing your old friend the array type, `Array<Element>`!

Your challenge is to update the `Keeper` type to have this kind of interface. You'll probably want to include a private array inside `Keeper` and then provide methods and properties on `Keeper` to allow outside access to the array.

Section IV: Advanced Topics

You've made it to the final section of this book! In this section, you'll delve into some important but more advanced topics to round out your Swift apprenticeship:

- **Chapter 18, Access Control and Code Organization**: Swift gives you powerful tools for hiding complexity and organizing your code into easier to digest units. This chapter details how to do that.
- **Chapter 19, Custom Operators, Subscripts, Keypaths**: You'll learn how you can define your own operators and subscripts to make your types feel even more like built-in language constructs. You will also learn about type-safe keypaths introduced in Swift 4.
- **Chapter 20, Pattern Matching**: With pattern matching you can accomplish more — with less typing. You'll master all of its many forms in this chapter.
- **Chapter 21, Error Handling**: In the real world, some errors cannot be avoided. Handling them gracefully is what sets apart mediocre code from great code.
- **Chapter 22, Encoding and Decoding Types**: You will learn about the type serialization system introduced in Swift 4 with particular emphasis on the JSON format.
- **Chapter 23, Async Closures and Memory Management**: This chapter digs into the details of Swift memory management examining the relation between objects. It shows you how you avoid common leaks.
- **Chapter 24, Value Types and Reference Types**: Value semantics have a clear advantage over reference semantics in terms of the local reasoning but can lead to inefficiency for large objects. This chapter shows you how to get the best of both worlds.
- **Chapter 25, Protocol-Oriented Programming**: From the standard library to user authored generics, Swift is a protocol-based language. In this chapter you'll see how to get all of the benefits associated with object-oriented programming while being able to avoid most of the difficulties.

Chapter 18: Access Control and Code Organization

By Eli Ganim

Swift types can be declared with properties, methods, initializers, and even other nested types. These elements can be thought of as the **interface** to your code.

As code grows in complexity, controlling this interface becomes an important part of software design. You may wish to create methods that serve as "helpers" to your code, or properties that are designed to keep track of internal states that you don't want as part of your code's interface.

Swift solves these problems with a feature area known as **access control**, which lets you control the viewable interface of your code. Access control lets you, the library author, hide implementation complexity from users.

This hidden internal state is sometimes referred to as **the invariant**, which your public interface should always maintain. Preventing direct access to the internal state of a model and maintaining the invariant is a fundamental software design concept known as **encapsulation**. In this chapter, you will learn what access control is, the problems it solves, and how to apply it.

Problems introduced by lack of access control

Imagine for a moment you are writing a banking library. This library would help serve as the foundation for your customers (other banks) to write their banking software.

In a playground, start with the following protocol:

```
/// A protocol describing core functionality for an account
protocol Account {
  associatedtype Currency

  var balance: Currency { get }
```

```
  func deposit(amount: Currency)
  func withdraw(amount: Currency)
}
```

This code contains `Account`, a protocol that describes what any account should have — the ability to deposit, withdraw, and check the balance of funds.

Now add a conforming type with the code below:

```
typealias Dollars = Double

/// A U.S. Dollar based "basic" account.
class BasicAccount: Account {

  var balance: Dollars = 0.0

  func deposit(amount: Dollars) {
    balance += amount
  }

  func withdraw(amount: Dollars) {
    if amount <= balance {
      balance -= amount
    } else {
      balance = 0
    }
  }
}
```

This conforming class, `BasicAccount`, implements `deposit(amount:)` and `withdraw(amount:)` by simply adding or subtracting from the balance (typed in `Dollars`, an alias for `Double`).

Although this code is very straightforward, you may notice a slight issue. The `balance` property in the `Account` protocol is designed to be read-only — in other words, it only has a `get` defined. However, the implementation of `BasicAccount` requires `balance` to be declared as a variable so that the value can be updated when funds are deposited or withdrawn.

Nothing can prevent other code from directly assigning new values for `balance`:

```
// Create a new account
let account = BasicAccount()

// Deposit and withdraw some money
account.deposit(amount: 10.00)
account.withdraw(amount: 5.00)

// ... or do evil things!
account.balance = 1000000.00
```

Oh no! Even though you carefully designed the `Account` protocol to only be able to `deposit` or `withdraw` funds, the implementation details of `BasicAccount` that allow it to update its own balance could be used by *any* code.

Fortunately, you can use access control to limit the scope at which your code is visible to other types, files, or even software modules!

> **Note:** Access control is not a security feature that protects your code from malicious hackers. Rather, it lets you express intent by generating helpful compiler errors if a user attempts directly access implementation details that may compromise the invariant.

Introducing access control

You can add access modifiers by placing a modifier keyword in front of a property, method or type declaration.

Add the access control modifier `private(set)` to the definition of `balance` in `BasicAccount`:

```
private(set) var balance: Dollars
```

The access modifier above is placed before the property declaration, and includes an optional `get`/`set` modifier in parentheses. In this example, the setter of `balance` is made `private`.

You'll cover the details of `private` shortly, but you can see it in action already: your code no longer compiles!

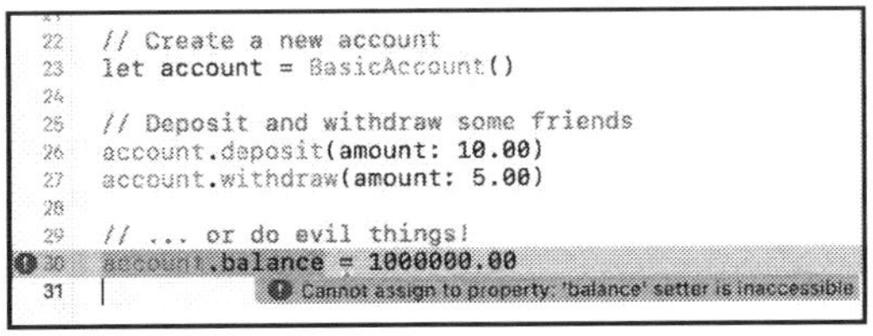

By adding `private` to the property setter, the property has been made inaccessible to the consuming code.

This demonstrates the fundamental benefit of access modifiers: access is restricted to code that *needs* or *should* have access, and restricted from code that doesn't. Effectively, access control allows you to control the code's accessible interface while defining whatever properties, methods or types you need to implement the behavior you want.

The `private` modifier used in the brief example above is one of several access modifiers available to you in Swift:

- **`private`**: Accessible only to the defining type, all nested types and extensions on that type within the same source file.
- **`fileprivate`**: Accessible from anywhere within the source file in which it's defined.
- **`internal`**: Accessible from anywhere within the *module* in which it's defined. This is the **default** access level.
- **`public`**: Accessible from anywhere within the module in which it is defined, as well as another software module that imports this module.
- **`open`**: The same as `public`, with the additional ability of being able to be *overridden* by code in another module.

Next, you will learn more about these modifiers, when to use them, and how to apply them to your code.

Private

The `private` access modifier restricts access to the entity it is defined in, as well as any nested type within it — also known as the "lexical scope". Extensions on the type within the same source file can also access the entity.

To demonstrate, continue with your banking library by extending the behavior of `BasicAccount` to make a `CheckingAccount`:

```
class CheckingAccount: BasicAccount {
  private let accountNumber = UUID().uuidString

  class Check {
    let account: String
    var amount: Dollars
    private(set) var cashed = false

    func cash() {
      cashed = true
    }

    init(amount: Dollars, from account: CheckingAccount) {
      self.amount = amount
      self.account = account.accountNumber
    }
  }
}
```

CheckingAccount has an accountNumber declared as private. CheckingAccount also has a nested type Check which can read the private value of accountNumber in its initializer.

> **Note:** In this example, the UUID class is used to generate unique account numbers. This class is part of Foundation, so don't forget to import it!

Checking accounts should be able to write and cash checks as well. Add the following methods to CheckingAccount:

```
func writeCheck(amount: Dollars) -> Check? {
  guard balance > amount else {
    return nil
  }

  let check = Check(amount: amount, from: self)
  withdraw(amount: check.amount)
  return check
}

func deposit(_ check: Check) {
  guard !check.cashed else {
    return
  }

  deposit(amount: check.amount)
  check.cash()
}
```

While CheckingAccount can still make basic deposits and withdrawals, it can now also write and deposit checks! The method writeCheck(amount:) checks for sufficient balance before withdrawing the amount and creating the check, and deposit(_:) will not deposit the check if it has already been cashed.

Give this code a try in your playground by having John write a check to Jane:

```
// Create a checking account for John. Deposit $300.00
let johnChecking = CheckingAccount()
johnChecking.deposit(amount: 300.00)

// Write a check for $200.00
let check = johnChecking.writeCheck(amount: 200.0)!

// Create a checking account for Jane, and deposit the check.
let janeChecking = CheckingAccount()
janeChecking.deposit(check)
janeChecking.balance // 200.00
```

```
// Try to cash the check again. Of course, it had no effect on
// Jane's balance this time :]
janeChecking.deposit(check)
janeChecking.balance // 200.00
```

This code works great, of course; the *real* story is what this code *can't* do. Remember that access control lets you control the interface to your code. Look at what the autocomplete window shows as the interface for `CheckingAccount`:

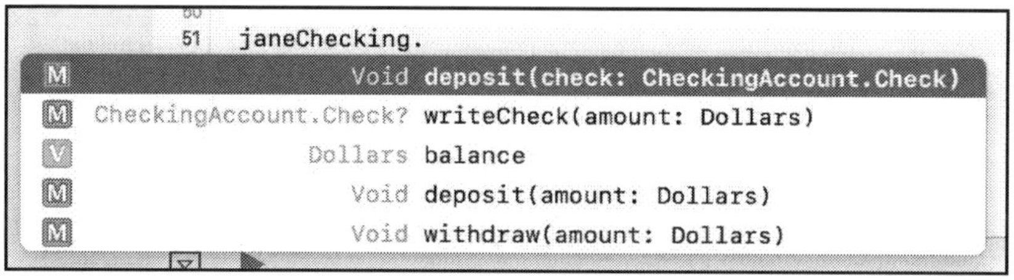

The `accountNumber` is treated as an implementation detail of `CheckingAccount`, and isn't visible to consuming code.

Likewise, `Check` makes the setter for `cashed` private and requires consumers to use `cash()` instead:

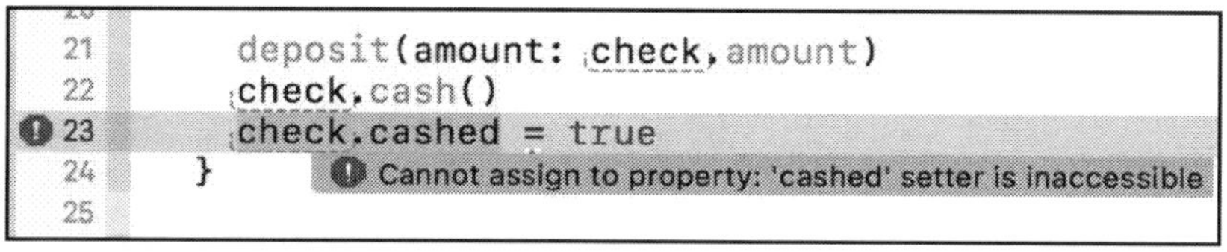

This interface gives `Check` a way for consumers to mark a check as cashed, but not the other way around! In other words, it is not possible to un-cash a check.

Finally, even though `accountNumber` was not visible on `CheckingAccount`, the number is made accessible by anyone holding a `Check`:

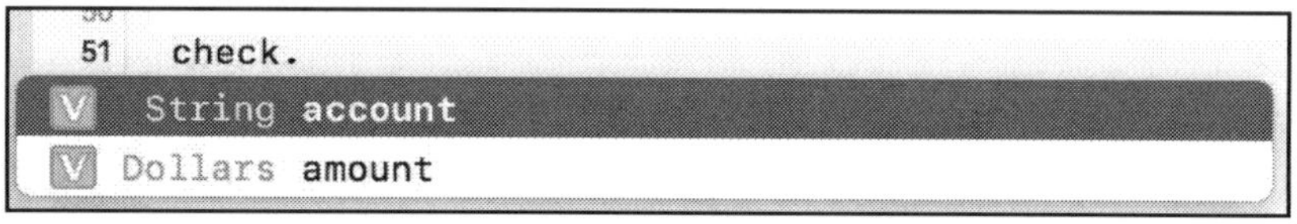

While the `account` property got its value from the `CheckingAccount`, that's but another implementation detail. The important thing is that access modifiers let the code shape its own interface regardless of the code used to implement it.

Playground sources

Before jumping into the rest of this chapter, you'll need to learn a new feature of Swift playgrounds: source files.

In Xcode, make sure the Project Navigator is visible by going to **View\Navigators\Show Project Navigator**. Under the playground tree you'll see a slightly dimmed folder named **Sources**:

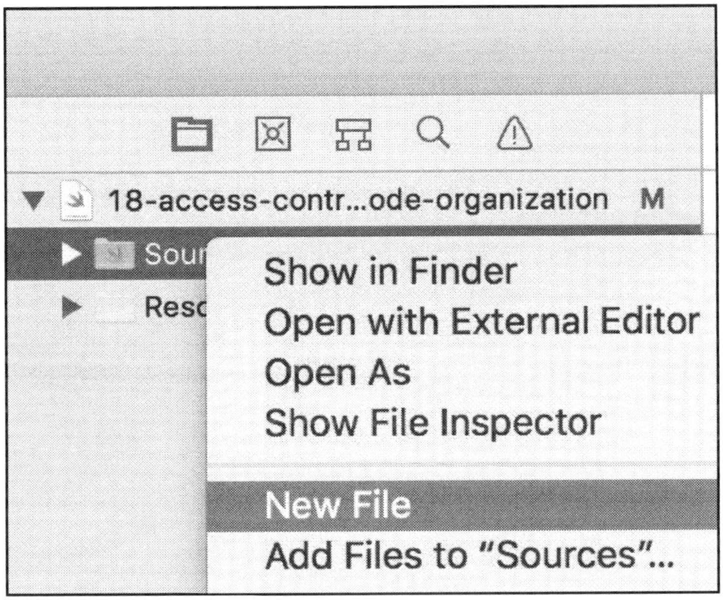

Right-click on the folder, select **New File** and name the file **Account.swift**. Move the `Account` protocol, the `BasicAccount` class, and the `Dollars` typealias all to this file.

Create one more source file and name it **Checking.swift**. Move `CheckingAccount` into this file.

That's it! The important things to note about the Sources folder is that the code within it is treated as a separate module from the code within your playground.

You can comment out the rest of the code in your playground for now. It won't be able to "see" the code you just moved until later in this chapter.

Fileprivate

Closely related to `private` is `fileprivate`, which permits access to any code written in the same **file** as the entity, instead of the same lexical scope and extensions within the same file, which `private` provided.

You'll use the two new files you just created to try this out!

Right now, nothing is preventing a haphazard coder who doesn't read the documentation from creating a `Check` on their own. In your safe code, you want a `Check` to only originate from `CheckingAccount` so that it can keep track of balances.

In the `Check` class, try adding the `private` modifier to the initializer:

```
private init(amount: Dollars, from account: CheckingAccount)
{ //...
```

While this prevents bad code from creating a `Check`, you'll notice it also prevents `CheckingAccount` from creating one as well. `private` entities can be accessed from anything *within* lexical scope, but in this case `CheckingAccount` is one step *outside* the scope of `Check`. Fortunately, this is where `fileprivate` is very useful.

Replace the initializer instead with `fileprivate`:

```
fileprivate init(amount: Dollars, from account: CheckingAccount)
{ //...
```

Great! Now `CheckingAccount` can still write checks, but you can't create them from anywhere else.

The `fileprivate` modifier is ideal for code that is "cohesive" within a source file; that is, code that is closely related or serves enough of a common purpose to have shared but protected access. `Check` and `CheckingAccount` are great examples of two cohesive types.

Internal, public, and open

With `private` and `fileprivate` you were able to protect code from being accessed by other types and files. These access modifiers *modified* access from the default access level of **internal**.

The `internal` access level means that an entity can be accessed from anywhere within the software *module* in which it's defined. To this point in the book, you've written all of your code in a single playground file, which means it's all been in the same module.

When you added code to the Sources directory in your playground, you effectively created a module which your playground consumed. The way playgrounds are designed in Xcode, all files in the Sources directory are part of one module, and everything in the playground is another module that *consumes* the module in the Sources folder.

Internal

Back in your playground, uncomment the code that handles John writing checks to Jane:

```
// Create a checking account for John. Deposit $300.00
let johnChecking = CheckingAccount()
johnChecking.deposit(amount: 300.00)
// ...
```

Because `CheckingAccount` has no access modifier specified, it is treated as `internal` and is thus inaccessible to the playground which consumes the module in which it's defined.

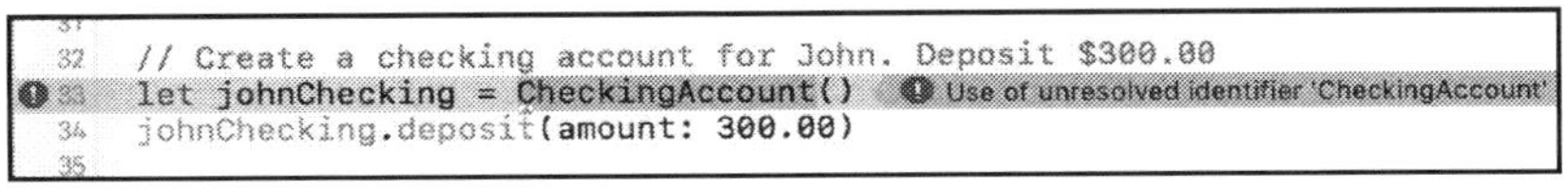

The result is that Swift displays a build error trying to use the `CheckingAccount` type.

To remedy this, you will have to learn about the `public` and `open` access modifiers.

> **Note**: Because `internal` is the default access level, you never need to explicitly declare your code `internal`. Whether you use `internal` keyword in your definitions is a matter of style and preference.

Public

To make `CheckingAccount` visible to your playground, you'll need to change the access level from `internal` to `public`. An entity that is `public` can be seen and used by code outside the module in which it's defined.

Add the `public` modifier to class `CheckingAccount`:

```
public class CheckingAccount: BasicAccount {
```

You'll also need to add `public` to `BasicAccount` since `CheckingAccount` subclasses it:

```
public class BasicAccount: Account
```

The playground will now recognize `CheckingAccount`, yet you're still not able to instantiate it.

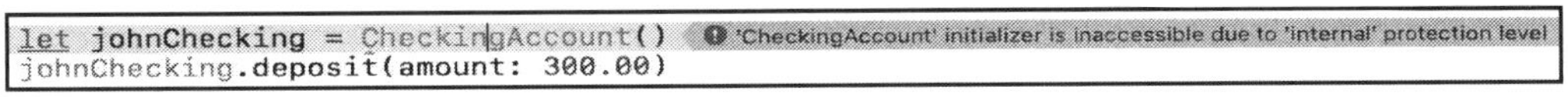

While the type itself is now public, its members are still internal and thus unavailable outside of the module. You'll need to add `public` modifiers to all the entities you want to be part of your module's interface.

Start by adding a public initializer to `BasicAccount` and `CheckingAccount`:

```
// In BasicAccount:
public init() { }

// In CheckingAccount:
public override init() { }
```

Next, in BasicAccount, add public to balance, deposit(amount:) and withdraw(amount:). You'll also need to make the Dollars typealias public, as this typealias is now used in public methods.

Finally, in CheckingAccount, add public to writeCheck(amount:), deposit(_:) and class Check.

Save all files; you'll find that everything builds and runs!

> **Note:** Even though BasicAccount adopts Account, you may notice that the playground can't see Account, nor does it know that BasicAccount conforms to it. To consuming modules, protocol conformance will be invisible if the protocol itself is not accessible.

Open

Now that CheckingAccount and its public members are visible to the playground, you can use your banking interface as designed.

Well — almost! The banking library should provide a set of common accounts such as checking accounts, but also be open to extensibility for any special kind of account a bank may have.

In your playground, create an interest-accumulating SavingsAccount that subclasses BasicAccount:

```
class SavingsAccount: BasicAccount {
  var interestRate: Double

  init(interestRate: Double) {
    self.interestRate = interestRate
  }

  func processInterest() {
    let interest = balance * interestRate
    deposit(amount: interest)
  }
}
```

While BasicAccount is declared public and is accessible to the playground, Swift will show a build error when trying to subclass BasicAccount:

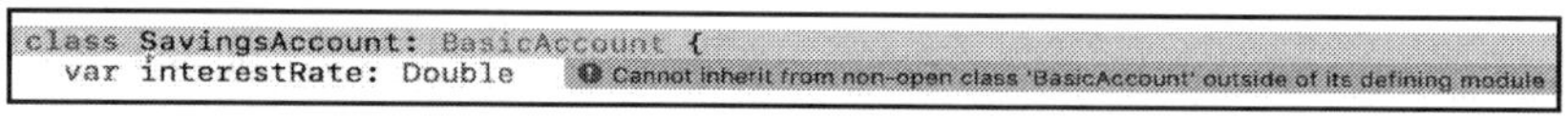

For a class, method or property to be overridden by code in another module, it is required to be declared `open`. Open **Account.swift** and replace the `public` access modifier for class `BasicAccount` with `open`:

```
open class BasicAccount: Account { //..
```

Do you see it all coming together? The interfaces you've crafted using `public` and `open` permit subclassing of `BasicAccount` to provide new types of accounts. `withdraw(amount:)` and `deposit(amount:)`, because they're public, can be used by those subclasses. The implementations of `withdraw(amount:)` and `deposit(amount:)` are safe from being overridden because they're only public, not open!

Imagine if you could override `withdraw(amount:)` and `deposit(amount:)`:

```
override func deposit(amount: Dollars) {
    // LOL
    super.deposit(amount: 1_000_000.00)
}
```

Oh noes!

If you're creating a library, you often want to restrict the ability to override methods and properties so you can avoid otherwise surprising behavior. The `open` access modifier allows you to explicitly control what other modules do to your code.

Mini-exercises

1. Create a struct `Person` in a new Sources file. This struct should have `first`, `last` and `fullName` properties that are readable but not writable by the playground.

2. Create a similar type, except make it a class and call it `ClassyPerson`. In the playground, subclass `ClassyPerson` with class `Doctor` and make a doctor's `fullName` print the prefix `"Dr."`.

Organizing code into extensions

A theme of access control is the idea that your code should be loosely coupled and highly cohesive. Loosely coupled code limits how much one entity knows about another, which in turn makes different parts of your code less dependent on others. Highly cohesive code, as you learned earlier, helps closely related code work together to fulfill a task.

Swift features such as access modifiers, when used with extensions, can help you both organize your code as well as encourage good software design.

Extensions by behavior

An effective strategy in Swift is to organize your code into extensions by behavior. You can even apply access modifiers to extensions themselves, which will help you categorize entire sections of code as `public`, `internal`, or `private`.

Begin by adding some basic fraud protection to `CheckingAccount`. Add the following properties to `CheckingAccount`:

```
private var issuedChecks: [Int] = []
private var currentCheck = 1
```

These will keep track of checks that have been written by the checking account.

Next, add the following private extension:

```
private extension CheckingAccount {
  func inspectForFraud(with checkNumber: Int) -> Bool {
    return issuedChecks.contains(checkNumber)
  }

  func nextNumber() -> Int {
    let next = currentCheck
    currentCheck += 1
    return next
  }
}
```

These two methods can be used by `CheckingAccount` to determine the number of a check that is being written, as well as check to ensure it has been in fact issued by the account.

Notably, this extension is marked `private`. A `private` extension implicitly marks all of its members as `private` as well. These fraud protection tools are meant to be used by the `CheckingAccount` only — you definitely don't want other code incrementing the `currentCheck` number!

Putting these two methods together also ties together two related and cohesive methods. It's clear to yourself and anyone else maintaining the code that these two are *cohesive* and help solve a common task.

Extensions by protocol conformance

Another effective technique is to organize your extensions based on protocol conformance. You've already seen this technique used in Chapter 16, "Protocols". As an example, let's make `CheckingAccount` conform to `CustomStringConvertible` by adding the following extension:

```
extension CheckingAccount: CustomStringConvertible {
  public var description: String {
    return "Checking Balance: $\(balance)"
  }
}
```

This extension implements `CustomStringConvertible`, and more importantly:

- Makes it obvious `description` is part of `CustomStringConvertible`
- *Doesn't* help conform to other protocols
- Can easily be removed without doing collateral damage to the rest of `CheckingAccount`
- Is easy to grok!

Key points

- Access control modifiers are `private`, `fileprivate`, `internal`, `public`, and `open`. The `internal` access level is the default.
- Modifiers can be used to control your code's visible interface and hide complexity.
- `private` and `fileprivate` protect code from being accessed by code in other types or files, respectively.
- `public` and `open` allow code to be accessed from another module. The `open` modifier additionally allows entities to be overridden by other modules.
- When access modifiers are applied to extensions, all members of the extension receive that access level.
- Extensions that mark protocol conformance cannot have access modifiers.

Challenges

Challenge 1: Singleton pattern

A **singleton** is a design pattern that restricts the instantiation of a class to one object.

Use access modifiers to create a singleton class `Logger`. This `Logger` should:

- Provide shared, public, global access to the single `Logger` object.

- Not be able to be instantiated by consuming code
- Have a method `log()` that will print a string to the console

Challenge 2: Stack

Declare a generic type `Stack`. A stack is a LIFO (last-in-first-out) data structure that supports the following operations:

- `peek`: returns the top element on the stack without removing it. Returns `nil` if the stack is empty.
- `push`: adds an element on top of the stack.
- `pop`: returns and removes the top element on the stack. Returns `nil` if the stack is empty.
- `count`: returns the size of the stack.

Ensure that these operations are the only exposed interface. In other words, additional properties or methods needed to implement the type should not be visible.

Challenge 3: Character battle

Utilize something called a **static factory method** to create a game of Wizards vs. Elves vs. Giants.

Add a file **Characters.swift** in the Sources folder of your playground.

To begin:

- Create an enum `GameCharacterType` that defines values for `elf`, `giant`, and `wizard`.
- Create a class protocol `GameCharacter` that has properties `name`, `hitPoints` and `attackPoints`. Implement this protocol for every character type.
- Create a struct `GameCharacterFactory` with a single static method `make(ofType: GameCharacterType) -> GameCharacter`.
- Create a global function `battle` that pits two characters against each other — with the first character striking first! If a character reaches 0 hit points, they have lost.

Notes:

- The playground should not be able to see the concrete types that implement `GameCharacter`.
- Elves have 3 hit points, and 10 attack points. Wizards have 5 hit points and 5 attack points. Giants have 10 hit points and 3 attack points.

- The playground should know none of the above!

In your playground, you should use the following scenario as a test case:

```
let elf = GameCharacterFactory.make(ofType: .elf)
let giant = GameCharacterFactory.make(ofType: .giant)
let wizard = GameCharacterFactory.make(ofType: .wizard)

battle(elf, vs: giant) // Giant defeated!
battle(wizard, vs: giant) // Giant defeated!
battle(wizard, vs: elf) // Elf defeated!
```

Chapter 19: Custom Operators, Subscripts and Keypaths

By Cosmin Pupăză

You've learned the basics of **operator overloading** in Chapter 16, "Protocols", where you implemented the `Equatable` and `Comparable` protocols and added custom behavior to standard operators.

However, there are certain cases when overloading standard operators is simply not enough. This chapter will show you how to create custom operators from scratch and define your very own **subscripts**, a special case of computed properties. You will use subscripts to declare your own shortcuts for accessing the elements of custom types and provide **keypaths** as dynamic references for properties of objects.

Custom operators

You declare your own operators when you want to define a custom behavior no other standard operator is designed for. Think of **exponentiation**, for example. You could overload the multiplication operator since exponentiation means repeated multiplication, but it would be confusing: Operators are designed to do only one type of operation, and you use the same operator to do two different things in this case.

So you'll define your own exponentiation operator, first only for a certain type and then extend it by making it **generic**. Before doing that, you need to know a little bit of theory about operator types. Time to dive in!

Types of operators

There are three major types of operators: unary, binary and ternary.

- **Unary** operators work with only one operand and are defined either as **postfix**, if they appear after the operand, or **prefix**, if they appear before the operand. The logical not operator is a unary prefix operator and the forced unwrapping operator is a unary postfix one; you've learned about them in Chapter 3, "Basic Control Flow" and Chapter 6, "Optionals".
- **Binary** operators work with two operands and are **infix** because they appear between the operands. All the arithmetic operators (+, −, *, /, %), comparison operators (==, != , <, >, <=, >=) and most of the logical ones (&&, ||) are binary infix.
- **Ternary** operators work with three operands. You've learned about the conditional operator in Chapter 3, "Basic Control Flow". This is the only ternary operator in Swift.

Exponentiation operator

The exponentiation operator is a custom one, so you get to choose its name yourself. It's usually best to stick to the characters /, =, −, +, !, *, %, <, >, &, |, ^ and ?, although many other Unicode characters are allowed. Keep in mind you'll have to type it often, so the fewer keystrokes, the better. Since exponentiation is repeated multiplication under the hood, it would be nice to choose something which reflects that, so use ** for the operator's name.

Now for the operator's type. Swift doesn't let you declare custom ternary operators, so you are stuck with the prefix, postfix and infix ones. The ** operator works with two operands, so it's an infix operator.

Here's what the operator's signature looks like:

```
infix operator **
```

Nothing fancy here: the operator's name and type bundled into one line of code with the `operator` keyword. As for the operator's implementation, a naive one looks like this:

```
func **(base: Int, power: Int) -> Int {
  precondition(power >= 2)
  var result = base
  for _ in 2...power {
    result *= base
  }
  return result
}
```

The function takes two arguments of type Int and uses loops, ranges and wildcards to return the first argument raised to the power of the second one. Note the multiplication assignment operator in action.

> **Note**: You use the **wildcard pattern** to discard the loop's values. You will learn more about it and other pattern matching techniques in Chapter 20, "Pattern Matching".

Now test your brand-new operator:

```
let base = 2
let exponent = 2
let result = base ** exponent
```

Compound assignment operator

Most built-in operators have a corresponding **compound assignment** version. Do the same for the exponentiation operator:

```
infix operator **=

func **=(lhs: inout Int, rhs: Int) {
  lhs = lhs ** rhs
}
```

The operator's name is **= and it is infix, just like the exponentiation operator created earlier. It has no return type and instead uses the inout keyword in front of the type of the operand you are modifying. You've already seen inout in action in Chapter 5, "Functions". The function changes the inout parameter directly because it's passed by reference.

This is how the operator works:

```
var number = 2
number **= exponent
```

Your custom operator is really cool and all, but it only works for Int. Time to make it generic!

Mini-exercises

1. Implement a custom multiplication operator for strings so that the following code works:

```
let baseString = "abc"
let times = 5
var multipliedString = baseString ** times
```

2. Implement the corresponding multiplication assignment operator so that the following code runs without errors:

```
multipliedString **= times
```

Generic operators

You want the exponentiation operator to work for all kind of integer types. Update your operator implementations as follows:

```
func **<T: BinaryInteger>(base: T, power: Int) -> T {
  precondition(power >= 2)
  var result = base
  for _ in 2...power {
    result *= base
  }
  return result
}

func **=<T: BinaryInteger>(lhs: inout T, rhs: Int) {
  lhs = lhs ** rhs
}
```

Notice the `BinaryInteger` type constraint on the generic parameter. This constraint is required here as the *= operator used in the function body isn't available on any type `T`, but it is available on all types that conform to the `BinaryInteger` protocol. The function's body is the same as before, since the generic operator does the same thing as its non-generic equivalent.

Your previous code should still work. Now that the operator is generic, test it with some types other than `Int`:

```
let unsignedBase: UInt = 2
let unsignedResult = unsignedBase ** exponent

let base8: Int8 = 2
let result8 = base8 ** exponent
```

```
let unsignedBase8: UInt8 = 2
let unsignedResult8 = unsignedBase8 ** exponent

let base16: Int16 = 2
let result16 = base16 ** exponent

let unsignedBase16: UInt16 = 2
let unsignedResult16 = unsignedBase16 ** exponent

let base32: Int32 = 2
let result32 = base32 ** exponent

let unsignedBase32: UInt32 = 2
let unsignedResult32 = unsignedBase32 ** exponent

let base64: Int64 = 2
let result64 = base64 ** exponent

let unsignedBase64: UInt64 = 2
let unsignedResult64 = unsignedBase64 ** exponent
```

The exponentiation operator now works for all integer types: `Int`, `UInt`, `Int8`, `UInt8`, `Int16`, `UInt16`, `Int32`, `UInt32`, `Int64` and `UInt64`.

> **Note**: You can also use the `pow(_:_:)` function from the `Foundation` framework for exponentiation, but it doesn't work for all the above types. It does, however, handle negative and fractional exponents and is written to be O(log) instead of O(n) as in the naive implementation.

Precedence and associativity

Your shiny new custom operator seems to work just fine, but if you use it in a complex expression Swift won't know what to do with it:

```
2 * 2 ** 3 ** 2 // Does not compile!
```

In order to understand this expression, Swift needs the following information about your operator:

- **Precedence**: Should the multiplication be done before or after the exponentiation?
- **Associativity**: Should the consecutive exponentiations be done left to right, or right to left?

Without this information, the only way to get Swift to understand your code is to add parentheses.

```
2 * (2 ** (3 ** 2))
```

These parentheses are telling Swift that the exponentations should be done before the multiplication, and from right to left. If this is always the case, you can define this behavior using a **precedence group**.

Change your operator definition to the following:

```
precedencegroup ExponentiationPrecedence {
  associativity: right
  higherThan: MultiplicationPrecedence
}

infix operator **: ExponentiationPrecedence
```

Here, you're creating a precedence group for your exponentiation operator, telling Swift it is right-associative and has higher precedence than multiplication.

Swift will now understand your expression, even without parentheses:

```
2 * 2 ** 3 ** 2
```

Maybe that is a good thing, maybe it is not. You may choose to make `associativity: none` and force users to make things explicit with parenthesis.

That's it for custom operators. Time for some fun with subscripts!

Subscripts

You've already used **subscripts** in Chapter 7, "Arrays, Dictionaries, Sets" to retrieve the elements of arrays and dictionaries. It's high time you learned to create your very own subscripts. Think of them as overloading the `[]` operator in order to provide shortcuts for accessing elements of a collection, class, structure or enumeration.

The subscript syntax is as follows:

```
subscript(parameterList) -> ReturnType {
  get {
    // return someValue of ReturnType
  }

  set(newValue) {
    // set someValue of ReturnType to newValue
  }
}
```

As you can see, subscripts behave both like functions and computed properties:

- The subscript's prototype looks like a function's signature: It has a parameter list and a return type, but instead of the `func` keyword and the function's name, you use the `subscript` keyword. Subscripts may have variadic parameters, but can't use `inout` or default parameters and can't throw errors. You will learn more about errors in Chapter 21, "Error Handling".
- The subscript's body looks like a computed property: it has both a getter and a setter. The setter is optional, so the subscript can be either read-write or read-only. You can omit the setter's `newValue` default parameter; its type is the same as the subscript's return type. Only declare it if you want to change its name to something else.

Enough theory! Add a subscript to a `Person` class defined as follows:

```
class Person {
  let name: String
  let age: Int

  init(name: String, age: Int) {
    self.name = name
    self.age = age
  }
}
```

The `Person` class has two stored properties: `name` of type `String` and `age` of type `Int`, along with a designated initializer to kick things off.

Now suppose I want to create a version of myself right now, as follows:

```
let me = Person(name: "Cosmin", age: 31)
```

It would be nice to access my characteristics with a subscript like this:

```
me["name"]
me["age"]
me["gender"]
```

If you run this, Xcode would output the following error:

```
Type "Person" has no subscripts members
```

Whenever you use the square brackets operator, you actually call a subscript under the hood. Your class doesn't have any subscripts defined by default, so you have to declare them yourself.

Add the following code to the Person class with an extension like this:

```
extension Person {
  subscript(key: String) -> String? {
    switch key {
      case "name":
        return name
      case "age":
        return "\(age)"
      default:
        return nil
    }
  }
}
```

The subscript returns an optional string based on the key you provide: you either return the key's corresponding property's value or nil if you don't use a valid key. The switch must be exhaustive, so you need a default case. The subscript is read-only, so its entire body is a getter — you don't need to explicitly state that with the get keyword.

The above test code works now:

```
me["name"]
me["age"]
me["gender"]
```

and outputs:

```
Cosmin
31
nil
```

Subscript parameters

You don't have to use names for the subscript's parameters when calling the subscript even if you don't use *underscores* when declaring them. Add **external parameter names** if you want to be more specific like this:

```
subscript(key key: String) -> String? {
  // original code
}
```

The parameter's name appears in the subscript call now:

```
me[key: "name"]
me[key: "age"]
me[key: "gender"]
```

Use descriptive names for external parameters instead of their local counterparts if you want to add more context to the subscript:

```
subscript(property key: String) -> String? {
  // original code
}

me[property: "name"]
me[property: "age"]
me[property: "gender"]
```

Subscripts are easy to use and implement. They live somewhere between computed properties and functions. However, take care not to overuse them. Unlike computed properties and functions, subscripts have no name to make their intentions clear. Subscripts are almost exclusively used to access the elements of a collection, so don't confuse the readers of your code by using them for something unrelated and unintuitive!

Keypaths

Keypaths enable you to store references to properties. For example, this is how you model the tutorials on our website:

```
class Tutorial {
  let title: String
  let author: Person
  let type: String
  let publishDate: Date

  init(title: String, author: Person, type: String, publishDate:
Date) {
    self.title = title
    self.author = author
    self.type = type
    self.publishDate = publishDate
  }
}

let tutorial = Tutorial(title: "Object Oriented Programming in
Swift", author: me, type: "Swift", publishDate: Date())
```

> **Note**: You need to import the `Foundation` framework in order to work with the `Date` type.

Each tutorial has a certain title, author, type and publishing date. Using keypaths, you can get the tutorial's title like this:

```
let title = \Tutorial.title
let tutorialTitle = tutorial[keyPath: title]
```

You first use a *backslash* to create a keypath for the `title` property of the `Tutorial` class and then access its corresponding data with the `keyPath(_:)` subscript.

Keypaths can access properties several levels deep:

```
let authorName = \Tutorial.author.name
var tutorialAuthor = tutorial[keyPath: authorName]
```

Appending keypaths

You can make new keypaths by **appending** to existing ones like this:

```
let authorPath = \Tutorial.author
let authorNamePath = authorPath.appending(path: \.name)
tutorialAuthor = tutorial[keyPath: authorNamePath]
```

You use the `appending(path:)` method to add a new keypath to the already defined `authorPath` one and infer the keypath's base type.

Setting properties

Keypaths can change property values. Suppose you set up your very own jukebox to play your favorite song:

```
class Jukebox {
  var song: String

  init(song: String) {
    self.song = song
  }
}

let jukebox = Jukebox(song: "Nothing else matters")
```

You declare the `song` property as a variable because your best friend comes to visit and wants to listen to her favorite song instead:

```
let song = \Jukebox.song
jukebox[keyPath: song] = "Stairway to heaven"
```

You use the `song` keypath to change the song for your friend and everyone is happy now!

As you can see, using keypaths is more involved than using properties. With keypaths, accessing a property becomes a two-step process:

1. First, you decide which property you need and create a keypath.
2. Then, you pass this keypath to an instance using the keypath subscript to access the selected property.

The benefit of this process is that it allows you to parameterize the properties you use in your code. Instead of hard coding them, you can store them in variables as keypaths. You could even leave it up to your users to decide which properties should be used!

Key points

1. Remember the **custom operators** mantra when creating brand new operators from scratch: With great power comes great responsibility. Makes sure the additional cognitive overhead of a custom operator introduces pays for itself.
2. Choose the appropriate type for custom operators: *postfix*, *prefix*, or *infix*.
3. Don't forget to define any related operators, such as compound assignment operators, for custom operators.
4. Use **subscripts** to overload the square brackets operator for classes, structures and enumerations.
5. Use **keypaths** to create dynamic references to properties.

Where to go from here?

If you are still in the mood for overloading Swift's standard operators, there's even more to come. You will learn to use and overload the pattern matching operator for the **expression pattern** in the next chapter. You can also make use of keypaths in your own apps by implementing the type safe key value observing mechanism.

Challenges

Challenge 1

Modify the following subscript implementation so that it compiles in a playground:

```
extension Array {
  subscript(index: Int) -> (String, String)? {
    guard let value = self[index] as? Int else {
      return nil
    }

    switch (value >= 0, abs(value) % 2) {
      case (true, 0):
        return ("positive", "even")
      case (true, 1):
        return ("positive", "odd")
      case (false, 0):
        return ("negative", "even")
      case (false, 1):
        return ("negative", "odd")
      default:
        return nil
    }
  }
}
```

Challenge 2

Write a subscript that computes the character at a certain index in a string. Why is this considered harmful?

Challenge 3

Implement the exponentiation generic operator for float types so that the following code works:

```
let exponent = 2
let baseDouble = 2.0
var resultDouble = baseDouble ** exponent
let baseFloat: Float = 2.0
var resultFloat = baseFloat ** exponent
let base80: Float80 = 2.0
var result80 = base80 ** exponent
let baseCG: CGFloat = 2.0
var resultCG = baseCG ** exponent
```

> **Note**: You should import the `CoreGraphics` framework in order to work with `CGFloat`

Challenge 4

Implement the exponentiation assignment generic operator for float types so that the following code works:

```
resultDouble **= exponent
resultFloat **= exponent
result80 **= exponent
resultCG **= exponent
```

Chapter 20: Pattern Matching

By Ben Morrow

In this chapter, you'll learn about proper golf attire: how to pair a striped shirt with plaid shorts:

No, just playing! This is *not* your grandfather's pattern matching.

Actually, you've already seen pattern matching in action. In Chapter 4, "Advanced Control Flow", you used a `switch` statement to match numbers and strings in different cases. These are examples of pattern matching. That's a simple example, but there's a lot more to explore on the topic.

You're going to dive deep into the underlying mechanisms and understand more about how the Swift compiler interprets the code you type.

Swift is a multi-paradigm language that lets you build full featured, production ready, object-oriented software. In addition, the designers of Swift borrowed some tricks from more functional style languages like Haskell and Erlang. Pattern matching is a staple of those functional languages. It saves you from having to type much longer and less readable statements to evaluate conditions.

Suppose you have a coordinate with *x-*, *y-*, and *z-* axis values:

```
let coordinate = (x: 1, y: 0, z: 0)
```

Both of these code snippets will achieve the same result:

```
// 1
if (coordinate.y == 0) && (coordinate.z == 0) {
  print("along the x-axis")
}

// 2
if case (_, 0, 0) = coordinate {
  print("along the x-axis")
}
```

The first option digs into the internals of a tuple and has a long equatable comparison. It also uses the logical && operator to make sure both conditions are true.

The second option, using pattern matching, is concise and readable.

The following sections will show you how — and when — to use patterns in your code.

Introducing patterns

Patterns provide rules to match values. You can use patterns in `switch` cases, as well as in `if`, `while`, `guard`, and `for` statements. You can also use patterns in variable and constant declarations.

Believe it or not, you've already seen another good example of patterns with that `coordinate` tuple declaration. You construct a tuple by separating values with commas between parentheses, like `(x, y, z)`. The compiler will understand that pattern is referring to a tuple of 3 values: *x*, *y* and *z*. Tuples have the structure of a composite value.

Single values also have a structure. The number `42` is a single value and by its very nature is identifiable.

The structure of a value is defined by a pattern. Pattern matching lets you check values against each other.

> **Note**: The structure of a value is not referring to the `struct` type. They are different concepts even though we use the same word in English. That's the paucity of language!

Basic pattern matching

In this section, you'll see some common uses for pattern matching.

if and guard

Throughout the book so far, you've used plain old `if` and `guard` statements. You can transform them into pattern matching statements by using a `case` condition. The example below shows how you use an `if` statement with a `case` condition:

```
func process(point: (x: Int, y: Int, z: Int)) -> String {
  if case (0, 0, 0) = point {
    return "At origin"
  }
  return "Not at origin"
}

let point = (x: 0, y: 0, z: 0)
let response = process(point: point) // At origin
```

In that code, all three axes are matched to zero values.

A `case` contition in a `guard` statement achieves the same effect:

```
func process(point: (x: Int, y: Int, z: Int)) -> String {
  guard case (0, 0, 0) = point else {
    return "Not at origin"
  }
  // guaranteed point is at the origin
  return "At origin"
}
```

In a `case` condition, you write the pattern first followed by an equals sign, =, and then the value you want to match to the pattern. `if` statements and `guard` statements work best if there is a single pattern you care to match.

switch

If you care to match multiple patterns, the `switch` statement is your best friend.

You can rewrite `processPoint()` like this:

```
func process(point: (x: Int, y: Int, z: Int)) -> String {
  // 1
  let closeRange = -2...2
  let midRange = -5...5
  // 2
  switch point {
  case (0, 0, 0):
    return "At origin"
  case (closeRange, closeRange, closeRange):
    return "Very close to origin"
  case (midRange, midRange, midRange):
    return "Nearby origin"
  default:
    return "Not near origin"
  }
}

let point = (x: 15, y: 5, z: 3)
let response = process(point: point) // Not near origin
```

This code introduces a couple of new concepts:

1. You can match against ranges of numbers.
2. The `switch` statement allows for multiple cases to match patterns.

The `switch` statement also provides an advantage over the `if` statement because of its exhaustiveness checking. The compiler guarantees that you have checked for all possible values by the end of a switch statement.

Also recall that a `switch` statement will exit with the first `case` condition that matches. That's why the `midRange` condition is placed second. Even though the `midRange` condition would match a `closeRange` value, it won't be evaluated unless the previous condition fails. The `default` case is the catch-all. If there hasn't been a match in all the other cases, the `default` case will execute.

Mini exercise

Given the population of a group of people, write a `switch` statement that prints out a comment for different ranges of group sizes: single, a few, several, and many.

for

A `for` loop churns through a collection of elements. Pattern matching can act like a filter:

```
let groupSizes = [1, 5, 4, 6, 2, 1, 3]
for case 1 in groupSizes {
  print("Found an individual") // 2 times
}
```

In this example, the array provides a list of workgroup sizes for a school classroom. The implementation of the loop only runs for elements in the array that match the value `1`. Since students in the class are encouraged to work in teams instead of by themselves, you can isolate the people who have not found a partner.

Patterns

Now that you've seen some basic examples of pattern matching, let's talk about the patterns on which you can match.

Wildcard pattern

Revisit the example you saw at the beginning of this chapter, where you wanted to check if a value was on the *x*-axis, for the `(x, y, z)` tuple coordinate:

```
if case (_, 0, 0) = coordinate {
  // x can be any value. y and z must be exactly 0.
  print("On the x-axis") // Printed!
}
```

The pattern in this `case` condition matches any value of *x* component and exactly `0` for the *y* and *z* components.

Value-binding pattern

The value-binding pattern sounds more sophisticated than it turns out to be in practice. You simply use `var` or `let` to declare a variable or a constant while matching a pattern. You can then use the value of the variable or constant inside the execution block:

```
if case (let x, 0, 0) = coordinate {
  print("On the x-axis at \(x)") // Printed: 1
}
```

The pattern in this `case` condition matches any value on the *x*-axis, and then binds its *x* component to the constant named `x` for use in the execution block.

If you wanted to bind multiple values, you could write `let` multiple times or, even better, move the `let` outside the tuple:

```
if case let (x, y, 0) = coordinate {
  print("On the x-y plane at (\(x), \(y))") // Printed: 1, 0
}
```

By putting the `let` on the outside of the tuple, the compiler will bind all the unknown constant names it finds.

Identifier pattern

The identifier pattern is even simpler than the value-binding pattern. The identifier pattern is the constant or variable name itself; in the example above, that's the `x` in the pattern. You're telling the compiler, "When you find a value of `(something, 0, 0)`, assign the `something` to `x`."

This description feels intertwined with what you've seen before because the identifier pattern is a sub-pattern of the value-binding pattern.

Tuple pattern

You've already been using another bonus pattern — did you recognize it? The tuple isn't just a series of comma-separated values between parentheses: it's actually comma-separated patterns. In the example tuple pattern, `(something, 0, 0)`, the interior patterns are (*identifier*, *expression*, *expression*).

You'll learn about expression patterns at the end of this chapter. For now, the important takeaway is that the tuple pattern combines many patterns into one and helps you write terse code.

Enumeration case pattern

In Chapter 15, "Enumerations" you saw how you could match the member values of an enumeration:

```
enum Direction {
  case north, south, east, west
}

let heading = Direction.north

if case .north = heading {
```

```
  print("Don't forget your jacket") // Printed!
}
```

As you can imagine, the enumeration case pattern matches the value of an enumeration. In this example, `case .north` will only match on the `.north` value of the enumeration.

The enumeration case pattern has some magic up its sleeve. When you combine it with the value binding pattern you can extract associated values from an enumeration:

```
enum Organism {
  case plant
  case animal(legs: Int)
}

let pet = Organism.animal(legs: 4)

switch pet {
case .animal(let legs):
  print("Potentially cuddly with \(legs) legs") // Printed: 4
default:
  print("No chance for cuddles")
}
```

In that code, the associated value for `.animal` is bound to the constant named `legs`. You reference the `legs` constant in the `print` call inside the execution block of that condition.

Associated values are locked away in enumeration values until you use the value-binding pattern to extract them.

Mini exercise

In Chapter 15, "Enumerations" you learned that an optional is an enumeration under the hood. An optional is either `.some(value)` or `.none`. You just learned how to extract associated values from optionals. Given the following array of optionals, print the names that are not `nil` with a `for` loop:

```
let names: [String?] =
  ["Michelle", nil, "Brandon", "Christine", nil, "David"]
```

Optional pattern

Speaking of optionals, there is also an optional pattern. The optional pattern consists of an identifier pattern followed immediately by a question mark. You can use this pattern in the same places you would use enumeration case patterns.

You can rewrite the solution to the mini exercise as:

```
for case let name? in names {
  print(name) // 4 times
}
```

Optional patterns are **syntactic sugar** for enumeration case patterns containing optional values. Syntactic sugar simply means a nicer way of writing the same thing.

"Is" type-casting pattern

By using the `is` operator in a case condition, you check if an instance is of a particular type. One example where this would be useful would be parsing JSON you downloaded from a server. In case you're not familiar, JSON is basically an array full of all different types, which you can write as `[Any]` in Swift.

Therefore you'll need to check if each value is of a particular type:

```
let array: [Any] = [15, "George", 2.0]

for element in array {
 switch element {
 case is String:
   print("Found a string") // 1 time
 default:
   print("Found something else") // 2 times
 }
}
```

With this code, you find out that one of the elements is of type `String`. But you don't have access to the value of that `String` in the implementation. That's where the next pattern comes to the rescue.

"As" type-casting pattern

The `as` operator combines the `is` type casting pattern with the value-binding pattern. Extending the example above, you could write a case like this:

```
for element in array {
 switch element {
 case let text as String:
   print("Found a string: \(text)") // 1 time
 default:
   print("Found something else") // 2 times
 }
}
```

So when the compiler finds an object that it can cast to a `String`, the compiler will bind the value to the `text` constant.

Advanced patterns

You've blazed through all the above patterns! What you've learned so far in this chapter will carry you quite far in life. In this section, you'll learn about some modifier tricks that can help you consolidate your code even further.

Qualifying with where

You can specify a `where` condition to further filter a match by checking a unary condition in line. In Chapter 4, "Advanced Control Flow" you saw an example like this:

```
for number in 1...9 {
  switch number {
  case let x where x % 2 == 0:
    print("even") // 4 times
  default:
    print("odd") // 5 times
  }
}
```

If the number in the code above is divisible evenly by two, the first case is matched.

You can utilize `where` in a more sophisticated way with enumerations. Imagine you're writing a game where you want to save the player's progress for each level:

```
enum LevelStatus {
  case complete
  case inProgress(percent: Double)
  case notStarted
}

let levels: [LevelStatus] = [.complete, .inProgress(percent:
0.9), .notStarted]

for level in levels {
  switch level {
  case .inProgress(let percent) where percent > 0.8 :
    print("Almost there!")
  case .inProgress(let percent) where percent > 0.5 :
    print("Halfway there!")
  case .inProgress(let percent) where percent > 0.2 :
    print("Made it through the beginning!")
  default:
    break
```

```
  }
}
```

In this code, one level in the game is currently in progress. That level matches the first case as 90% complete and prints `"Almost there!"`.

Chaining with commas

In Chapter 4, "Advanced Control Flow" you learned how to match more than one pattern in a single case condition. Here's an example similar to what you saw in that chapter:

```
func timeOfDayDescription(hour: Int) -> String {
  switch hour {
  case 0, 1, 2, 3, 4, 5:
    return "Early morning"
  case 6, 7, 8, 9, 10, 11:
    return "Morning"
  case 12, 13, 14, 15, 16:
    return "Afternoon"
  case 17, 18, 19:
    return "Evening"
  case 20, 21, 22, 23:
    return "Late evening"
  default:
    return "INVALID HOUR!"
  }
}
let timeOfDay = timeOfDayDescription(hour: 12) // Afternoon
```

Here you see several identifier patterns matched in each case condition. You can use the constants and variables you bind in preceding patterns in the patterns that follow after each comma. Here's a refinement to the cuddly animal test:

```
if case .animal(let legs) = pet, case 2...4 = legs {
  print("potentially cuddly") // Printed!
} else {
  print("no chance for cuddles")
}
```

The first pattern, before the comma, binds the associated value of the enumeration to the constant `legs`. In the second pattern, after the comma, the value of the `legs` constant is matched against a range.

Swift's `if` statement is surprisingly capable. An `if` statement can have multiple conditions, separated by commas. Conditions fall into one of three categories:

- **Simple logical test** E.g.: `foo == 10 || bar > baz`.

- **Optional binding** E.g.: `let foo = maybeFoo`.
- **Pattern matching** E.g.: `case .bar(let something) = theValue`.

Conditions are evaluated in the order they are defined. At runtime, no conditions following a failing condition will be evaluated. Here is a contrived example of a complicated `if` statement:

```
enum Number {
  case integerValue(Int)
  case doubleValue(Double)
  case booleanValue(Bool)
}

let a = 5
let b = 6
let c: Number? = .integerValue(7)
let d: Number? = .integerValue(8)

if a != b {
  if let c = c {
    if let d = d {
      if case .integerValue(let cValue) = c {
        if case .integerValue(let dValue) = d {
          if dValue > cValue {
            print("a and b are different") // Printed!
            print("d is greater than c") // Printed!
            print("sum: \(a + b + cValue + dValue)") // 26
          }
        }
      }
    }
  }
}
```

Nesting all those if statements one inside the other is called a “pyramid of doom”. Instead, you can use the unwrapped and bound values immediately after consecutive commas:

```
if a != b,
   let c = c,
   let d = d,
   case .integerValue(let cValue) = c,
   case .integerValue(let dValue) = d,
   dValue > cValue {
  print("a and b are different") // Printed!
  print("d is greater than c") // Printed!
  print("sum: \(a + b + cValue + dValue)") // Printed: 26
}
```

So now you see that pattern matching can be combined with simple logical conditions and optional binding within a single `if` statement. Your code is looking more elegant already!

Custom tuple

In this chapter you saw how a tuple pattern could match a three-dimensional coordinate, (x, y, z). You can create a just-in-time tuple expression at the moment you're ready to match it.

Here's a tuple that does just that:

```
let name = "Bob"
let age = 23

if case ("Bob", 23) = (name, age) {
  print("Found the right Bob!") // Printed!
}
```

Here the name and age constants are combined into a tuple and are evaluated together.

Another such example involves a login form with a username and password field. The user might not fill all the fields out before clicking Submit. In this case, you'd want to show a specific error message to the user indicating which field is missing.

```
var username: String?
var password: String?

switch (username, password) {
case let (username?, password?):
  print("Success! User: \(username) Pass: \(password)")
case let (username?, nil):
  print("Password is missing. User: \(username)")
case let (nil, password?):
  print("Username is missing. Pass: \(password)")
case (nil, nil):
  print("Both username and password are missing")  // Printed!
}
```

Each case checks of one of the possible submissions. You write the success case first because if it is true, there is no need to check the rest of the cases. `switch` statements in Swift do not fall through, so if the first case condition is true, the rest of the conditions will not be evaluated.

Fun with wildcards

One fun way to use the wildcard pattern is within the definition of a `for` loop:

```
for _ in 1...3 {
  print("hi") // 3 times
}
```

This code performs its action three times. The underscore _ means that you don't care to use each value from the sequence. If you ever find yourself needing to repeat an action, this is a clean way to write the code.

Validate that an optional exists

```
let user: String? = "Bob"
guard let _ = user else {
  print("There is no user.")
  fatalError()
}
print("User exists, but identity not needed.") // Printed!
```

In this code, you check to make sure `user` has a value. You use the underscore to indicate that, right now, you don't care what value it contains.

Even though you *can* do something, doesn't mean you *should*. The best way to validate an optional where you don't care about the value is like so:

```
guard user != nil else {
  print("There is no user.")
  fatalError()
}
```

Here, `user != nil` does the same thing as `let _ = user` but the intent is clearer.

Organize an if-else-if

```
struct Rectangle {
  let width: Int
  let height: Int
  let color: String
}

let view = Rectangle(width: 15, height: 60, color: "Green")
switch view {
case _ where view.height < 50:
  print("Shorter than 50 units")
case _ where view.width > 20:
  print("Over 50 tall, & over 20 wide")
```

```
case _ where view.color == "Green":
  print("Over 50 tall, at most 20 wide, & green") // Printed!
default:
  print("This view can't be described by this example")
}
```

You could write this code as a chain of `if` statements. By using the `switch` statement, it is clear that each condition is a case. Notice that each case uses an underscore with a qualifying `where` clause.

Programming exercises

As you continue learning Swift, you may one day apply for a position where you'll get to use Swift at work. The classic company interview questions are the Fibonacci and FizzBuzz algorithms. Pattern matching can come in handy for both of these challenges.

> **Note:** These algorithms are call-intensive. If you're following along in a playground, you should start a new playground and use it for the rest of this chapter. That way the playground won't stutter under the processing load.

Fibonacci

In the Fibonacci sequence, every element is the sum of the two preceding elements. The sequence starts with 0, 1, 1, 2, 3, 5, 8 ...

Here's how you could find the 15th number of the Fibonacci sequence:

```
func fibonacci(position: Int) -> Int {
  switch position {
  // 1
  case let n where n <= 1:
    return 0
  // 2
  case 2:
    return 1
  // 3
  case let n:
    return fibonacci(position: n - 1) + fibonacci(position: n -
2)
  }
}

let fib15 = fibonacci(position: 15) // 377
```

1. If the current sequence position is less than two, the function will return `0`.
2. If the current sequence position is equal to two, the function will return `1`.
3. Otherwise, the function will use recursion to call itself and sum up all the numbers. This code is also an example of a way to avoid the `default` case in a `switch` statement. The `let n` case matches all values, so the `default` case is not needed.

FizzBuzz

In the FizzBuzz algorithm, your objective is to print the numbers from 1 to 100, except:

- On multiples of three, print `"Fizz"` instead of the number.
- On multiples of five, print `"Buzz"` instead of the number.
- On multiples of both three and five, print `"FizzBuzz"` instead of the number.

```
for i in 1...100 {
  // 1
  switch (i % 3, i % 5) {
  // 2
  case (0, 0):
    print("FizzBuzz", terminator: " ")
  case (0, _):
    print("Fizz", terminator: " ")
  case (_, 0):
    print("Buzz", terminator: " ")
  // 3
  case (_, _):
    print(i, terminator: " ")
  }
}
print("")
```

Here's what's going on:

1. You construct a tuple in the `switch` expression.
2. Each of the cases checks a result of the modulo operation. The underscore means you don't care and it matches any value.
3. In this code, you learn another equivalent way to avoid writing the `default` case of a `switch` statement. A tuple pattern with all underscores, `(_, _)`, matches any value.

The `terminator` parameter of the `print` call tells the compiler to end each line with a space character instead of a new line. All the numbers in the algorithm will get printed on one line in your debug area. The final `print("")` call adds an empty string with a new line so that the code you add in the future will start printing on a new line.

Now you know how to beat those job interview questions in a surprisingly elegant fashion using pattern matching. You can thank me later for your new Swift job!

Expression pattern

With all the pattern matching skills you've developed so far, you're finally ready to learn what's underneath the hood. The expression pattern is simple, but oh, so powerful.

In the beginning of this chapter, you saw the example tuple pattern `(x, 0, 0)`. You learned that, internally, the tuple is a comma-separated list of patterns. You also learned that the `x` is an identifier pattern, while the `0`'s are examples of the expression pattern. So the internal patterns of this tuple are (*identifier*, *expression*, *expression*).

The expression pattern compares values with the ~= pattern matching operator. The match succeeds when a comparison returns `true`. If the values are of the same type, the common == equality operator will perform the comparison instead. You've already learned how to implement `Equatable` and == for your own named types back in Chapter 16, "Protocols".

When the values aren't of the same type or the type doesn't implement the `Equatable` protocol, the ~= pattern matching operator will be used. For instance, the compiler uses the ~= operator to check whether an integer value falls within a range. The range is certainly not an integer, so the compiler cannot use the == operator. However, you can conceptualize the idea of checking whether an `Int` is within a range. That's where the ~= pattern matching operator comes in:

```
let matched = (1...10 ~= 5) // true
```

As in the definition of a case condition, the pattern is required to be on the left-hand side of the operator, and the value on the right-hand side of the operator. Here's what the equivalent case condition looks like:

```
if case 1...10 = 5 {
  print("In the range")
}
```

This `if case` statement is functionally equivalent to using the ~= operator in the previous example.

Overloading ~=

You can overload the ~= operator to provide your own custom expression matching behavior. You'll implement a pattern match between an array and an integer to check if the integer is an element of the array. A value of 2 should match the pattern `[0, 1, 2, 3]`. With the standard library, you'll get an error on this code:

```
let list = [0, 1, 2, 3]
let integer = 2

let isInArray = (list ~= integer) // Error!

if case list = integer { // Error!
  print("The integer is in the array")
} else {
  print("The integer is not in the array")
}
```

Sure, you could check if the integer is in the array like this:

```
let isInList = list.contains(integer) // true
```

But it would be nice to use pattern matching so that you could check for a match within a `switch` statement.

You can implement the missing pattern matcher with this code:

```
// 1
func ~=(pattern: [Int], value: Int) -> Bool {
  // 2
  for i in pattern {
    if i == value {
      // 3
      return true
    }
  }
  // 4
  return false
}
```

Here's what's happening:

1. The function takes an array of integers as its `pattern` parameter and an integer as its `value` parameter. The function returns a `Bool`.
2. In the implementation, a `for` loop iterates through each element in the array.
3. If the value is equal to the current array element, the function immediately returns `true` and no more code is run within the function implementation.
4. If the `for` loop finishes without any matches, then the function returns `false`.

Now that the pattern matching operator has been overloaded, the expression patterns you saw earlier now match correctly with no errors.

```
let isInArray = (list ~= integer) // true

if case list = integer {
  print("The integer is in the array") // Printed!
} else {
  print("The integer is not in the array")
}
```

You are now a pattern matching ninja! With your mastery of patterns, you're empowered to write clear and concise code that reads well.

Key points

- A pattern represents the structure of a value.
- Pattern matching can help you write more readable code than the alternative logical conditions.
- Pattern matching is the only way to extract associated values from enumeration values.

Challenges

Challenge 1

Given this code, write an `if` statement that shows an error if the user is not yet 21 years old:

```
enum FormField {
  case firstName(String)
```

```
  case lastName(String)
  case emailAddress(String)
  case age(Int)
}
let minimumAge = 21
let submittedAge = FormField.age(22)
```

Challenge 2

Given this code, find the planets with liquid water using a `for` loop:

```
enum CelestialBody {
  case star
  case planet(liquidWater: Bool)
  case comet
}

let telescopeCensus = [
  CelestialBody.star,
  CelestialBody.planet(liquidWater: false),
  CelestialBody.planet(liquidWater: true),
  CelestialBody.planet(liquidWater: true),
  CelestialBody.comet
]
```

Challenge 3

Given this code, find the albums that were released in 1974 with a `for` loop:

```
let queenAlbums = [
  ("A Night at the Opera", 1974),
  ("Sheer Heart Attack", 1974),
  ("Jazz", 1978),
  ("The Game", 1980)
]
```

Challenge 4

Given this code, write a `switch` statement that will print out whether the monument is located in the northern hemisphere, the southern hemisphere, or on the equator.

```
let coordinates = (lat: 192.89483, long: -68.887463)
```

Chapter 21: Error Handling

By Janie Clayton

All programmers, especially skilled ones, need to worry about error handling. It isn't about being a bad programmer — it's about acknowledging that you don't control everything.

In this chapter, you'll learn the fundamentals of error handling: what it is, how you implement it and when you need to worry about it.

What is error handling?

Error handling is the art of failing gracefully. You have complete control of your code, but you don't have complete control of anything outside of your code. This includes user input, network connections and any external files your app needs to access.

Imagine you're in the desert and you decide to surf the internet. You're miles away from the nearest Wi-Fi spot. You have no cellular signal. You open your internet browser. What happens? Does your browser hang there forever with a spinning wheel of death, or does it immediately alert you to the fact that you have no internet access?

These are things you need to consider when you're designing the user experience for your apps, as well as the interfaces of your classes and structs. Think about what can go wrong and how you want your app to respond to it.

First level error handling with optionals

Before you deep dive into the error handling protocols and blocks, start with the simplest error-handling mechanism possible. In programming, it's important to use the simplest solution at your disposal. There is no point in complicating things, when your problem could be solved by changing one line of code.

Failable initializers

When you attempt to initialize an object, it may fail. For example, if you're converting a `String` into an `Int` there is no guarantee it'll work.

```
let value = Int("3")            // Optional(3)
let failedValue = Int("nope") // nil
```

If you make your own raw representable enumeration type, the compiler will write a **failable initializer** for you. To see it at work, try the following:

```
enum PetFood: String {
  case kibble, canned
}

let morning = PetFood(rawValue: "kibble")  // Optional(.kibble)
let snack = PetFood(rawValue: "fuuud!")    // nil
```

As you can see, failable initializers return optionals instead of regular instances. The return value will be `nil` if initialization failed.

You can create failable initializers yourself. Try it out:

```
struct PetHouse {
  let squareFeet: Int

  init?(squareFeet: Int) {
    if squareFeet < 1 {
      return nil
    }
    self.squareFeet = squareFeet
  }
}

let tooSmall = PetHouse(squareFeet: 0) // nil
let house = PetHouse(squareFeet: 1)    // Optional(Pethouse)
```

To make a failable initializer, you simply name it `init?(...)` and return `nil` if it fails. By using a failable initializer, you can *guarantee* that your instance has the correct attributes or it will never exist.

Optional chaining

Have you ever been working with Xcode when you've gotten a prompt from the compiler that something is wrong and you are supposed to add `!` to a property? The compiler is telling you that you are dealing with an optional value and it is suggesting that you deal with this optional value by force unwrapping it.

Sometimes force unwrapping or using an implicitly unwrapped optional is just fine. If you are dealing with `@IBOutlets` in your UI, you know that those UI elements must exist after the view loads, because if they don't there is something terribly wrong with your application. In general, force unwrap or using implicitly unwrapped optionals is appropriate only when an optional *must* contain a value. In all other cases, you're asking for trouble!

```
class Pet {
  var breed: String?

  init(breed: String? = nil) {
    self.breed = breed
  }
}

class Person {
  let pet: Pet

  init(pet: Pet) {
    self.pet = pet
  }
}

let delia = Pet(breed: "pug")
let olive = Pet()

let janie = Person(pet: olive)
let dogBreed = janie.pet.breed! // This is bad! Will cause a
crash!
```

In this simple example, Olive was not given a breed. She was a rescue from the pound, so her breed is unknown. But she's still a sweetheart.

If you assume that her breed has been set and force unwrap this property, it will cause the program to crash. There's a better way of handling this situation.

```
if let dogBreed = janie.pet.breed {
  print("Olive is a \(dogBreed)")
} else {
  print("Olive's breed is unknown.")
}
```

This is pretty standard optional handling, but you can take advantage of this structure to do some pretty complex operations. This can be incredibly helpful if you have a lot of complicated data structures with many optional properties. Comment out what you have so far and start over with the following types:

```
class Toy {

  enum Kind {
    case ball
    case zombie
    case bone
    case mouse
  }

  enum Sound {
    case squeak
    case bell
  }

  let kind: Kind
  let color: String
  var sound: Sound?

  init(kind: Kind, color: String, sound: Sound? = nil) {
    self.kind = kind
    self.color = color
    self.sound = sound
  }
}

class Pet {

  enum Kind {
    case dog
    case cat
    case guineaPig
  }

  let name: String
  let kind: Kind
  let favoriteToy: Toy?

  init(name: String, kind: Kind, favoriteToy: Toy? = nil) {
    self.name = name
    self.kind = kind
```

```
    self.favoriteToy = favoriteToy
  }
}

class Person {
  let pet: Pet?

  init(pet: Pet? = nil) {
    self.pet = pet
  }
}
```

A lot of raywenderlich.com team members own pets — but not all. Some pets have a favorite toy and others don't. Even further into this, some of these toys make noise and others don't.

For example, Tammy Coron has an evil cat that is plotting to kill her.

This cat's favorite toy to chew on (besides Tammy) is a catnip mouse. This toy doesn't make any noise.

Ray has another team member, Felipe Marsetti, who lives in a condo and isn't allowed to have pets.

```
let janie = Person(pet: Pet(name: "Delia", kind: .dog,
favoriteToy: Toy(kind: .ball, color: "Purple", sound: .bell)))
let tammy = Person(pet: Pet(name: "Evil Cat Overlord",
kind: .cat, favoriteToy: Toy(kind: .mouse, color: "Orange")))
let felipe = Person()
```

You want to check to see if any of the team members has a pet with a favorite toy that makes a sound. You can use **optional chaining** for this; it's a quick way to walk through a chain of optionals by adding a `?` after every property or method that can return `nil`. If any of the values in the chain was `nil`, the result will be `nil` as well. So instead of having to test every optional along the chain, you simply test the result!

For example:

```
if let sound = janie.pet?.favoriteToy?.sound {
  print("Sound \(sound)")
} else {
  print("No sound.")
}
```

Janie's pet fulfills all of the conditions and therefore the sound can be accessed.

Try accessing the sound with Tammy and Felipe:

```
if let sound = tammy.pet?.favoriteToy?.sound {
  print("Sound \(sound)")
} else {
  print("No sound.")
}

if let sound = felipe.pet?.favoriteToy?.sound {
  print("Sound \(sound)")
} else {
  print("No sound.")
}
```

During each stage of this chain, the compiler checks whether or not each optional property is present. Since Tammy's cat's toy does not have a sound, the process bails out after `favoriteToy?`. Since Felipe doesn't have a pet at all, the process bails out after `pet?`.

This is an awful lot of repetitive code. What if you wanted to iterate through the entire array of team members to find this information?

Map and flatMap

Let's say you want to create an array of pets that are owned by the team. First off, you need to create an array of team members:

```
let team = [janie, tammy, felipe]
```

You want to iterate through this array and extract all pet names. You could use a `for` loop, but you've already learned a better way to do this: `map`.

```
let petNames = team.map { $0.pet?.name }
```

This creates a new array of pet names by pulling out the pet name from each team member in the array. You want to see what these values are, so why not print them out?

```
for pet in petNames {
  print(pet)
}
```

The compiler generates a warning. Look at the output for this `print` statement:

```
Optional("Delia")
Optional("Evil Cat Overlord")
nil
```

Ew! That doesn't look right. Instead of having a nice list of names, you have a bunch of optional values and even a `nil`! This won't do at all.

You could take this array, filter it and then call `map` again to unwrap all the values that are not `nil`, but that seems rather convoluted. Iterating through an array of optional values that you need to unwrap and ensure are not `nil` is a very common operation.

There is a better way to accomplish this task: `flatMap`. Try out the following:

```
let betterPetNames = team.flatMap { $0.pet?.name }

for pet in betterPetNames {
  print(pet)
}
```

You should see a far more useful and user friendly output:

```
Delia
Evil Cat Overlord
```

In general, `flatMap` does a regular `map` operation and then "flattens", or simplifies, the results. In this case, you're using `flatMap` to flatten the return type `[Optional<String>]` into the simpler type `[String]`. Another common use of `flatMap` is to turn an array of arrays into a single array.

So far you have learned how to do some informal error handling. Up next, you'll learn about the `Error` protocol to do some formal error handling.

Error protocol

Swift includes the `Error` protocol, which forms the basis of the error-handling architecture. Any type that conforms to this protocol can be used to represent errors.

The `Error` protocol can be implemented by any type you define, but it's especially well-suited to enumerations. As you learned in Chapter 15, enumerations are types with a fixed set of instances. This is ideal for representing specific error types.

Create a new playground. You are going to start your own bakery and use it to learn how to throw and handle errors using the `Error` protocol.

Add this code to your playground:

```
class Pastry {
  let flavor: String
  var numberOnHand: Int

  init(flavor: String, numberOnHand: Int) {
    self.flavor = flavor
    self.numberOnHand = numberOnHand
  }
}

enum BakeryError: Error {
  case tooFew(numberOnHand: Int)
  case doNotSell
  case wrongFlavor
}
```

The `Error` protocol tells the compiler that this enumeration can be used to represent errors that can be thrown. At a bakery, you might not have enough of each item the customer wants, or it could be the wrong flavor, or you may not sell it altogether.

Throwing errors

This is kind of cool, but what does your program do with these errors? It throws them, of course! That's the actual terminology you'll see: **throwing** errors, and then **catching** them.

Add this class to your playground:

```
class Bakery {
  var itemsForSale = [
    "Cookie": Pastry(flavor: "ChocolateChip", numberOnHand: 20),
    "PopTart": Pastry(flavor: "WildBerry", numberOnHand: 13),
    "Donut" : Pastry(flavor: "Sprinkles", numberOnHand: 24),
    "HandPie": Pastry(flavor: "Cherry", numberOnHand: 6)
  ]

  func orderPastry(item: String,
                   amountRequested: Int,
                   flavor: String)  throws  -> Int {
    guard let pastry = itemsForSale[item] else {
      throw BakeryError.doNotSell
    }
    guard flavor == pastry.flavor else {
      throw BakeryError.wrongFlavor
    }
    guard amountRequested <= pastry.numberOnHand else {
      throw BakeryError.tooFew(numberOnHand:
pastry.numberOnHand)
    }
    pastry.numberOnHand -= amountRequested

    return pastry.numberOnHand
  }
}
```

First off you need to have some items to sell. Each item needs to have a flavor and an amount on hand. When the customer orders a pastry from you, they need to tell you what pastry they want, what flavor they want, and how many they want. Customers can be incredibly demanding. :]

First, you need to check if you even carry what the customer wants. If the customer tries to order albatross with wafers, you don't want the bakery to crash. After you verify that the bakery actually carries the item the customer wants, you need to check if you have the requested flavor and if you have enough of that item to fulfill the customer's order.

As this example shows, you throw errors using `throw`. The errors you throw must be instances of a type that conforms to `Error`. A function (or method) that throws errors and does not immediately handle them must make this clear by adding `throws` to its declaration.

Next, try out your bakery:

```
let bakery = Bakery()
bakery.orderPastry(item: "Albatross",
                   amountRequested: 1,
                   flavor: "AlbatrossFlavor")
```

The code above does not compile. What's wrong? Oh right — you need to catch the error and do something with it.

Handling errors

After your program throws an error, you need to handle that error. There are two ways to approach this problem: You can handle your errors immediately, or you can bubble them up to another level.

To choose your approach, you need to think about where it makes the most sense to handle the error. If it makes sense to handle the error immediately, then do so. If you're in a situation where you have to alert the user and have her take action, but you're several function calls away from a user interface element, then it makes sense to bubble up the error until you reach the point where you can alert the user.

It's entirely up to you when to handle the error, but *not* handling it isn't an option. Swift requires you to handle your error at some point in the chain, or your program won't compile.

Replace the previous line of code with this:

```
do {
    try bakery.orderPastry(item: "Albatross",
                           amountRequested: 1,
                           flavor: "AlbatrossFlavor")
} catch BakeryError.doNotSell {
  print("Sorry, but we don't sell this item")
} catch BakeryError.wrongFlavor {
  print("Sorry, but we don't carry this flavor")
} catch BakeryError.tooFew {
  print("Sorry, we don't have enough items to fulfill your
order")
}
```

Code that can throw errors must always be inside a **do** block which creates a new scope. Even more, the exact points where errors can be thrown must be marked with **try**. The `try` above doesn't actually do anything. It serves as a reminder so that whoever reads your code can easily understand what can go wrong.

You're now catching each error condition and providing useful feedback to the user about why you can't fulfill their order.

Not looking at the detailed error

If you don't really care about the details of the error you can use `try?` to wrap the result of a function (or method) in an optional. The function will then return `nil` instead of throwing an error. No need to setup a `do {} catch {}` block. For example:

```
let remaining = try? bakery.orderPastry(item: "Albatross",
                                        amountRequested: 1,
                                        flavor:
"AlbatrossFlavor")
```

This is nice and short to write, but the downside is that you don't get any details if the request fails.

Stoping your program on an error

Sometimes you know for sure that your code is not going to fail. For example, if know you just restocked the cookie jar, you know you will be able to order a cookie. Add:

```
do {
  try bakery.orderPastry(item: "Cookie",
                         amountRequested: 1,
                         flavor: "ChocolateChip")
}
catch {
  fatalError()
}
```

Swift gives you a short way to write the same thing:

```
try! bakery.orderPastry(item: "Cookie", amountRequested: 1,
flavor: "ChocolateChip")
```

It's delicious syntactic sugar, but know that your program will halt if the no error assumption is violated. So, just as with implicitly unwrapped optionals, you need to be extra careful when using `try!`.

Advanced error handling

Cool, you know how to handle errors! That's neat, but how do you scale your error handling to the larger context of a complex app?

PugBot

The sample project you'll work with in this second half of the chapter is **PugBot**. The PugBot is cute and friendly, but sometimes it gets lost and confused. As the programmer of the PugBot, it's your responsibility to make sure it doesn't get lost on the way home from your PugBot lab.

You'll learn how to make sure your PugBot finds its way home by throwing an error if it steers off course.

First, you need to set up an enum containing all of the directions in which your `PugBot` will move:

```
enum Direction {
  case left
  case right
  case forward
}
```

You'll also need an error type to indicate what can go wrong:

```
enum PugBotError: Error {
  case invalidMove(found: Direction, expected: Direction)
  case endOfPath
}
```

Here, associated values are used to further explain what went wrong. With any luck, you'll be able to use these to rescue a lost `PugBot`!

Last but not least, create your PugBot class:

```
class PugBot {
  let name: String
  let correctPath: [Direction]
  private var currentStepInPath = 0

  init(name: String, correctPath: [Direction]) {
    self.correctPath = correctPath
    self.name = name
  }

  func turnLeft() throws {
    guard currentStepInPath < correctPath.count else {
      throw PugBotError.endOfPath
    }
    let nextDirection = correctPath[currentStepInPath]
    guard nextDirection == .left else {
      throw PugBotError.invalidMove(found: .left,
                                    expected: nextDirection)
    }
    currentStepInPath += 1
  }

  func turnRight() throws {
    guard currentStepInPath < correctPath.count else {
      throw PugBotError.endOfPath
    }
    let nextDirection = correctPath[currentStepInPath]
    guard nextDirection == .right else {
      throw PugBotError.invalidMove(found: .right,
                                    expected: nextDirection)
    }
    currentStepInPath += 1
  }
```

```
  func moveForward() throws {
    guard currentStepInPath < correctPath.count else {
      throw PugBotError.endOfPath
    }
    let nextDirection = correctPath[currentStepInPath]
    guard nextDirection == .forward else {
      throw PugBotError.invalidMove(found: .forward,
                                    expected: nextDirection)
    }
    currentStepInPath += 1
  }

  func reset() {
    currentStepInPath = 0
  }
}
```

When creating a PugBot, you tell it how to get home by passing it the correct directions. The three movement methods cause the PugBot to move. If at any point the program notices the PugBot isn't doing what it's supposed to do, it throws an error.

Give your PugBot a test:

```
let pug = PugBot(name: "Pug",
                 correctPath:
[.forward, .left, .forward, .right])

func goHome() throws {
  try pug.moveForward()
  try pug.turnLeft()
  try pug.moveForward()
  try pug.turnRight()
}

do {
  try goHome()
} catch {
  print("PugBot failed to get home.")
}
```

Every single command in goHome must pass for the method to complete successfully. The moment an error is thrown, your PugBot will stop trying to get home and will stay put until you come and rescue it.

Handling multiple errors

Since you're a smart developer, you've noticed that you're not handling errors in goHome. Instead, you've marked that function with throws as well, leaving the error handling up to the caller of the function.

You might benefit from a function that can move the PugBot and handle errors at the same time, so you don't have to handle errors every time you move the PugBot.

```
func moveSafely(_ movement: () throws -> ()) -> String {
  do {
    try movement()
    return "Completed operation successfully."
  } catch PugBotError.invalidMove(let found, let expected) {
    return "The PugBot was supposed to move \(expected), but
moved \(found) instead."
  } catch PugBotError.endOfPath {
    return "The PugBot tried to move past the end of the path."
  } catch {
    return "An unknown error occurred"
  }
}
```

This function takes a movement function (like goHome) or a closure containing movement function calls as a parameter, calls it and handles any errors that might be thrown.

You might notice that you have to add a default case at the end. What gives? You've exhausted the cases in your PugBotError enum, so why is the compiler hassling you?

Unfortunately, at this point, Swift's do-try-catch system isn't type-specific. There's no way to tell the compiler that it should only expect PugBotErrors. To the compiler, that isn't exhaustive, because it doesn't handle each and every possible error that it knows about, so you still need to have a default case.

Now you can use your function to handle movement in a safe manner:

```
pug.reset()
moveSafely(goHome)

pug.reset()
moveSafely {
  try pug.moveForward()
  try pug.turnLeft()
  try pug.moveForward()
  try pug.turnRight()
}
```

Thanks to trailing closure syntax, your movement calls are cleanly wrapped in the call to moveSafely(_:). Here, your PugBot will find her way home safely.

Rethrows

A function that takes a throwing closure as a parameter has to make a choice: either catch every error, or be a throwing function itself.

Let's say you want a utility function to perform a certain movement, or set of movements, several times in a row. You could define this function as follows:

```
func perform(times: Int, movement: () throws -> ()) rethrows {
  for _ in 1...times {
    try movement()
  }
}
```

Notice the `rethrows` here. This function does not handle errors like `moveSafely`, but instead leaves the error handling up to the caller of the function, like `goHome`. By using `rethrows` instead of `throws`, this function indicates that it will only rethrow errors thrown by the function passed into it, but never errors of its own.

Key points

- A type can conform to the **Error** protocol to work with Swift's error-handling system.
- Any function that can throw an error, or calls a function that can throw an error, has to be marked with **throws** or **rethrows**.
- When calling an error-throwing function, you must embed the function call in a **`do`** block. Within that block, you **`try`** the function, and if it fails, you **`catch`** the error.

Where to go from here?

Handling errors is a necessary part of programming. You never know when things will go wrong, and it's important to make sure that the end users of your app — as well as anyone else using your code — have a great, error-handled experience!

With `try` and `throws` and other language features, Swift makes it very explicit where things can go wrong. It's up to you now to *try* writing error-free code, but to keep in mind where failures can happen and make sure you signal those problems when they occur.

Challenges

Challenge 1

`CGAffineTransform` is a transform type used by Core Graphics to scale and rotate graphical elements. You can obtain an inverse transform by calling the `inverted()` method.

Just as dividing by zero will fail, inverting a singular transform can fail. When this happens, `CGAffineTransform` does nothing to warn you except print a message to the console. You can do better.

The following code checks whether a transform can be inverted or will fail:

```
extension CGAffineTransform {
  var isInvertable: Bool {
     return abs(a*d - b*c) > CGFloat.ulpOfOne
   }
 }

CGAffineTransform().isInvertable  // false
CGAffineTransform.identity.isInvertable // true
```

Use the following code to make viewing transforms easy:

```
extension CGAffineTransform: CustomStringConvertible {
  public var description: String {
    return [a,b,c,d,tx,ty].reduce("") { $0 + " \($1)" }
  }
}
```

Write a method on `CGAffineTransform` named `safeInverted()` that returns an optional type. If the transform can be inverted it returns the new transform. Otherwise it returns `nil`.

Test your method with `let scaleByTwo = CGAffineTransform.identity.scaledBy(x: 2, y: 2)` and observe the values you get back.

Challenge 2

Use optional chaning to safely invert the transform and then invert it again. Much like taking the reciprocal of the same number, you should wind up with the same number.

Challenge 3

Change your design to throw `MathError.singular` if the transform can't be inverted. Name this new method `checkedInverted()` so it can co-exist nicely with your `safeInverted()` method. Test it out.

Challenge 4

Note the return types of `safeInverted()` and `checkedInverted()`. How do they differ?

Chapter 22: Encoding and Decoding Types

By Eli Ganim

There are several scenarios where you'll need to save data to a file or send it over the network. In this chapter, you'll learn how to achieve these tasks by converting your instances to another representation, like a string or a stream of bytes. This process is called encoding, also known as **serialization**.

The reverse process of turning the data into an instance is called decoding, or **deserialization**.

Imagine you have an instance you want to write to a file. The instance itself cannot be written as-is to the file, so you need to encode it into another representation, such as a stream of bytes:

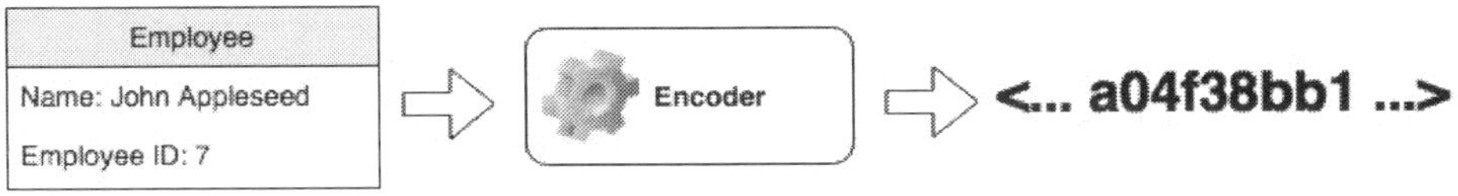

Once the data is encoded and saved to a file, you can turn it back into an instance whenever you want by using a decoder:

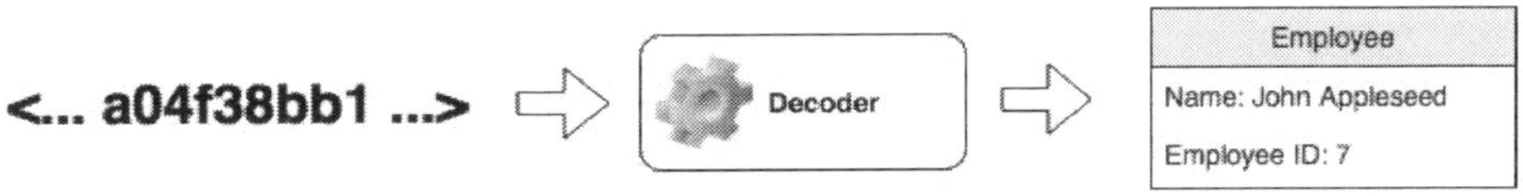

Encodable and Decodable protocols

The `Encodable` protocol is used by types that can be encoded to another representation. It declares a single method:

```
func encode(to: Encoder) throws
```

...which the compiler generates for you if all the stored properties of that type conform to `Encodable` as well. You'll learn more about this later on in the chapter.

The `Decodable` protocol is used by types that can be decoded. It declares just a single initializer:

```
init(from decoder: Decoder) throws
```

You will know when and how to implement these methods by the end of this chapter.

What is Codable?

`Codable` is a protocol that a type can conform to, to declare that it can be encoded and decoded. It's basically an alias for the `Encodable` and `Decodable` protocols.

```
typealias Codable = Encodable & Decodable
```

Automatic encoding and decoding

There are many types in Swift which are codable out of the box: `Int`, `String`, `Date`, `Array` and many other types from the Standard Library and the Foundation framework. If you want your type to be codable, the simplest way to do it is by conforming to `Codable` and making sure all its stored properties are also codable.

For example, let's say you own a toy factory and you have this struct to store employee data:

```
struct Employee {
    var name: String
    var id: Int
}
```

All you need to do to be able to encode and decode this type is to conform to the `Codable` protocol, like so:

```
struct Employee: Codable {
    var name: String
    var id: Int
}
```

Wow, that was easy. You were able to do it because both `name` (`String`) and `id` (`Int`) are codable.

This works well when you're only using types that are already `Codable`. But what if your type includes other custom types as properties? For example, looking at your `Employee` struct, assume that it also has a `favoriteToy` property:

```
struct Employee: Codable {
    var name: String
    var id: Int
    var favoriteToy: Toy
}

struct Toy: Codable {
    var name: String
}
```

By making sure `Toy` also conforms to `Codable`, you maintain the overall conformance to `Codable` for `Employee` as well.

All collections types, like `Array` and `Dictionary` are also codable if they contain codable types.

Encoding and decoding custom types

There are several representations you can encode to or decode from, such as XML or a Property List. In this section, you'll learn how to encode to and decode from JSON, by using Swift's `JSONEncoder` and `JSONDecoder` classes.

JSON stands for JavaScript Object Notation, and is one of the most popular ways to serialize data. It's easily readable by humans and easy for computers to parse and generate.

For example, if you were to encode an instance of type `Employee` to JSON, it might look something like this:

```
{ "name": "John Appleseed", "id": 7 }
```

You can easily understand how the `Employee` instance looked before it was serialized into JSON.

JSONEncoder and JSONDecoder

Once you have a codable type, you can use `JSONEncoder` to convert your type to `Data` which can be either written to a file or sent over the network. Assume you have this employee instance:

```
let toy1 = Toy(name: "Teddy Bear");
let employee1 = Employee(name: "John Appleseed", id: 7,
favoriteToy: toy1)
```

John's birthday is coming up and you want to give him his favorite toy as a gift. You need to send over this data to the Gifts department. Before you can do that, you need to encode it like this:

```
let jsonEncoder = JSONEncoder()
let jsonData = try jsonEncoder.encode(employee1)
```

You'll notice that you need to use `try` because `encode(_:)` might fail and throw an error.

If you try to print `jsonData` like this:

```
print(jsonData)
```

You'll see that Xcode omits the data and only provides the number of bytes in `jsonData`. This is fine, because `jsonData` contains an unreadable representation of `employee1`. If you would like to create a readable version of this JSON as a string, you can use `String`'s initializer:

```
let jsonString = String(data: jsonData, encoding: .utf8)
print(jsonString)
// {"name":"John Appleseed","id":7,"favoriteToy":{"name":"Teddy
Bear"}}
```

Now you can send `jsonData` or `jsonString` over to the gifts department using their special gift API.

If you want to decode the JSON data back into an instance, you need to use `JSONDecoder`:

```
let jsonDecoder = JSONDecoder()
let employee2 = try jsonDecoder.decode(Employee.self, from:
jsonData)
```

Note that you need to tell the decoder what type to decode the JSON to, because the compiler can't figure this out on its own.

Renaming properties with CodingKeys

It turns out that the gifts department API requires that the employee ID appear as `employeeId` instead of `id`. Luckily, Swift provides a solution to this kind of problem.

CodingKey protocol, CodingKeys enum

The `CodingKeys` enum, which conforms to `CodingKey` protocol, lets you rename specific properties in case the serialized format doesn't match the requirements of the API.

Add the nested enumeration `CodingKeys` like this:

```
struct Employee: Codable {
  var name: String
  var id: Int
  var favoriteToy: Toy

  enum CodingKeys: String, CodingKey {
    case id = "employeeId"
    case name
    case favoriteToy
  }
}
```

There are several things to note here:

1. `CodingKeys` is a nested enumeration in your type.
2. It has to conform to `CodingKey`.
3. You also need `String` as the raw type, since the keys are always strings.
4. You have to include all properties in the enumeration, even if you don't plan to rename them.
5. By default, this enumeration is created by the compiler, but when you need to rename a key you need to implement it yourself.

Now if you print the JSON, you'll see that the stored property `id` key has changed to `employeeId`.

```
{ "employeeId": 7, "name": "John Appleseed", "favoriteToy":
{"name":"Teddy Bear"}}
```


Manual encoding and decoding

You try to send the data over to the gifts department, and again the data gets rejected. This time they claim that the information of the gift you want to send to the employee should not be inside a nested type, but rather as a property called `gift`. So the JSON should actually look like this:


```
{ "employeeId": 7, "name": "John Appleseed", "gift": "Teddy
Bear" }
```


In this case you can't use `CodingKeys`, since you need to alter the structure of the JSON and not just rename properties. You need to write your own encoding and decoding logic.

The encode function

As mentioned earlier in the chapter, `Codable` is actually just a typealias for the `Encodable` and `Decodable` protocols. You need to implement `encode(to: Encoder)` and describe how to encode each property.

It might sound complicated, but it's pretty simple. First, update `CodingKeys` to use the key `gift` instead of `favoriteToy`:

```
enum CodingKeys: String, CodingKey {
  case id = "employeeId"
  case name
  case gift
}
```

Then, you need to remove `Employee`'s conformance to `Codable` and then add this extension:

```
extension Employee: Encodable {
  func encode(to encoder: Encoder) throws {
    var container = encoder.container(keyedBy: CodingKeys.self)
    try container.encode(name, forKey: .name)
    try container.encode(id, forKey: .id)
    try container.encode(favoriteToy.name, forKey: .gift)
  }
}
```

First you get back the `container` of the encoder. This is a view into the storage of the encoder that you can access with keys. Note how you choose which properties to encode for which keys. Importantly, you flatten `favoriteToy.name` down to the `.gift` key.

If you stop now, you should get an error that says:

```
'Employee' does not conform to expected type 'Decodable'
```

This is because you removed the conformance to `Codable` and only added conformance to `Encodable`. For now you can comment out the code that decodes `jsonString` to `employee2`.

If you print `jsonString` once more, this is what you'll get:

```
{"name":"John Appleseed","gift":"Teddy Bear","employeeId":7}
```

Success!

The decode function

Once the data arrives at the gifts department, they need to be able to convert this JSON back to an instance in their system. For this they'll need a decoder.

Add the following code to your playground to make `Employee` conform to `Decodable` (and thus also `Codable`):

```
extension Employee: Decodable {
  init(from decoder: Decoder) throws {
    let values = try decoder.container(keyedBy: CodingKeys.self)
    name = try values.decode(String.self, forKey: .name)
    id = try values.decode(Int.self, forKey: .id)
    let gift = try values.decode(String.self, forKey: .gift)
    favoriteToy = Toy(name: gift)
  }
}
```

Here you're pretty much doing the opposite of what you did in the `encode` method using the decoder's keyed storage container.

Key points

- You need to encode (or **serialize**) an instance before you can save it to a file or send it over the web.

- Your type should conform to the `Codable` protocol to make it codable. If all properties are codable, then the type is automatically codable as well.
- JSON is the most common encoding in modern applications and web services, and you can use `JSONEncoder` and `JSONDecoder` to encode and decode your types to and from JSON.

Where to go from here?

You can now use your new skills to serialize all your types and send them over the network to the world. In the next chapters, you'll cover more advanced topics like memory management and protocol-oriented programming.

Challenges

1. Given the structures below:

```
struct Spaceship {
  var name: String
  var crew: [Spaceman]
}

struct Spaceman {
  var name: String
  var race: String
}
```

Make the necessary modifications to make `Spaceship` codable.

2. It appears that the spaceship's interface is different than that of the outpost on Mars. The Mars outpost expects to get the spaceship's name as **spaceship_name**. Make the necessary modifications so encoding the structure would return the JSON in the correct format.

3. You received a transmission from planet Earth about a new spaceship. This is the incoming message:

```
{"spaceship_name":"USS Enterprise", "captain":{"name":"Spock",
"race":"Human"}, "officer":{"name": "Worf", "race":"Klingon"}}
```

Write a custom decoder to convert this JSON into a `Spaceship`. Note that in your type there are no ranks, just an array of crewmen. This means you'll need to use different keys for encoding and decoding.

Chapter 23: Asynchronous Closures and Memory Management

By Cosmin Pupăză

You've learned the basics of memory management in Chapter 14, "Advanced Classes", where you explored the class lifecycle and **automatic reference counting** or ARC. In most cases, memory management works out of the box in Swift and you don't have to worry about it.

However, there are certain cases when ARC can't infer what the proper relationships is between objects and you need to tell it. In this chapter, you'll revisit the concept of **reference cycles** and learn how to resolve them for classes and closures. You will also learn to manage asynchronous code with **Grand Central Dispatch** and use **capture lists** in closures to capture values from the enclosing scope.

Before you start breaking reference cycles, it's very important to understand how they are created.

Reference cycles for classes

Two class instances which hold a **strong reference** to each other create a **strong reference cycle** that leads to a **memory leak**. That's because each instance keeps the other one alive, so their reference counts never reach zero.

For example, our website has a lot of high quality programming tutorials and each of them is edited by a specific editor. You can model these tutorials with the following class:

```
class Tutorial {
  let title: String
  var editor: Editor?

  init(title: String) {
```

```
    self.title = title
  }

  deinit {
    print("Goodbye Tutorial \(title)!")
  }
}
```

In addition to a title propery, a tutorial might have a editor so it is marked optional. You might have additional properties such as creation date, category, body text and so on, but leave them out for this example to keep things simple. Remember from Chapter 14, "Advanced Classes", that Swift calls the **deinitializer** automatically right before it releases the object from memory and its reference count becomes zero.

You've defined an editor for each tutorial, but you haven't declared the `Editor` class yet. Here's what it looks like:

```
class Editor {
  let name: String
  var tutorials: [Tutorial] = []

  init(name: String) {
    self.name = name
  }

  deinit {
    print("Goodbye Author \(name)!")
  }
}
```

Each editor has a name and a list of tutorials they have edited. The `tutorials` property is an array so you can add to it.

Now define a brand new tutorial for publishing and an editor to bring it up to the site's high quality standards:

```
do {
  let tutorial: Tutorial = Tutorial(title: "Memory management")
  let editor: Editor = Editor(name: "Ray")
}
```

These are placed in a scope (created with `do {}`) so that as soon as they go out of scope they are deallocated. Everything is working fine. But what happens if you replace with code that makes a relationship between the two objects as so:

```
do {
  let tutorial: Tutorial = Tutorial(title: "Memory management")
  let editor: Editor = Editor(name: "Ray")
```

```
    tutorial.editor = editor
    editor.tutorials.append(tutorial)
  }
```

Although both objects go out of scope, deinitializers never get called and nothing gets printed to the console — bummer! That's because you've just created a reference cycle between the tutorial and its corresponding editor. You don't actually release the objects from memory, even though you don't need them anymore.

Now that you understand how reference cycles happen, it's time to break them. Weak references to the rescue!

Weak references

Weak references don't play any part in the **reference count** of a certain object. You declare them as optionals, so they become `nil` once the reference count reaches zero.

A tutorial doesn't always have an editor assigned, so it makes perfect sense to model it as a weak reference. Change the property's declaration in the `Tutorial` class to the following:

```
weak var editor: Editor?
```

You break the reference cycle with the `weak` keyword; both deinitializers run and print the following output to the console now:

```
Goodbye Tutorial Memory management!
Goodbye Editor Ray!
```

> **Note**: You can't define a weak reference as a constant because it will be set to `nil` at some point during runtime. If fact, if you clear the `tutorials` array from an editor the reference in the tutorial automatically becomes `nil`. Very cool!

There's one more way to break reference cycles between class instances: unowned references.

Unowned references

Unowned references behave much like weak ones: they don't increase the object's reference count. However, unlike weak references, they **always** expect to have a value — you can't declare them as optionals. It doesn't makes sense for a tutorial to exist without an author.

Modify the `Tutorial` class as shown below:

```
class Tutorial {
  let title: String
  let author: Author
  weak var editor: Editor?

  init(title: String, author: Author) {
    self.title = title
    self.author = author
  }
  deinit {
    print("Goodbye Author \(title)!")
  }
}
```

Add the following `Author` class as well:

```
class Author {
  let name: String
  var tutorials: [Tutorial] = []

  init(name: String) {
    self.name = name
  }

  deinit {
    print("Goodbye Author \(name)!")
  }
}
```

This *guarantees* that tutorials always have an author. Because of that, it is not declared as optional. On the other hand, an authors `tutorials` is a variable so that it can be added to after initialization.

There is still an error in your code however. The previously created tutorial doesn't yet have an author, so modify its declaration as follows:

```
do {
  let author = Author(name: "Cosmin")
  let tutorial = Tutorial(title: "Memory management", author:
author)
  author.tutorials.append(author)
}
```

Only the editor is released instead of all of the objects. You've just created another another reference cycle, this time between the tutorial and its corresponding author.

Each tutorial on the website has an author. There are no anonymous authors here! The tutorial's `author` property is the perfect match for an unowned reference since it's never `nil`. Change the property's declaration in the `Tutorial` class to the following:

```
class Tutorial {
  unowned let author: Author
  // original code
}
```

You break the reference cycle with the `unowned` keyword and all the `deinit` methods run and print the following output to the console now:

```
Goodbye Author Cosmin!
Goodbye Tutorial Memory management!
Goodbye Editor Ray!
```

That's it for reference cycles for classes. Time to move on to reference cycles with closures.

Reference cycles for closures

You've learned in Chapter 8, "Collection Iteration with Closures" that closures capture values from the enclosing scope. You create a reference cycle if you assign a closure which captures a class instance to a property, since closures are reference types under the hood.

For example, add a property that computes the tutorial's description to the `Tutorial` class like this:

```
lazy var createDescription: () -> String = {
  return "\(self.title) by \(self.author.name)"
}
```

Recall from Chapter 11, "Properties" that you define a **lazy property** to ensure you don't assign it until you use it for the very first time, and that `self` is only available after initialization.

Now print the tutorial's description to the console. Add the following code right after the `tutorial` object's declaration:

```
print(tutorial.createDescription())
```

You've created another strong reference cycle between the tutorial object and the closure by capturing `self`, so only the author's `deinit` method runs. In order to break it, you need to know a thing or two about capture lists.

> **Note:** Swift requires you use `self` inside closures, as a reminder that a reference to the current object is being captured. The only exception to this rule is in the case of **non escaping** closures, which you'll learn about just a bit later.

Capture lists

A **capture list** is an array of variables which are captured by a closure. You use the `in` keyword to separate the variables between square brackets from the rest of the closure's body. If the closure has both a parameter list and a capture list, the capture list comes first.

Consider the following code snippet:

```
var counter = 0
var closure = { print(counter) }
counter = 1
closure()
```

The closure prints the `counter` variable's updated value, as expected, because the closure captured a reference to the `counter` variable.

If you want to show the original value instead, define a capture list for the closure.

```
counter = 0
closure = { [counter] in print(counter) }
counter = 1
closure()
```

The closure will now copy the value of `counter` into a new local constant with the same name. As a result, the original value `0` is printed.

When dealing with objects, remember that "constant" has a different meaning for reference types. With reference types, a capture list will cause the closure to capture and store the current *reference* stored inside the captured variable. Changes made to the object through this reference will still be visible outside of the closure.

Now that you understand how capture lists work, it's time to see how you can use them to break reference cycles for closures.

Unowned self

The closure which determines the tutorial's description captures a strong reference of `self` and creates a reference cycle. Since the closure doesn't exist after you release the `tutorial` object from memory, `self` will never be `nil` so you can change the strong reference to an unowned one using a capture list.

```
lazy var createDescription: () -> String = {
  [unowned self] in
  return "\(self.title) by \(self.author.name)"
}
```

This breaks the reference cycle. All the `deinit` methods work as before and output the following to the console:

```
Memory management by Cosmin
Goodbye Editor Ray!
Goodbye Author Cosmin!
Goodbye Tutorial Memory management!
```

Asynchronous code uses closures to do work and another source of reference cycle creation. Time to look at those next.

Handling asynchronous closures

Modern operating environments are **multi-threaded**. This means work can happen simultaneously on multiple **threads of execution**. For example, all networking operations execute in a background thread so they don't block the user interface that happens on the main thread. In practice, working in multi-threaded environments can be very tricky. For example, just as one thread is writing some data, another thread might be trying to read it and get a half-baked value, but only very occasionally, making it very difficult to diagnose.

In order to avoid **race conditions** like this, **synchronization** becomes necessary. Although Swift does not yet have a native concurrency model, you can use a framework called **Grand Central Dispatch** or GCD to simplify many of these issues. GCD is an abstraction on top of threads that makes doing background work less error-prone.

> **Note:** Swift initialization of global data and reference counting are **thread safe** so you don't need to worry about those fundamental things.

Since GCD lets you pass around closures, and those closures may contain references to objects, you need to be aware of what is getting passed around so as not to create unintended cycles. The ownership principles discussed earlier work *exactly the same* as with synchronous code. The danger comes that since the order of completion changes from run to run, you need to be extra careful not to access an unowned reference that may have disappeared.

GCD

Instead of exposing raw threads to you, GCD provides the concept of a **work queue**. You put work on a queue using a closure and that closure in its body can in turn dispatch work onto another GCD queue. If a queue is **serial** it performs closures on it sequentially. If a queue is **concurrent** it can dispatch multiple closures at the same time. GCD queues are thread safe — you can add closures to a queue from any other queue.

You'll create a dispatch function `execute` which runs a closure on the background queue to perform a lengthy calculation and then passes the result to a closure on the main queue when it completes. The data is copied, not shared, to avoid data race conditions.

First of all, define some functions you'll need:

```
func log(message: String) {
  let thread = Thread.current.isMainThread ? "Main"
               : "Background"
  print("\(thread) thread: \(message)")
}

func addNumbers(upTo range: Int) -> Int {
  log(message: "Adding numbers...")
  return (1...range).reduce(0, +)
}
```

`log(message:)` uses the ternary operator to checks if the current thread is either the main or the background queue and logs a message to the console accordingly.

`addNumbers(upTo:)` calculates the sum of a given range of numbers. You'll use this to represent a complicated task that must be run on a background thread.

To run tasks on a background queue, you first need to create a queue:

```
let queue = DispatchQueue(label: "queue")
```

Here you created a **serial queue**, where tasks execute one at a time in **FIFO** (first in first out) order. If you defined a **concurrent queue** you'd have to deal with all of the issues of concurrency, which is beyond the scope of this book. Work dispatched from a specific serial queue doesn't need to know about simultaneous interference from another closure on the same serial queue. Concurrent queues and sharing common data between queues is another story and does require consideration.

Next, create a method like so:

```
// 1
func execute<Result>(backgroundWork: @escaping () -> Result,
                     mainWork: @escaping (Result) -> ()) {
  // 2
```

```
    queue.async {
      let result = backgroundWork()
      // 3
      DispatchQueue.main.async {
        mainWork(result)
      }
    }
  }
```

There's quite a lot going on here, so take it in steps:

1. You make the function generic because the `backgroundWork` closure returns a generic result while the `mainWork` closure works with that result. You mark both closures with the `@escaping` attribute because they **escape** the function: you use them asynchronously, so they get called after the function returns. Closures are non-escaping by default. Non-escaping means that when the function using the closure returns it will never be used again.
2. You run the `backgroundWork` closure asynchronously on the serial queue previously defined and store its return value.
3. You dispatch the `mainWork` closure asynchronously on the main queue and you use the `backgroundWork` closure's result as its argument.

You can't run asynchronous code in a playground out of the box; you must enable the playground's **asynchronous mode** first:

```
PlaygroundPage.current.needsIndefiniteExecution = true
```

You'll also need to import the `PlaygroundSupport` framework to work with the `PlaygroundPage` class.

Time to see your new method in action:

```
execute(backgroundWork: { addNumbers(upTo: 100) },
        mainWork:       { log(message: "The sum is \($0)") })
```

Here you add the numbers on the background thread and print the result to the console on the main thread. This outputs the following:

```
Background thread: Adding numbers...
Main thread: The sum is 5050
```

Now that you know how GCD works, it's time to see how to deal with reference cycles for asynchronous code.

Weak self

There are certain times when you can't capture `self` as an unowned reference because it may become `nil` at some point while running an asynchronous task. For example, an editor edits a certain tutorial and submits the editing feedback on the tutorial's card as follows:

```
extension Editor {
  func feedback(for tutorial: Tutorial) -> String {
    let tutorialStatus: String
    // Should use the tutorial.content here, really. :]
    // Instead, flip a coin
    if arc4random_uniform(10) % 2 == 0 {
      tutorialStatus = "published"
    } else {
      tutorialStatus = "rejected"
    }
    return "Tutorial \(tutorialStatus) by \(self.name)"
  }
}
```

This editor isn't doing a very good job, and decides to publish or reject a tutorial at random.

Add the `editTutorial()` method to the `Editor` extension:

```
func editTutorial(_ tutorial: Tutorial) {
  queue.async() {
    [unowned self] in
    let feedback = self.feedback(for: tutorial)
    DispatchQueue.main.async {
      print(feedback)
    }
  }
}
```

This method uses the same GCD code as the `execute(backgroundWork: mainWork:)` one you've used before. The editing happens on a background thread and the resulting feedback prints on the main thread.

Although there is no reference cycle happening in this case, because you decided you did not want `feedback` to extend the lifetime of a `Editor` object, you declared `self` as `unowned`. However, this code isn't safe! If, for some reason, the editor went out of scope before `editTutorial` had completed, `self.feedback` would crash when it eventually executed.

The strong weak pattern

To allow editors to disappear if they go out of scope but properly perform the edit if they are still around when closure executes, you can create a temporary *strong* reference to `self`. Update `editTutorial` as follows:

```
func editTutorial(_ tutorial: Tutorial) {
  queue.async() {
    [weak self] in

      guard let strongSelf = self else {
        print("I no longer exist so no feedback for you!")
        return
      }
    DispatchQueue.main.async {
      print(strongSelf.feedback(for: tutorial))
    }
  }
}
```

This code is all or nothing. If the editor has gone away by the time the closure runs, it will print a snarky message. If `strongSelf` is not `nil` it will stick around until the print statement finishes.

Key points

- Use a **weak reference** to break a strong reference cycle if a reference may become `nil` at some point in its lifecycle.
- Use an **unowned reference** to break a strong reference cycle when you know a reference **always** has a value and will **never** be `nil`.
- You **must** use `self` inside a closure's body. This is the way the Swift compiler hints to you that you need to be careful not to make a circular reference.
- **Capture lists** define how you capture values and references in closures.
- The **strong weak pattern** extends an object's lifecycle for asynchronous closures.
- An **escaping closure** can be used later after the corresponding function returns.

Where to go from here?

Now that you know the basics of asynchronous closures and memory management, it's time to apply them in your apps.

It is important to understand the relationships between the different objects and closures to prevent leaks.

A fundamental tenant of Swift is to understand your object graph. While it does not work in playgrounds, you may want to check out the visual debugger feature in Xcode 9 that allows you to explore your object graph graphically at runtime.

Challenges

Challenge 1

Break the strong reference cycle in the following code:

```
class Person {
  let name: String
  let email: String
  var car: Car?

  init(name: String, email: String) {
    self.name = name
    self.email = email
  }

  deinit {
    print("Goodbye \(name)!")
  }
}

class Car {
  let id: Int
  let type: String
  var owner: Person?

 init(id: Int, type: String) {
   self.id = id
   self.type = type
 }

 deinit {
   print("Goodbye \(type)!")
 }
```

```
}

var owner: Person? = Person(name: "Cosmin",
                            email: "cosmin@whatever.com")
var car: Car? = Car(id: 10, type: "BMW")

owner?.car = car
car?.owner = owner

owner = nil
car = nil
```

Challenge 2

Break the strong reference cycle in the following code:

```
class Customer {
  let name: String
  let email: String
  var account: Account?

  init(name: String, email: String) {
    self.name = name
    self.email = email
  }

  deinit {
    print("Goodbye \(name)!")
  }
}

class Account {
  let number: Int
  let type: String
  let customer: Customer

  init(number: Int, type: String, customer: Customer) {
    self.number = number
    self.type = type
    self.customer = customer
  }

  deinit {
    print("Goodbye \(type) account number \(number)!")
  }
}

var customer: Customer? = Customer(name: "George",
                                   email: "george@whatever.com")
var account: Account? = Account(number: 10, type: "PayPal",
                                customer: customer!)
```

```
customer?.account = account

account = nil
customer = nil
```

Chapter 24: Value Types and Value Semantics

By Alexis Gallagher

Swift supports two kinds of types: value types and reference types. Structs and enums are value types; classes and functions are reference types. These types differ in their behavior.

The behavior you've come to expect from value types is the result of **value semantics**. When a type supports value semantics, you can reason about a variable's value by looking only at that variable, since interactions with other variables cannot affect it.

The type *guarantees the independence of variables*, which rules out a large class of bugs. This is why most Swift standard library types support value semantics, why many Cocoa types are imported to offer value semantics, and why you should use value semantics when appropriate.

That said, value semantics are not always the appropriate choice, and they can require some subtle handling to support correctly.

This chapter will define value semantics, show how to test for it, explain where it's suitable, and show how to build types with value semantics using value types, reference types, or some mix of the two. A deft mixed type can offer the best of both worlds, with the simple interface of value semantics and the efficiency of reference types under the hood.

Value types vs. reference types

Value and reference types differ in their **assignment behavior**, which is just the name for *what Swift actually does* whenever you assign a value to a variable. You assign values all the time; for example, whenever you assign to global variables, local variables, or to properties. You also assign whenever you call a function, effectively assigning a value to the function's parameter.

Reference types

Reference types use **assign-by-reference**. When a variable is of a reference type, assigning an instance to the variable sets that variable to refer to that instance. If another variable was already referring to that instance, then both of those variables post-assignment now refer to the *same* instance, like so:

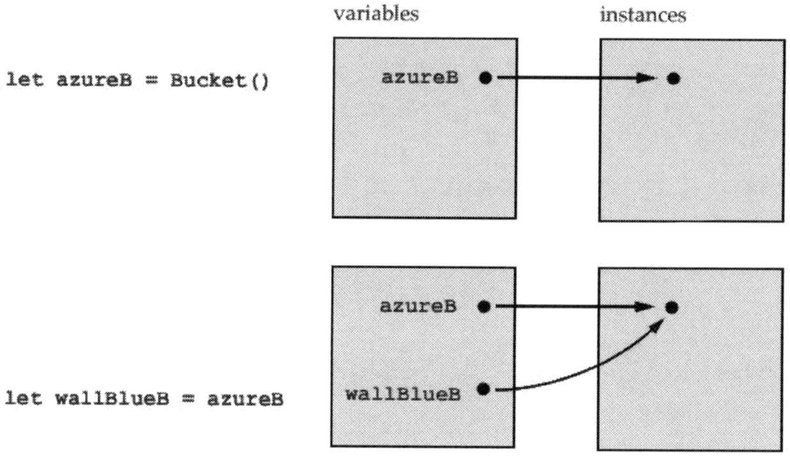

Since both variables point to the same instance, you can use one variable to change that instance and see the effect of the change in the other.

Suppose you're running a paint shop, selling paint to landscape artists and housepainters and building. You are building an inventory app to keep track of your paint. You start out with a simple color and paint abstraction:

```
struct Color: CustomStringConvertible {
  var red, green, blue: Double

  var description: String {
    return "r: \(red) g: \(green) b: \(blue)"
  }
}

// Preset colors
extension Color {
  static var black = Color(red: 0, green: 0, blue: 0)
  static var white = Color(red: 1, green: 1, blue: 1)
  static var blue  = Color(red: 0, green: 0, blue: 1)
  static var green = Color(red: 0, green: 1, blue: 0)
  // more ...
}

// Paint bucket abstraction
class Bucket {
```

```
  var color: Color
  var isRefilled = false

  init(color: Color) {
    self.color = color
  }

  func refill() {
    isRefilled = true
  }
}
```

Landscape artists like painting the sky, so you have a bucket of blue paint in the shop with the label "azure" on the side. Housepainters also like that color, but they call it "wall blue". On the other side of that same bucket, you have another label that says "wall blue".

The code in your inventory app reflects this:

```
let azurePaint = Bucket(color: .blue)
let wallBluePaint = azurePaint
wallBluePaint.isRefilled // => false, initially
azurePaint.refill()
wallBluePaint.isRefilled // => true, unsurprisingly!
```

When you call `azurePaint.refill()`, you also refill `wallBluePaint`, because the two variables both refer to the same instance.

In fact, the two variables now *depend on each other*. The value of any variable is simply the value of the instance it refers to. These two variables refer to the same instance, so the value of each variable depends on the value of the other variable. Changing one might change the other. The two variables are two names for the same bucket.

Value types

Value types, however, use **assign-by-copy**. Assigning an instance to a variable of a value type *copies* the instance and sets the variable to hold that new instance. So after every assignment, a variable holds an instance which it owns all to itself.

Here's how this looks:

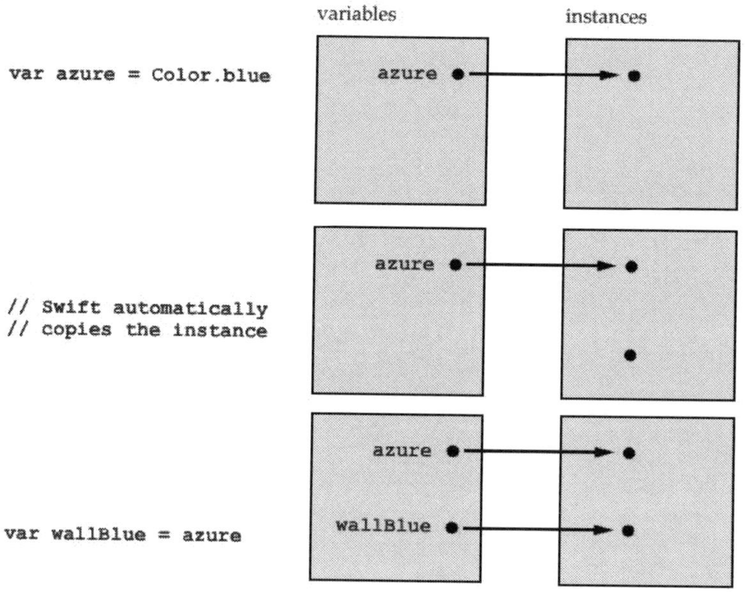

In the example above, `Color` is a value type, so assigning a value to `wallBlue` creates a copy of the instance held by `azure`.

Now each variable is independent, so you never need to worry that another variable might change it. For instance, suppose the tastes of housepainters change, and they decide that a good wall should be a much darker shade of blue. If you call a method `wallBlue.darken()` to change what color is meant by `wallBlue`, that has no effect on what is meant by `azure`.

```
extension Color {
  mutating func darken() {
    red *= 0.9; green *= 0.9; blue *= 0.9
  }
}

var azure = Color.blue
var wallBlue = azure
azure  // r: 0.0 g: 0.0 b: 1.0
wallBlue.darken()
azure  // r: 0.0 g: 0.0 b: 1.0 (unaffected)
```

To continue the metaphor, instead of being different names for the same bucket of paint, where the bucket's contents can change, these value-type variables are more like names printed on color sample swatches. Each name is independently associated with just one color, because it is a name for the color itself.

Defining value semantics

What's nice about about primitive value types like `Color` or `Int` is not the assign-by-copy behavior itself, but rather the *guarantee* this behavior creates.

This guarantee is that the *only* way to affect a variable's value is through that variable itself. If a type promises that, then the type supports value semantics.

To test if a type supports value semantics, consider it in a snippet like the following:

```
var x = MysteryType()
var y = x
exposeValue(x) // => initial value derived from x
// {code here which uses only y}
exposeValue(x) // => final value derived from x
// Q: are the initial and final values different?
```

If the code which "uses only `y`" can affect the value of `x`, then `MysteryType` does not support value semantics.

One benefit of value semantics is that they aid **local reasoning**, since to find out how a variable got its value you only need to consider the history of interactions with that variable. When using value semantics, you work in a simple world, where variables have values and those variables do not affect each other.

When to prefer value semantics

When should you design a type to support value semantics?

While they are convenient, whether value semantics are appropriate depends on what the type is supposed to model.

Value semantics are good for representing inert, descriptive data. For example: numbers; strings; physical quantities like angle, length, and color; mathematical objects like vectors and matrices; pure binary data; collections of such values; and finally, large rich structures made from such values, like media.

Reference semantics are good for representing distinct items in your program or in the world. For example: constructs within your program such as specific buttons or memory buffers; an object which plays a specific role in coordinating certain other objects; or a particular person or physical object in the real world.

The underlying logic here is that the referenceable items are all *objects*, meaning they all have a distinct identity. Two people could be alike in all physical attributes, but they are still distinct *people*. Two buffers could hold equal byte patterns, but they are still distinct *buffers*.

But the items on the value semantics list are all *values*. They lack identity, so it is meaningless to talk about two things being equal but distinct. If we agree `x` equals five, there is no further question about which five it equals. Five is five.

A common pattern is to see a model type like `Person` defined as a reference type to reflect that it is an object with identity, while it is loaded with various value properties like `age`, `hairColor`, and so on, which describe that object.

When a program must represent many distinct items (like `Persons`), or when different parts of a program need to coordinate around the same item (like the device's screen or the `UIApplication` instance itself), reference types are the natural tool for representing those items.

Reference types are used throughout UIKit because one of the main things running application code needs to refer to is other pieces of code. So you have `UIView` which describes a view on screen, `UIScreen` for the screen, `NSNotificationCenter` for objects providing framework services, and so on.

Implementing value semantics

But say you *do* want value semantics. If you're defining a type, how do you enforce it? The approach depends on the details of the type. In this section, you will consider the various cases one by one.

Case 1. Primitive value types

Primitive value types like `Int` support value semantics automatically. This is because assign-by-copy ensures each variable holds its own instance (so no other variable can affect the instance), and because the instance itself is structurally independent. That is, the instance defines its own value independently of any other instance, so no other instance could affect its value.

The intuition here is that an `Int` is directly represented by a pattern of bits, which is copied whole with no reference to anything external.

Case 2. Composite value types

Composite value types, like `structs` or `enums`, also follow a simple rule: a `struct` will support value semantics if all its stored properties support value semantics.

This rule can be proved by looking at how Swift does the instance copying. When Swift copies the instance of a `struct`, it creates a copy instance as if it's directly assigning all the stored properties of the original instance into the properties of the copy instance.

This is a direct assignment in that it does not invoke any property observers.

Since you are assigning a struct, which is a value type, the assigned-to variable will hold a copy of the assigned instance. And since the instance's properties have value semantics, the copy instance's properties will be the only variables that can modify *their* instances. So from this you can see the assigned-to variable is the only way to modify its instance, or any other instance it depends on, and therefore is the only way to modify its own value. This proves the rule.

If the type is an enumeration, it's analogous: the instance copy is defined to have the same enumeration member, and it is as if that member's associated values are directly assigned from the associated values of the existing instance.

Incidentally, since an `Array<Element>` provides the same semantics as a `struct` with a property of type `Element`, this case also tells you whether arrays support value semantics. They do, but only if their element type does.

Case 3. Reference types

Reference types can also have value semantics.

To see how, recall that a type has value semantics if the only way to affect a variable's value is through that variable. In general, you can change the value of a variable of a reference type in only two ways, either by assigning to the variable so it refers to a different instance or by modifying the instance itself.

The first way works through the variable, so it is allowed by value semantics. But the second way — modifying the instance — could be effected through another variable, so this must be prevented to preserve value semantics.

So the solution is straightforward: to define a reference type with value semantics, you must define it to be *immutable*; that is, built so it is impossible to change the instance's value after initialization. To achieve this, it suffices to ensure that all its stored properties are constant, and that they in turn all use types with value semantics.

Many of the basic UIKit utility types adopt this pattern. For instance, consider this code handling a `UIImage`:

```
var a = UIImage(named:"smile.jpg")
var b = a
computeValue(b) // => something
doSomething(a)
computeValue(b) // => same thing!
```

Because `UIImage` is immutable, there is no possible function `doSomething(a)` which will cause `computeValue(b)` to change the value it returns. One could ask if `b` refers to a copy of, or a reference to, `a`'s instance. But the deeper point is that it doesn't matter.

The `UIImage` type has dozens of properties (`scale`, `capInsets`, `renderingMode`, etc.), but since they are all read-only, there is no way to modify an instance, and therefore no way for one variable to affect another. But if one of its properties were *not* constant, then setting that property would mutate the instance and spoil the invariant. This structural sharing of a common instance would not be safe.

`UIImage` along with many of the Cocoa types are defined as immutable for this reason, because an immutable reference type has value semantics.

Case 4. Value types containing mutable reference types

The final case is mixed types; that is, value types containing mutable reference types. This is the subtlest case but perhaps the most valuable, since it allows combining the simple programming model of value types with the efficiency benefits of reference types.

To see why this fails, look again at the instance copying rule. When a mixed-type instance is copied, all of its properties are directly assigned. But since any reference-type property is assigned by reference to the copy, the copy instance's property and the original instance's property will now refer to the *same* shared instance. The instance and its copy are distinct from each, but their values depend on each other because of this structural sharing of a property that affects both their values.

An example and a diagram will explain this best. Returning to your paint shop example, imagine you want a type to define a plan for a painting project, a plan which specifies the bucket that provides the main color and also specifies the accent color to be used for small touches:

```
struct PaintingPlan // a value type, containing ...
{
  // a value type
  var accent = Color.white
  // a mutable reference type
  var bucket = Bucket(color: .blue)
}
```

You might want to define your plan for a piece of artwork by starting with a plan for housepainting, and then modify it. Since `PaintingPlan` is a struct — a value type — you might hope to do this by assigning a new variable and then modifying that variable.

Unfortunately, since it's a `struct` that contains a reference type, the assignment does not create a truly independent copy. When you change the color in the house plan you change the color in the art plan, since they share the same bucket.

```
var artPlan = PaintingPlan()
var housePlan = artPlan
artPlan.bucket.color // => blue
```

```
// for house-painting only we fill the bucket with green paint
housePlan.bucket.color = Color.green
artPlan.bucket.color // => green. oops!
```

This is due to implicit structural sharing of the paint bucket instance:

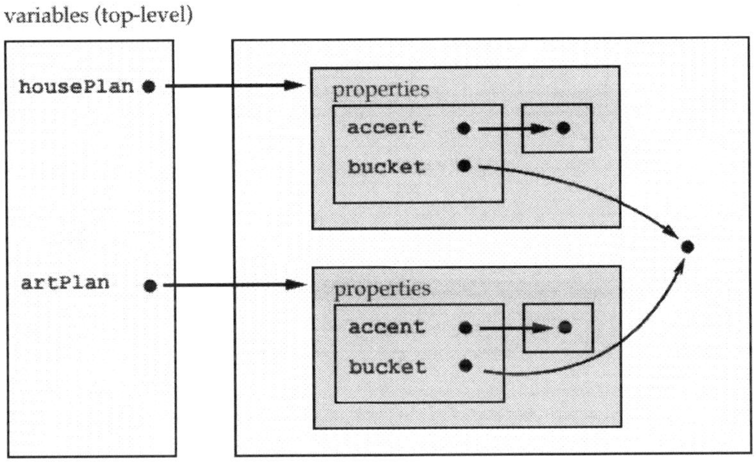

Because of this structural sharing, `PaintingPlan` is a value type but lacks value semantics.

Copy-on-write to the rescue

What's the fix? The first step lies in recognizing that value semantics is defined relative to an access level. Value semantics depends on what changes you can make and see with a variable, which in turn depends on the access level of the setters and mutating functions of the variable's type. So a type may provide value semantics to all client code (which can access `internal` or `public` members, for example) while not providing value semantics to code which can access its `private` members.

So the trick to preserving value semantics in a mixed type is to define the type such that its *users* are never able to see the effects of mutation on the contained reference-type property. This example makes the mutable reference type `private` and provides an interface that controls reads and writes:

```
struct PaintingPlan // a value type, containing ...
{
  // a value type
  var accent = Color.white
  // a private reference type, for "deep storage"
  private var bucket = Bucket()
```

```
    // a pseudo-value type, using the deep storage
    var bucketColor: Color {
      get {
        return bucket.color
      }
      set {
        bucket = Bucket(color: newValue)
      }
    }
  }
```

To code that can access private members, this struct contains the mutable reference-type property `bucket`, spoiling value semantics. But to a client with `internal` access or higher, the type behaves just like a struct that has value semantics, with two properties `accentColor` and `bucketColor`.

Reading `bucketColor` simply invokes the computed property getter which reads from the private reference-type property `bucket`, which acts as the *backing storage*. Apple sometimes also calls this *indirect storage*, or *deep storage*. Assigning to `bucketColor` invokes the computed property setter, which is designed to preserve the independence of `PaintingPlan` values. Whenever a user modifies `bucketColor`, the setter creates a distinct new instance of indirect storage, a new `Bucket`, to back it.

The effect is that assigning a value of `PaintingPlan` does not immediately copy the backing storage at the moment of assignment, as with a simple value type. Instances will in fact share their backing storage for a while. But every instance appears as if it always had its own backing store, since it privately creates its own unique backing store as soon as one is needed.

This pattern is called *copy-on-write (COW)*, because the system only copies the backing store at the moment when you try to write to the variable.

But what's the point of that?

The point is performance. Suppose the backing store is very large. When you only read from variables, the instances can all share the same backing store, using less storage and sparing the computational cost of copying it.

But once you use a variable to mutate an instance — to write to it — only then does the system do the work of copying the backing store, to ensure the modification does not affect other variables. This minimizes immediate storage and compute costs, deferring them only until they are needed.

If the backing store is large enough to deserve this optimization, then it is almost certainly worth applying a further optimization, and performing an in-place mutation of the backing store if it is not shared elsewhere. This is cheaper than creating a new store and throwing away the old one.

For this to work, your value type needs a way to tell if it uniquely refers to a given backing store. The standard library function `isKnownUniquelyReferenced` provides just the thing for that:

```
struct PaintingPlan // a value type, containing ...
{
  // ... as above ...

  // a computed property facade over deep storage
  // with copy-on-write and in-place mutation when possible
  var bucketColor: Color {
    get {
      return bucket.color
    }
    set {
      if isKnownUniquelyReferenced(&bucket) {
        bucket.color = bucketColor
      } else {
        bucket = Bucket(color: newValue)
      }
    }
  }
}
```

The Swift standard library uses this technique extensively.

In fact, many of the Swift value types are not primitive value types, but are mixed types which only seem like primitive value types because they provide value semantics, relying on efficient copy-on-write implementations to do so. The Swift language itself relies on copy-on-write, sometimes deferring the copying of instances until the compiler can deduce that it is needed by a mutation.

Beyond copy-on-write

In the future, Swift will take such optimizations even farther. Although copy-on-write types remove some unnecessary copying of the backing store, they do not remove them all. For example, Swift now allows mutation via certain unlikely uses of `inout` parameters and closures, and the Swift runtime must defensively copy instances to keep memory safe in case of these uses.

To remove the need for these copies Swift will disallow these uses entirely as part of a new "law of exclusivity." This law essentially requires that only one piece of code be able to write to a variable at a time. Here, "at a time" does not refer to multithreaded concurrency but to a notion of "formal access duration" defined mostly by lexical expression structure.

For instance, suppose you define a variable `i` and a function which takes a closure and potentially mutates its argument:

```
func mightModify(x: inout Int, andRun f: () -> ()) { }
var i: Int = 0
```

It would be legal to call the function passing in a closure which did not touch `i`, for instance with `mightModify(x: &i, andRun: {})`. But it would be illegal to call the function with `mightModify(x: &i, andRun: { i += 1 })`. This is because the closure captures `i` and modifies it, and the function itself takes `i` as an `inout` parameter so it *also* might modify it. The compiler will complain that modification requires exclusive access.

At the time of publication of this book, the details of these rules are still under development, but the thinking can be found in the Swift Ownership Manifesto https://github.com/apple/swift/blob/master/docs/OwnershipManifesto.md. This document contains Apple's most painstakingly precise language describing notions of value. It also describes plans for other, opt-in storage annotations, like `shared`, `owned`, and `moveonly`, which will allow the compiler to remove heap allocations, reference counting, and other performance costs that now affect even highly optimized copy-on-write types.

The manifesto lays out the future of value semantics in Swift: providing the benefits of local reasoning while also enabling extreme efficiency when needed, via judicious restrictions on the language itself and a range of more manual features which developers can use as needed. The future of Swift is speed!

Recipes for value semantics

But in the present, to summarize, here is the recipe for determining if a type has value semantics or how to define your own such type:

For a reference type (a `class`):

- The type must be *immutable*, which requires that all its properties be constant. All its properties must be of types that have value semantics.

For a value type (a `struct` or `enum`):

- A primitive value type like `Int` always has value semantics.
- If you define a `struct` type with properties, that type will have value semantics if all of its properties have value semantics.
- Similarly, if you define an `enum` type with associated values, that type will have value semantics if all its associated values have value semantics.

For copy-on-write value types (a `struct` or `enum`):

1. Choose the "value-semantics access level", that is, the access level which will expose an interface that preserves value semantics.
2. Make note of all mutable reference-type properties, as these are the ones which spoil automatic value semantics. Set their access level below the value-semantics level.
3. Define all the setters and mutating functions at and above the value-semantics access level so that they never actually modify a shared instance of those reference-type properties, but instead assign a copy of the instance to the reference-type property.

Key points

Here are key points from this chapter:

- Value types and reference types differ in their *assignment behavior*. Value types use assign-by-copy; reference types use assign-by-reference. This describes whether a variable copies, or refers to, the instance being assigned to it.
- This assignment behavior affects not only variables but also function calls.
- Value types help you implement types with *value semantics*. A type has value semantics if assigning to a variable seems to create a completely independent instance. When this is the case, the only way to affect a variable's value is through the variable itself, and you can simply think about variables as if instances and references did not exist.
- Primitive value types and immutable reference types have value semantics automatically. Value types which contain reference types (i.e., mixed types) will only have value semantics if they are engineered to do so, for instance, by sharing only immutable properties, or privately copying shared components when they would be mutated.
- Structural sharing is when distinct instances both refer to a common backing instance that contributes to their value. This economizes storage since multiple instances can depend on one large shared instance. But if one instance can modify the shared backing instance, it can indirectly modify the value of other instances, so that the distinct instances are not fully independent, undermining value semantics.
- Copy-on-write is the optimization pattern where a type relies on structural sharing but also preserves value semantics by copying its backing instance only at the moment when it itself is mutated. This allows the efficiency of a reference type in the read-only case, while deferring the cost of instance copying in the read-write case.

- Reference types also have value semantics if you define them to be fully *immutable*, meaning that they cannot be modified after initialization. To do this it suffices that all their stored properties are read-only and of types that themselves have value semantics.

Where to go from here?

The best place to explore advanced implementations of value semantic types is in the Swift standard library, which relies on these optimizations extensively.

Apple, and many practitioners in the wider community, have written about value types and value-oriented programming more generally. Here are some relevant videos available online:

- WWDC 2016 session 207: What's New in Foundation for Swift https://developer.apple.com/videos/play/wwdc2016/207/. Apple.
- WWDC 2015 session 414: Building Better Apps with Value Typeshttps://developer.apple.com/videos/play/wwdc2015/414/. Apple.
- Controlling Complexity in Swift https://realm.io/news/andy-matuschak-controlling-complexity/. Andy Matuschak
- Value of Values https://www.infoq.com/presentations/Value-Values. Rich Hickey
- Value Semantics (not Value Types)https://academy.realm.io/posts/swift-gallagher-value-semantics/. Your humble author.

These talks offer a perspective complementary to the one in this chapter, as none but the last is directly focused on the distinction between value types (defined by assignment behavior) and value semantics (defined by independence of variable values).

A related literature is the writing on persistent data structures, also known as purely functional data structures. These are data structures which make extensive use of structural sharing, not just to economize on storage for read-only copies, but also to represent all the variations of a value produced over its mutational history.

An old classic on this is *Purely Functional Data Structures* by Chris Okasaki. More recently, the Clojure language has made extensive use of hash array mapped tries. It would be interesting to consider how to implement them in Swift.

Challenges

Challenge 1

Build a new type, `Image`, that represents a simple image. It should also provide mutating functions that apply modifications to the image. Use copy-on-write to economize use of memory in the case where a user defines a large array of these identical images, and does not mutate any of them.

To get you started, assume you are using the following Pixels class for the raw storage.

```
private class Pixels {
  let storageBuffer: UnsafeMutableBufferPointer<UInt8>

  init(size: Int, value: UInt8) {
    let p = UnsafeMutablePointer<UInt8>.allocate(capacity: size)
    storageBuffer = UnsafeMutableBufferPointer<UInt8>(start: p,
count: size)
    storageBuffer.initialize(from: repeatElement(value, count:
size))
  }

  init(pixels: Pixels) {
    let otherStorage = pixels.storageBuffer
    let p  = UnsafeMutablePointer<UInt8>.allocate(capacity:
otherStorage.count)
    storageBuffer = UnsafeMutableBufferPointer<UInt8>(start: p,
count: otherStorage.count)
    storageBuffer.initialize(from: otherStorage)
  }

  subscript(offset: Int) -> UInt8 {
    get {
      return storageBuffer[offset]
    }
    set {
      storageBuffer[offset] = newValue
    }
  }

  deinit {
    storageBuffer.baseAddress!.deallocate(capacity:
self.storageBuffer.count)
  }
}
```

Your image should be able to set and get individual pixel values as well as set all the values at once. Typical usage:

```
var image1 = Image(width: 4, height: 4, value: 0)

// test setting and getting
image1[0,0] // -> 0
image1[0,0] = 100
image1[0,0] // -> 100
image1[1,1] // -> 0

// copy
var image2 = image1
image2[0,0] // -> 100
image1[0,0] = 2
image1[0,0] // -> 2
image2[0,0] // -> 100 because of copy-on-write

var image3 = image2
image3.clear(with: 255)
image3[0,0] // -> 255
image2[0,0] // -> 100 thanks again, copy-on-write
```

Challenge 2

If you were Apple and wanted to modify `UIImage` to replace it with a value type that had the mutating functions described above, could you do this in a way that is backward compatible with code which uses the existing `UIImage` API?

Challenge 3

Consider the test snippet used to determine if a type has value semantics. What would you need to do in order to define an automatic means to test if a type supports value semantics? If someone handed you a type, could you know for sure if it offers value semantics? What if you could not see its implementation? Could the compiler be expected to know?

Chapter 25: Protocol-Oriented Programming

By Janie Clayton

Apple has declared Swift to be a *protocol-oriented programming language*. This declaration was made possible by the introduction of **protocol extensions**.

Although protocols have been in Swift since the very beginning, this announcement, and the protocol-heavy standard library changes Apple made, affects the way you think about your types. Extending protocols is the key to an entirely new style of programming!

In brief, **protocol-oriented programming** emphasizes coding to protocols, instead of to specific classes, structs or enums. It does this by breaking the old rules of protocols and allowing you to write *implementations* for protocols on the protocols themselves.

This chapter introduces you to the power of protocol extensions and protocol-oriented programming. Along the way, you'll learn how to use default implementations, type constraints, mixins and traits to vastly simplify your code.

Introducing protocol extensions

You briefly saw extensions in the previous chapters. They let you add additional members to a type:

```
extension String {
  func shout() {
    print(uppercased())
  }
}

"Swift is pretty cool".shout()
```

Here, you're extending the `String` type itself to add a new method. You can extend any type, including ones that you didn't write yourself. You can have any number of extensions on a type.

You can define a *protocol* extension using the following syntax:

```
protocol TeamRecord {
  var wins: Int { get }
  var losses: Int { get }
  var winningPercentage: Double { get }
}

extension TeamRecord {
  var gamesPlayed: Int {
    return wins + losses
  }
}
```

Similar to the way you extend a class, struct or enum, you use the keyword `extension` followed by the name of the protocol you are extending. Within the extension's braces, you define all the additional members of the protocol.

The biggest difference in the definition of a protocol extension, compared to the protocol itself, is that the extension includes the actual *implementation* of the member. In the example above, you define a new computed property named `gamesPlayed` that combines `wins` and `losses` to return the total number of games played.

Although you haven't written code for a concrete type that's adopting the protocol, you can use the members of the protocol within its extension. That's because the compiler knows that any type conforming to `TeamRecord` will have all the members required by `TeamRecord`.

Now you can write a simple type that adopts `TeamRecord`, and use `gamesPlayed` without the need to reimplement it.

```
struct BaseballRecord: TeamRecord {
  var wins: Int
  var losses: Int

  var winningPercentage: Double {
    return Double(wins) / Double(wins + losses)
  }
}

let sanFranciscoSwifts = BaseballRecord(wins: 10, losses: 5)
sanFranciscoSwifts.gamesPlayed // 15
```

Since `BaseballRecord` conforms to `TeamRecord` you have access to `gamesPlayed`, which was defined in the protocol extension.

You can see how useful protocol extensions can be to define "free" behavior on a protocol — but this is only the beginning. Next, you'll learn how protocol extensions can provide implementations for members of the protocol itself.

Default implementations

A protocol defines a contract for any type that adopts it. If a protocol defines a method or a property, any type that adopts the protocol *must* implement that method or property. Consider another example of a `TeamRecord` type:

```
struct BasketballRecord: TeamRecord {
  var wins: Int
  var losses: Int
  let seasonLength = 82

  var winningPercentage: Double {
    return Double(wins) / Double(wins + losses)
  }
}
```

Both `BasketballRecord` and `BaseballRecord` have identical implementations of `winningPercentage`. You can imagine that most of the `TeamRecord` types will implement this property the same way. That could lead to a lot of repetitive code.

Fortunately, Swift has a shortcut:

```
extension TeamRecord {
  var winningPercentage: Double {
    return Double(wins) / Double(wins + losses)
  }
}
```

While this is much like the protocol extension you defined in the previous example, it differs in that `winningPercentage` is a member of the `TeamRecord` protocol itself, whereas `gamesPlayed` wasn't. Implementing a member of a protocol in an extension creates a **default implementation** for that member.

You've already seen default arguments to functions, and this is similar: If you don't implement `winningPercentage` in your type, it will use the default implementation provided by the protocol extension.

In other words, you no longer need to explicitly implement `winningPercentage` on types that adopt `TeamRecord`:

```
struct BasketballRecord: TeamRecord {
  var wins: Int
  var losses: Int
  let seasonLength = 82
}

let minneapolisFunctors = BasketballRecord(wins: 60, losses: 22)
minneapolisFunctors.winningPercentage
```

Default implementations let you add a capability to a protocol while greatly reducing repeated or "boilerplate" code.

A default implementation doesn't prevent a type from implementing a protocol member on its own. Some team records may require a slightly different formula for the winning percentage, such as a sport that includes ties as a possible outcome:

```
struct HockeyRecord: TeamRecord {
  var wins: Int
  var losses: Int
  var ties: Int

  // Hockey record introduces ties, and has
  // its own implementation of winningPercentage
  var winningPercentage: Double {
    return Double(wins) / Double(wins + losses + ties)
  }
}
```

Now, if you call `winningPercentage` on a `TeamRecord` that's a `HockeyRecord` value type, it will calculate the winning percentage as a function of wins, losses and ties. If you call `winningPercentage` on another type that doesn't have its own implementation, it will fall back to the default implementation:

```
let chicagoOptionals = BasketballRecord(wins: 10, losses: 6)
let phoenixStridables = HockeyRecord(wins: 8, losses: 7, ties:
1)
```

```
chicagoOptionals.winningPercentage // 10 / (10 + 6) == 0.625
phoenixStridables.winningPercentage // 8 / (8 + 7 + 1) == 0.5
```

Mini-exercise

Write a default implementation on `CustomStringConvertible` that will simply remind you to implement `description` by returning `Remember to implement CustomStringConvertible!`.

Once you have your default implementation, you can write code like this:

```
struct MyStruct: CustomStringConvertible {}
print(MyStruct())
// should print "Remember to implement CustomStringConvertible!"
```

Understanding protocol extension dispatching

There's an important gotcha to keep in mind when defining protocol extensions. If a type *defines* a method or property in protocol extension, without *declaring* it in the protocol itself, **static dispatching** comes into play. This means the implementation of the property of method used depends on the type of the variable or constant — not the dynamic type of the instance.

Suppose you were to define a protocol similar to `TeamRecord` called `WinLoss`:

```
protocol WinLoss {
  var wins: Int { get }
  var losses: Int { get }
}
```

...and declared the following extension:

```
extension WinLoss {
  var winningPercentage: Double {
    return Double(wins) / Double(wins + losses)
  }
}
```

...which is adopted by the following type:

```
struct CricketRecord: WinLoss {
  var wins: Int
  var losses: Int
  var draws: Int

  var winningPercentage: Double {
    return Double(wins) / Double(wins + losses + draws)
  }
}
```

Observe what happens when you use the `winningPercentage` property:

```
let miamiTuples = CricketRecord(wins: 8, losses: 7, draws: 1)
let winLoss: WinLoss = miamiTuples

miamiTuples.winningPercentage // 0.5
winLoss.winningPercentage // 0.53 !!!
```

Even though `miamiTuples` and `winLoss` contain the same instance, you see different results. This is because static dispatching chooses an implementation based on the type of the constants: `CricketRecord` for `miamiTuples` and `WinLoss` for `winLoss`.

If `winningPercentage` were defined in the `WinLoss` protocol, the extension wouldn't add a new member, but instead simply provide a default implementation for a member already declared in the protocol. In this more common case, **dynamic dispatching** is used and the choice of implementation depends on the *actual* type of the instance, not the type of the constant or variable.

You've already seen dynamic dispatching in action in Chapter 14, as this is the dispatching method used for overridden properties and methods in class hierarchies.

Type constraints

For the protocol extensions on `TeamRecord`, you were able to use members of the `TeamRecord` protocol, such as `wins` and `losses`, within the implementations of `winningPercentage` and `gamesPlayed`. Much like in an extension on a struct, class or enum, you write code as if you were writing inside of the type you're extending.

When you write extensions on protocols, there's an additional dimension to consider: The adopting type could also be any number of *other* types. In other words, when a type adopts `TeamRecord`, it could very well also adopt `Comparable`, `CustomStringConvertible`, or even another protocol you wrote yourself!

Swift lets you write extensions used only when the type adopting a protocol is also another type that you specify. By using a **type constraint** on a protocol extension, you're able to use methods and properties from another type inside the implementation of your extension.

Take the following example of a type constraint:

```
protocol PostSeasonEligible {
  var minimumWinsForPlayoffs: Int { get }
}

extension TeamRecord where Self: PostSeasonEligible {
  var isPlayoffEligible: Bool {
    return wins > minimumWinsForPlayoffs
  }
}
```

You have a new protocol, `PostSeasonEligible`, that defines a `minimumWinsForPlayoffs` property. The magic happens in the extension of `TeamRecord`, which has a type constraint on `Self: PostSeasonEligible` that will apply the extension to all adopters of `TeamRecord` that *also* adopt `PostSeasonEligible`.

Applying the type constraint to the `TeamRecord` extension means that within the extension, `self` is known to be both a `TeamRecord` and `PostSeasonEligible`. That means you can use properties and methods defined on both of those types.

You can also use type constraints to create default implementations on specific type combinations. Consider the case of `HockeyRecord`, which introduced `ties` in its record along with another implementation of `winningPercentage`:

```
struct HockeyRecord: TeamRecord {
  var wins: Int
  var losses: Int
  var ties: Int

  var winningPercentage: Double {
    return Double(wins) / Double(wins + losses + ties)
  }
}
```

Ties are common to more than just hockey, so you could make that a protocol, instead of coupling it one specific sport:

```
protocol Tieable {
  var ties: Int { get }
}
```

With type constraints, you can also make a default implementation for `winningPercentage`, specifically for types that are both a `TeamRecord` and `Tieable`:

```
extension TeamRecord where Self: Tieable {
  var winningPercentage: Double {
    return Double(wins) / Double(wins + losses + ties)
  }
}
```

Now any type that is both a `TeamRecord` and `Tieable` won't need to explicitly implement a `winningPercentage` that factors in ties:

```
struct RugbyRecord: TeamRecord, Tieable {
  var wins: Int
  var losses: Int
  var ties: Int
}

let rugbyRecord = RugyRecord(wins: 8, losses: 7, ties: 1)
rugbyRecord.winningPercentage // 0.5
```

You can see that with a combination of protocol extensions and *constrained* protocol extensions, you can provide default implementations that make sense for very specific cases.

Mini-exercise

Write a default implementation on `CustomStringConvertible` that will print the win/loss record in the format `Wins - Losses` for any `TeamRecord` type. For instance, if a team is 10 and 5, it should return `10 - 5`.

Protocol-oriented benefits

You've seen a number of the benefits of protocol extensions, but what exactly are the benefits of protocol-oriented programming?

Programming to interfaces, not implementations

By focusing on protocols instead of implementations, you can apply code contracts to any type — even those that don't support inheritance. Suppose you were to implement `TeamRecord` as a base class.

```
class TeamRecordBase {
  var wins = 0
```

```
  var losses = 0

  var winningPercentage: Double {
    return Double(wins) / Double(wins + losses)
  }
}

// Will not compile: inheritance is only possible with classes.
struct BaseballRecord: TeamRecordBase {

}
```

At this point, you'd be stuck working with classes as long as you were working with team records. If you wanted to add ties to the mix, you'd either have to add ties to your subclass:

```
class HockeyRecord: TeamRecordBase {
  var ties = 0

  override var winningPercentage: Double {
    return Double(wins) / Double(wins + losses + ties)
  }
}
```

Or you'd have to create yet *another* base class and thus deepen your class hierarchy:

```
class TieableRecordBase: TeamRecordBase {
  var ties = 0

  override var winningPercentage: Double {
    return Double(wins) / Double(wins + losses + ties)
  }
}

class HockeyRecord: TieableRecordBase {
}

class CricketRecord: TieableRecordBase {
}
```

Likewise, if you wanted to work with any records that have wins, losses and ties, then you'd generally code against the lowest-common denominator base class:

```
extension TieableRecordBase {
  var totalPoints: Int {
    return (2 * wins) + (1 * ties)
  }
}
```

This forces you to "code to implementation, not interface." If you wanted to compare the records of two teams, all you care about is that there are wins and losses. With classes though, you'd need to operate on the specific base class that happens to define `wins` and `losses`.

I'm sure you don't want to hear what would happen if you suddenly needed to support divisional wins and losses on some sports! :]

With protocols, you don't need to worry about the specific type or even whether the thing is a class or a struct; all you care about is the existence of certain common properties and methods.

Traits, mixins, and multiple inheritance

Speaking of supporting one-off features such as a divisional win or loss, one of the real benefits of protocols is that they allow a form of multiple inheritance.

When creating a type, you can use protocols to decorate it with all the unique characteristics you want:

```
protocol TieableRecord {
  var ties: Int { get }
}

protocol DivisionalRecord {
  var divisionalWins: Int { get }
  var divisionalLosses: Int { get }
}

protocol ScoreableRecord {
  var totalPoints: Int { get }
}

extension ScoreableRecord where Self: TieableRecord, Self:
TeamRecord {
  var totalPoints: Int {
    return (2 * wins) + (1 * ties)
  }
}

struct NewHockeyRecord: TeamRecord, TieableRecord,
       DivisionalRecord, CustomStringConvertible, Equatable {
  var wins: Int
  var losses: Int
  var ties: Int
  var divisionalWins: Int
  var divisionalLosses: Int

  var description: String {
    return "\(wins) - \(losses) - \(ties)"
```

```
  }

  static func ==(lhs: NewHockeyRecord, rhs: NewHockeyRecord) ->
Bool {
    return lhs.wins == rhs.wins &&
           lhs.ties == rhs.ties &&
           lhs.losses == rhs.losses
  }
}
```

HockeyRecord is a TeamRecord and a TieableRecord, tracks divisional wins and losses, works with == and defines its own CustomStringConvertible description!

Using protocols in this way is described as using **traits** or **mixins**. These terms reflect that you can use protocols and protocol extensions to add, or mix in, additional behaviors, or traits, to a type.

Simplicity

When you write a computed property to calculate the winning percentage, you only need wins, losses and ties. When you write code to print the full name of a person, you only need a first and a last name.

If you were to write code to do these tasks inside of a more complex object, it could be easy to make the mistake of coupling it with unrelated code:

```
var winningPercentage: Double {
  var percent = Double(wins) / Double(wins + losses)

  // Oh no! Not relevant!
  above500 = percent > 0.5

  return percent
}
```

That above500 property might be needed for some reason in cricket, but not in hockey. However, that makes the function very specific to a particular sport.

You saw how simple the protocol extension version of this function was: it handled one calculation and that was it. Having simple default implementations that can be used throughout your types keeps the common code in one place.

You don't need to know that the type adopting a protocol is a HockeyRecord, or a StudentAthlete, or a class, struct or enum. Because the code inside your protocol extension operates only on the protocol itself, *any* type that conforms to that protocol will also conform to your code.

As you'll discover again and again in your coding life, simpler code means less buggy code. :]

Why Swift is a protocol-oriented language

You've learned about the capabilities of protocols and protocol extensions, but you may be wondering: What exactly does it mean that Swift is a *protocol-oriented* language?

Protocol extensions greatly affect your ability to write expressive and decoupled code — and many of the design patterns that protocol extensions enable are reflected in the Swift language itself.

To begin, you can contrast protocol-oriented programming with object-oriented programming. The latter is focused on the idea of *objects* and how they interact. Because of this, the class is at the center of any object-oriented language.

Though classes are a part of Swift, you'll find they are an *extremely* small part of the standard library. Instead, Swift is built primarily on a collection of structs and protocols. You can see the significance of this in many of Swift's core types, such as `Int` and `Array`. Consider the definition of `Array`:

```
// From the Swift standard library
public struct Array<Element> : RandomAccessCollection,
MutableCollection {
  // ...
}
```

The fact that `Array` is a struct means it's a value type, of course, but it also means that it can't be subclassed and it can't be a superclass. Instead of inheriting behaviors from common base classes, `Array` adopts protocols to define many of its more common capabilities.

`Array` is a `MutableCollection`, which is also a `Collection`. Thanks to protocol extensions, `Array` will get numerous properties and methods common to all `Collections` such as `first`, `count`, or `isEmpty` — simply by being a `Collection`. Thanks to many protocol extensions with generic constraints, you can `split()` an `Array` or find the `index(of:)` an element — if the type of that element conforms to `Equatable`.

These implementations are all defined within protocol extensions in the Swift standard library. By implementing them in protocol extensions, these behaviors can be treated as mix-ins, and do not need to be explicitly reimplemented on each adopting type.

This decoration of defined behaviors lets `Array` and `Dictionary` — yet another `Collection` — be similar in some respects and different in others. Had Swift used subclassing, `Dictionary` and `Array` would either share one common base class or none at all. With protocols and protocol-oriented programming, you can treat them *both* as a `Collection`.

With a design centered around protocols rather than specific classes, structs or enums, your code is instantly more portable and decoupled, because methods now apply to a range of types instead of one specific type. Your code is also more cohesive, because it operates only on the properties and methods within the protocol you're extending and its type constraints, and ignores the internal details of any type that conforms to it.

Understanding protocol-oriented programming is a powerful skill that will help you become a better Swift developer, and give you new ways to think about how to design your code.

> **Note:** More neutral-minded Swift developers will call Swift a "multi-paradigm" language. You've already seen inheritance and object-oriented techniques, and now protocol-oriented programming; Swift easily handles both!

Key points

- **Protocol extensions** let you write implementation code for protocols, and even write default implementations on methods required by a protocol.
- Protocol extensions are the primary driver for **protocol-oriented programming** and let you write code that will work on any type that conforms to a protocol.
- **Type constraints** on protocol extensions provide additional context and let you write more specialized implementations.
- You can decorate a type with **traits** and **mixins** to extend behavior without requiring inheritance.

Where to go from here?

Protocols and protocol oriented programming are at the foundation of the Swift language. The generics system, for example, uses protocols to specify with precision the type requirements of a generic type in use. If you have *m* data structures and *n* algorithms that operate on those data structures, in some languages, you need *m*n* blocks of code to implement them. With Swift, using protocols you only need to write *m+n* blocks with no repetition. Protocol-oriented programming gives you all of the advantages of typical object-oriented programming while dodging most of the pitfalls.

Next time you are faced with a programming task, see if you can figure out the underlying protocols at play. Doing so will lead you to a more flexible and extensible solution. Initially, you might find it easier to get something concrete working first and then extract the protocols. As you get more experienced, you may start seeing the protocols before you even begin coding just as easily as Neo can see the red dress.

Challenges

Challenge 1: Protocol extension practice

Suppose you own a retail store. You have food items, clothes and electronics. Begin with an `Item` protocol:

```
protocol Item {
  var name: String { get }
  var clearance: Bool { get }
  var msrp: Double { get }
  var totalPrice: Double { get }
}
```

Fulfill the following requirements using primarily what you've learned about protocol-oriented programming. In other words, minimize the code in your classes, structs or enums.

- Clothes do not have sales tax, but all other items have 7.5% sales tax.
- When on clearance, food items are discounted 50%, clothes are discounted 25% and electronics are discounted 5%.
- Items should implement `CustomStringConvertible` and return `name`. Food items should also print their expiration dates.

Challenge 2: Randomization

Write a protocol extension on `Sequence` named `randomized()` that will rearrange the elements in a somewhat random order. You can test out your implementation on an ordinary `Array`, which implements `Sequence`.

Hints:

- Your method signature should be `randomized() -> [Element]`. The type `[Element]` is an array of whatever type the `Sequence` holds, such as `String` or `Int`.
- You can call the `arc4random_uniform()` method like this: `arc4random_uniform(2)` to randomly generate a 1 or 0 for your randomization algorithm.

Conclusion

We hope you learned a lot about Swift in this book — and had some fun in the process! Swift is filled with language features and programming paradigms, and we hope you now feel comfortable enough with the language to move on to building bigger things.

With the language fundamentals under your belt, you're ready to crack your knuckles with iOS apps, macOS apps, the latest killer tvOS app and who knows what else!

If you have any questions or comments as you continue to use Swift, please stop by our forums at http://www.raywenderlich.com/forums.

Thank you again for purchasing this book. Your continued support is what makes the tutorials, books, videos, conferences and other things we do at raywenderlich.com possible — we truly appreciate it!

Wishing you all the best in your continued Swift adventures,

– Matt, Erik, Eli, Ben, Alexis, Janie, Cosmin, Steven, Chris and Ray F.

The *Swift Apprentice* team

27139917R10246

Printed in Poland
by Amazon Fulfillment
Poland Sp. z o.o., Wrocław